OLD AND NEW BIRMINGHAM.

"Ask Britain who gives her the spear and the shield,
The helmet, the sword—her defence in the field?
Ask Science (from Science the tribute is due)
Who gives her the lever, the wedge, and the screw?
Ask Ceres (for Ceres the claim will allow)
Who gives her the sickle, the scythe, and the plough?
'Tis Birmingham!"

—WILLIAM HAMPER

OLD AND NEW BIRMINGHAM:

A HISTORY OF
THE TOWN AND ITS PEOPLE.

BY

ROBERT K. DENT.

VOLUME III

"So describe,
That you shall fairly streets and buildings trace,
And all that gives distinction to the place."
—CRABBE.

Republished by
EP Publishing Limited
1973

Publisher's Notes

Volume I is a reprint of the first 33 chapters of 'Old and New Birmingham' covering the period up to 1760 and includes a new introduction by Dorothy H. McCulla.

Volume II includes chapters 34 to 60 and covers the period 1760–1832.

This Volume includes chapters 61 to 68 and the 10 chapters comprising part 2, and covers the period 1832–1880.

The work was originally published in weekly numbers between 1878 and 1880 by Houghton and Hammond, Scotland Passage, Birmingham.

Facsimiles of some of the original covers for this work are reproduced at the end of each volume.

This volume has been reproduced from Birmingham Public Library copy number 242137. The small corrections mentioned in the original errata have been corrected in this reprint.

Reprint © 1973 EP Publishing Limited

East Ardsley, Wakefield

Yorkshire, England

ISBN 0 85409 885 2

Please address all enquiries to EP Publishing Ltd.

(address as above)

Reprinted in Great Britain by

The Scolar Press Limited, Menston, Yorkshire

CONTENTS.

LIST OF ILLUSTRATIONS.

CHAPTER LXI.

THE THEATRE IN BIRMINGHAM, 1821-1830,

With Notices of other Amusements of the People.

Catalani in Birmingham—The "Theatrical Looker-on"—Edmund Kean, Macready, etc.—The Cheltenham Amateurs—Grimaldi—Live Properties—Mr. Power in *Frankenstein*—A novel Avalanche—A Military Spectacle—Another "Infant Roscius"—Mr. Warde's Address—The Juvenile Conductor—Realism—Equestrianism in the Theatre—Anecdote of Macready—The "African Roscius"—Kean the Younger—"I can't find Brummagem"—Miscellaneous Amusements.

OUR last chapter in the history of the local stage left the newly-rebuilt Theatre Royal in its first season, at the commencement of Mr. Alfred Bunn's managerial career. During the season of 1821, Mr. Vandenhoff, Mr. Mathews, Mr. W. C. Macready, Mrs. Bunn, and other celebrities appeared on the boards of our local theatre, but no particular event occurred worth chronicling. In the following March, two Concerts were given at the theatre, in which Madame Catalani and Mr. and Mrs. Yainciez took part. The prices of admission, were—Boxes, 10s., Pit, 7s., and Gallery, 5s. During the regular theatrical season of 1822, which commenced on the 20th of May, playgoers had the advantage of a locally-printed "guide, philosopher, and friend," to aid them in selecting 'what to see,' in the shape of a little weekly,—a mere duodecimo tract — entitled *The Theatrical Looker-On*, which proclaimed itself to be "nothing, if not critical." It had but a short-lived existence, extending only to the end of the one season, twenty-five numbers in all, commencing May 27, 1822, and finishing in November; it was edited, in part at least, by Mr. C. R. Cope. There was much scope for the exercise of its critical functions during this season; for in addition to the great Edmund Kean, (who appeared in "Macbeth," "Othello," "Richard III.," "A New Way to Pay Old Debts," Joanna Baillie's "De Montfort," and other pieces,) we had Mr. Young, in a round of Shakesperian characters, Munden, Harley,

Blanchard, Miss M. Tree, and an admirably selected general company.

The next season saw Mr. Macready here again, playing Wolsey to Mrs. Bunn's Queen Katharine; Farren also appeared, "for one night only," as *Ogleby*, in "The Clandestine Marriage," Elliston and Mr. and Mrs. Charles Kemble. Then came a series of much-lauded performances by "the celebrated Colonel Berkeley and the other Cheltenham Amateurs," for the benefit of the Deaf and Dumb Institution at Edgbaston, wholly uninteresting from a dramatic point of view. Following these, we had once more the veteran Grimaldi and his son, whose occasional visits to the town brought delight to all ages and ranks. On one of these occasions, we are told by Boz, in his memoirs of the celebrated clown, the manager had forgotten to provide suitable "properties" of the sawdust-stuffed goose and sausage order, to be purloined by the mirth-making Joe from the inevitable poulterer's shop, in the harlequinade. Of course the "business" could not proceed without these indispensable articles, and as there was no time to manufacture them in the ordinary way, the property-man had to sally forth into the market-place and buy some real poultry—and all alive too—so that the playgoers enjoyed the unusual sight of a clown playing with *live properties*. Whether the performance was repeated we cannot tell, but if so, the dumb, but by no means silent actors must have had anything but a pleasant time of it during the reign of misrule which characterised the harlequinade of an old-fashioned pantomime.

While on the subject of theatrical make-shifts, we may recall another droll incident which occurred at the Birmingham Theatre Royal, during Bunn's management. When Mrs. Shelley's

The comedian was continually urging upon the manager the necessity of providing for this sensational effect, but he invariably shelved the difficulty with, ' Oh ! we shall find something or other ;' and in this position matters remained on the day of the performance.   " Well," said Power

ALFRED BUNN.

strange story of *Frankenstein*, in its dramatic form, was the sensation, an Irish comedian—the celebrated Power—was starring in Birmingham, and he announced the piece for his benefit; but despite all his entreaties, Bunn refused to spend a penny upon its production, and there was one special scene,—the fall of an avalanche, burying beneath it the mysterious being of the play,— which certainly needed something like an expensive mounting, the more especially as that episode occupied the most prominent position in the bill.

at length, ruefully, " we shall have to change the piece, that's all."

" Change the piece ! nonsense !" responded the manager.

" But there's no avalanche, and we can't possibly finish the piece without it."

" Couldn't it be cut out ?"

" Impossible : we *must change the piece !*"

A few minutes pause on the part of the manager, and then he suddenly exclaimed " I have it !—but they must let down the green curtain instantly on the extraordinary effect. Hanging in the flies is the large elephant made for 'Blue Beard;' *we'll have it whitewashed."*

"What!" exclaimed Power.

"We'll have it whitewashed, continued Bunn coolly; "what is an avalanche but a vast mass of white? When Frankenstein is to be annihilated, the carpenters shall shove the whitened elephant over the flies—destroy you both in a moment— and down comes the curtain!"

It was a case of 'Hobson's choice;' and as poor Power had relied upon this great sensation to attract a large audience, he submitted to the inevitable. The huge whitewashed elephant tumbled over to the accompaniment of the customary stage thunder; the effect from the front was appalling, and the curtain fell amid thunders of applause.

It would seem strange to modern theatre-goers to hear of a representation of the charge of the Light Brigade, or the fall of Coomassie, in which none but those who had actually served in those engagements and could produce medals in proof of the fact should be allowed to appear; yet in 1824, such a representation of the great decisive battle of the present century,—Waterloo—was announced under those conditions. One hundred Waterloo veterans, all of whom were able to show medals, took part in the mimic warfare; whether they possessed any histrionic ability does not appear.

There was another "infant Roscius" in 1825, who astonished, if he did not edify, large audiences, at the Assembly Rooms of Dee's Royal Hotel. He is thus announced in the *Gazette* of that period :—

ROYAL HOTEL ASSEMBLY ROOMS, BIRMINGHAM.
On Monday, Tuesday, Thursday, and Friday, the 9th, 10th, 12th, and 13th of May, 1825—the celebrated Infant Roscius, only seven years and a quarter old, from the extreme pressure of the company, and from the most unbounded applause with which he has been received during the whole of his inimitable Performance, has induced him to select *four more Evenings' Amusement only,* entirely changing the whole of his Performance

from the last week, commencing with a *new introduction ;* and in the place of the Melo-drama the Infant Roscius will go through the much-admired and very humorous Comedy of *Pecks of Troubles* , or, *The Distress of the French Barber ;* the whole of his songs, and scenes in Macbeth, Pizarro, Merchant of Venice, Richard III, and Douglas, which will be entirely changed as usual, and conclude with the *Musical Glasses.*

In the same month the Theatre Royal was opened for the season, under the management of Mr. Warde, for whom the following address was written by the well-known song-writer, Thomas Haynes Bayly :

When a new Landlord takes a well-known Inn,
How should the Novice's career begin ?

If all the house is properly prepar'd,
Larder and cellar stocked, and beds well air'd ;
Servants engaged—all promising recruits,
From the head waiter down to Bob the Boots—
Surely the Host himself with smiles should wait
On the first Guests assembled at the gate ;
Present his bill of fare, and hope they'll find
Each little item perfect of its kind.

I am a Host to-night ; my hope now rests
On this, my Public House, and these my guests.
My constant aim shall be to meet your wishes,
I've ordered in a stock of tempting dishes ;
Old wine made mellow and improved by age,
New fruits just sent us from the London stage ;
The Comic trifle and the Tragic bowl,
" The feast of reason and the flow of soul ! "

My decorations, too, are quite complete,
Best rooms, and attics also, clean and neat ;
Each crevice freshly painted, washed, and burnish'd
And all my snug apartments newly furnish'd ;
In short, your Host thus humbly recommends
This House of Entertainment to his friends.

Yet hold—of Entertainment did I say ?
Hath not the Drama's sun-shine pass'd away ?
Is not poor dear Thalia almost mute ?
And sad Melpomene in disrepute ?
Because *recherché* people all dine late,
And think no food digestible till eight !
Doth not Dame Fashion drive her slaves about,
In an unvaried round, from rout to rout ?
To see the present ball reflect the past,
And every rout a ditto of the last ?
To be to-night, where nightly they have been,
While Shakespear's Dramas pass unheard—unseen.

And is our cause a bad one ? Must I stop,
Hopeless of patronage, and shut up shop ?
No, no ; my efforts have already met
Applauses here which I can ne'er forget ;
And shall I tremble, when success depends
Upon the favour of my former friends ?
Forbid it gratitude ! With true delight

I welcome those who grace these walls to-night.
Oh ! may the comic banquet I prepare
Exceed the promise of my bill of fare ;
May each part please when on the boards 'tis placed,
Not overdone, but sweeten'd to your taste ;
And may your present Landlord long remain,
Happy to see you " cut and come again."

Another precocious youngster was permitted to strut his little hour on the " Royal " stage during this season, and was, moreover, allowed to drive the conductor from his place in the orchestra, and, with the sublime impudence which appears to have characterised every " infant phenomenon," undertook to fill the vacated post himself. We read that he " led the orchestra on the violin in the celebrated overture to Lodoiska in a most masterly style (?) and afterwards appeared as Teddy O'Rourke, in the farce of the Irish Tutor, and performed the character with the skill and ability of a veteran of the stage." This " masterly " conductor and actor was just six years of age !

We meet with more sensational realism, too, this season, in the shape of " an Interlude from the Melo-drama of *Valentine and Orson*, called the Wild Man and the Bear, in which a real Bear, the property of Mr. Simpson . . . . . will exhibit his extraordinary performance." The evening's entertainment on this occasion con-cluded with " the Melo-drama of the Caravan ; . . . on which occasion *a Reservoir, contain-ing 2,000 cubic feet of real water* [was] introduced. " The last scene," continues the announcement, " exhibits a Waterfall and Lake of Water, into which the Dog Carlo is seen to plunge, and saves the life of the child Julio ! "

Following this came an equestrian company, with a stud of horses, performing " the grand and interesting Dramatic, Equestrian, and Military Spectacle, called the Invasion of Russia, or the burning of Moscow." But all these performances, calculated to " make the judicious grieve," were fully condoned by the liberal provision made for the cultured playgoer, in the engagement of Mr. Macready, Mr. Mathews, Miss Foote, and others.

Later in the year, however, this class of patrons would read with regret " that Mr. Ducrow has taken our theatre for a short period, and intends opening it with an Equestrian Performance on Monday next."

The most noteworthy incident of the season of 1826 is contained in the following paragraph, which will be read with interest by all admirers of the great artiste whom Birmingham claims as its own :

August 28, 1826.—It is pretty generally known that the receipts of the house on Monday last, the evening on which Mr. Macready took final leave of his Birmingham friends, prior to his departure for America, were early on the following morning abstracted from the treasury. It would appear that the villains, no doubt adepts in their vocation, and possessed of every necessary information, had concealed themselves within the walls of the house, until the time at which the watchmen upon the premises generally leave, and then, having unobstructed access to the stage, they forced open the door of the treasury, and finding the key of the iron chest, without further difficulty obtained possession of two hundred pounds, principally in silver, with which they escaped unobserved. The liberality of Mr. Macready on the occasion ought, for the honour of the profession of which he is so distinguished a member, to be universally known. Upon being made acquainted with the serious consequences with which the loss threatened the Manager, Mr. Macready not merely relinquished all claim upon the amount received, but even consented to perform a second night without remuneration. He accordingly sustained the character of Virginius, on the Thursday, to an audience nearly as numerous as on the first night, and the Manager was fully reimbursed. It is hardly necessary to say that the warmth with which Mr. Macready was received on his re-appearance, gave full assurance that his kind and dis-interested conduct was duly appreciated. Mr. Macready left on the following day for Cheltenham and Bristol, whence he proceeds to Liverpool, and embarks for New York on Friday. Two young men, strongly suspected of being parties in the robbery, are in custody, and have been remanded for further examination ; but how far the charge can be brought home to them is not yet known. A reward of twenty pounds has been offered on conviction of the depredators.

Italian Operas at " Theatre Prices," Liston, Braham, Miss A. Tree, " Arthur Matthison, the Pet of the Fancy," in the (? pugilistic) character of " Jocko," for the benefit of his friend Hector Simpson, (proprietor of the bear and dogs afore-mentioned.)—these are the chief features of the season of 1827. In January 1828 we had an

"African Roscius" among us, "whose successful performances in the round of Moorish and African characters in the Theatres Royal, Manchester, Liverpool, Brighton, Bristol, &c., have excited a considerable degree of interest in the Theatrical World," and who appeared in Birming-

24th of October we meet with our old friend Dobbs of the reaping machine, on the occasion of his benefit, when he introduced two songs of his own, entitled, "The Gun Trade" and "I can't find Brummagem," the latter of which is given entire by Dr. Langford, and, as it forms a curious

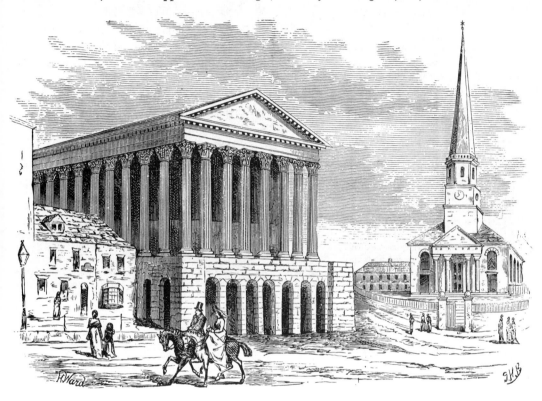

THE TOWN HALL;
As it first appeared; showing old houses adjoining, in Paradise Street.

ham for a few nights only, previous to his appearance at Covent Garden in the following month. The regular season of this year opened May 26th, with a visit from Mr. Macready, supported by a strong company; and in the following month we had Mr. T. P. ("Tippy") Cooke among us; in July we had Madame Vestris for three nights, and in the same year the younger Kean made his bow before a Birmingham audience in the character of *Romeo*.

We had also "one night" visits from Madame Catalani and "Paul Pry" Liston; and on the

and interesting illustration of our last chapter, we feel compelled to find a place for it here:

I CAN'T FIND BRUMMAGEM.

AIR—*Rob Roy M'Gregor, O!*

Full twenty years, and more, are past,
  Since I left Brummagem;
But I set out for home at last,
  To good old Brummagem.
But every place is altered so,
There's hardly a single place I know;
And it fills my heart with grief and woe
  For I can't find Brummagem.

As I walked down our street,
  As used to be in Brummagem,

I know'd nobody I did meet ;
　　They change their faces in Brummagem.
Poor old Spiceal Street's half gone.
And the poor Old Church stands all alone,
And poor old I stand here to groan,
　　For I can't find Brummagem.

But 'mongst the changes we have got,
　　In good old Brummagem,
They've made a market of the *Mott*,*
　　To sell the pigs in Brummagem.
But what has brought us most ill luck,
They've filled up poor old Pudding Brook,
Where in the mud I've often stuck,
　　Catching *jackbanils*† near Brummagem.

But what's more melancholy still
　　For poor old Brummagem,
They've taken away all Newhall-hill
　　Poor old Brummagem !
At Easter time, girls fair and brown,
Used to come rolly-polly down,
And show'd their legs to half the town ;
　　Oh ! the good old sights in Brummagem.

Down Peck Lane I walked alone,
　　To find out Brummagem ;
There was the *dungil*‡ down and gone !—
　　What, no rogues in Brummagem ?
They've taken it to the street called *Moor*,
A sign that rogues they get no fewer.
The rogue's won't like to go there' I'm sure,
　　While Peck Lane's in Brummagem.

I remember one John Growse,
　　A bucklemaker in Brummagem :
He built himself a country house,
　　To be out of the smoke of Brummagem :
But though John's country house stands still,
The town itself has walked up hill,
Now he lives beside of a smoky mill,
　　In the middle of the streets of Brummagem.

Amongst the changes that abound
　　In good old Brummagem,
May trade and happiness be found,
　　In good old Brummagem ;
And tho' no Newhall-hill we've got,
Nor Pudding Brook, nor any *Mott*,
May we always have enough to boil the pot,
　　In good old Brummagem.

The theatrical records of the last two years of
this decade are but a repetition of what has gone
before, Liston, Vandenhoff, Sally Booth, Macready, Charles and Fanny Kemble, and Braham,
all appeared during these two seasons; but the
attention of the people was probably too much

* The Moat.
† The common **Warwickshire** name for **Sticklebacks**.
‡ **The Dungeon.**

engrossed by the great political movements of that
period to give due support and patronage to
amusements, and so we allow the curtain once
more to fall upon the history of the player's art in
Birmingham.

The other amusements of the period were of
the usual type. We still find notes of the old
sport of " Cocking," and occasionally even of
bull-baiting. Madame Tussaud's wax-work exhibition found an unaccustomed home at the
Theatre in the winter of 1822 : and in the
" Garrick Room " in the same building the celebrated French giant Monsieur Jacques held his
receptions during the following February.

In 1823 we find a notice of a balloon ascent
by Mr. Sadler which seems to have proved an
unusual attraction to our townsmen, although
under somewhat unfavourable circumstances :

Oct. 20, 1823.—ASCENT OF MR. SADLER.—The hoist-
ing of a flag on the tower of St. Philip's Church, on
Monday morning, announced the intention of Mr. Sadler
to attempt an ascent with his balloon; and notwithstanding the very unfavourable state of the weather, thousands
of the inhabitants were observed in all directions making
their way towards the Crescent, the spot fixed upon for
the ascent, while a still denser stream of our population
directed their course towards Newhall Hill and other
eminences around, commanding a view of the Crescent,
and from which the ascent, though at some distance,
could be seen with the best possible effect. In these
situations the populace quietly remained during the pro-
cess of inflation, though the rain continued to descend in
torrents, and almost without intermission, during the
whole of the morning. As the hour fixed upon for the
ascent drew near, our streets became about wholly deserted,
and many of the shops, as well as the different warehouses, were closed, the attraction being too great to be
resisted, whether by master or servants ; indeed, since
the ascent of Mr. Sadler from Vauxhall in 1811, we do
not recollect any instance in which public curiosity was
more generally excited.

The Bull Ring appears to have ever been a
favourite locality for all curious exhibitions, and
in March, 1824, Birmingham sightseers were
attracted thither to see and hear a wonderful
" Speaking Doll," of French construction, which
was stated to be " the first attempt ever made,
with any degree of success, to form human
organization by means of mechanism."

In 1827 a large building of the Amphitheatre type was erected in Bradford Street, by the celebrated equestrian, Ryan, under the name of "The New Grand Arena." It was subsequently converted into a Baptist meeting-house, called "The Circus Chapel."

CHAPTER LXII.

THE BIRMINGHAM TRIENNIAL MUSICAL FESTIVALS
Second Period, from 1802 to 1829.

Mr. Joseph Moore—First Local Performance of the "Creation," 1802—Application to Lord Dudley for Venison—Mozart's Accompaniments to the "Messiah" first performed, 1805—Mrs. Billington—Dr. Crotch—Another difficulty respecting the Theatre—Madame Catalani—Miss Stephens—A New Departure—The Royal Household Band—Mozart's "Requiem"—Dress Ball—Royal Patronage—Costa—Erection of the Town Hall.

WE now return, "after many days," to the story of the Birmingham Musical Festivals. Adopting the plan of the able historian of the Festivals, Mr. J. Thackray Bunce, it will be remembered that our first chapter concluded with the last meeting of the eighteenth century. The present, embracing the second epoch in their history, carries us on to the last of the Festivals held in St. Philip's Church, previous to the erection of the Town Hall, which naturally enough forms the commencement of a third epoch.

The year 1802 unquestionably marked the commencement of a new era in the history of the Festivals, as it also marked the beginning of a useful career on the part of one whose name is indissolubly connected therewith. "Before that time," says Mr. Bunce, "the operations of the Committee though energetic and in the main well-directed, had not possessed the completeness, nor been attended by the success, which can only be secured by the labours of one qualified person, bent on realising in the performance of a great task the ambition of his life That person was found in our lamented townsman Mr. Joseph Moore. This gentleman had rendered much assistance in planning and conducting the Festival of 1799, but it was not until 1802 that he was placed virtually at the head of the Committee as their counsellor and director. From this time until the period of his death he devoted himself to the Birmingham Musical Festivals, and from the moment he undertook their control these meetings grew steadily in importance, both as regards their influence upon the development of musical art, and the assistance they afforded to the funds of the Hospital."*

The Festival of 1802 was remarkable as the first in which special attention was paid to the band and chorus. Both were considerably strengthened, the latter by selections from the metropolis and from provincial choral societies and the cathedral choirs of Worcester and Lichfield, and the former by the assistance of "the gentlemen of the Birmingham Private Concerts." Mr. F. Cramer was once more leader of the band, and the principal singers were Madame Dussek, Miss Tennant, Miss Mountain ; Messrs. Braham, Knyvett, Elliott, and Denman. The old custom of devoting two mornings to miscellaneous concerts was on this occasion broken through, and the patrons of the Festival had the pleasure of hearing for the first time in Birmingham, Haydn's oratorio of the "Creation," which excited an enthusiasm second only to that inspired by that divine masterpiece which had already become inseparable from the Birmingham celebrations, the "Messiah." Besides these two oratorios, the programme in-

* History of the Festivals, p. 77.

cluded a selection from Handel's "Acis and Galatea" and the usual miscellaneous concerts. The President for this year was the Earl of Dartmouth; the meeting commenced on the 2nd of September, and the result of Mr. Moore's able management was exemplified by an increase of more than £1,200 in the receipts, which amounted in all to £3,829, of which the Hospital received £2,380. Mr. Bunce throws considerable light upon the habits of our forefathers, from the minutes of the committee of this year. They appear to have bestowed great attention upon the commissariat department on this occasion, and at the same time to have endeavoured to keep down the charges within a reasonable limit. Accordingly they resolved that ordinaries should be prepared at the two principal taverns,—the Stork and the Shakespeare,—but that the charge should not exceed 5s. per head, "including malt liquor;" and further, that not more than ninepence per head should be charged for tea at the ball.

In order that there should be no stint of provisions, they directed their secretary "to write to Lord Dudley's steward, to ask whether his Lordship means to send any venison against the Oratorios." Presumably "his Lordship" did send the venison as requested—we had almost written *demanded*—for a similar request was made at the next Festival; and at a later date we find the demands of the Committee for a sufficient supply of this "savoury meat" extended to the Earl of Aylesford, and to Mr. Heneage Legge, of Aston Hall.

At the Festival of 1805 the band and chorus were still further increased, but the number of oratorios was again reduced to one,—the ever popular "Messiah," with (for the first time here) Mozart's accompaniments. In place of a second oratorio the Committee provided a selection from the "Creation," and the choicest *morceaux* of Handel's less-known works. For the second time the Birmingham Festival was graced with the presence of the greatest English soprano of that period. Mrs. Billington, who was supported by Miss Fanny Melville, and Mrs. Vaughan; the chief male singers being Messrs. Harrison, Vaughan, W. Knyvett, and Bartleman. For the first time, on this occasion, the announcements of the Festival contain the name of the conductor, that post being filled by Mr. Greatorex. The Festival commenced on the 2nd of October, with the Earl of Aylesford as president. The results again justified the wisdom of the Committee in allowing Mr. Moore so large a share of the control of affairs, the gross proceeds amounting to £4,222, (not less than £1,056 of which was received at the performance of the "Messiah,") and the profits yielded thereby to the Hospital being £2,202 17s. 11d.

Satisfactory as this result was, it was excelled, both as regards attractions and pecuniary returns, by the Festival of 1808, at which, for the third time, Mrs. Billington again appeared. As on the last previous occasion the meeting was deferred until the beginning of October; the oratorios were again the "Messiah" and the "Creation," the latter being compressed into two parts, in order to allow of an organ concerto by the eminent conductor, Dr. Crotch, and a short selection from "Jeptha," in which the powers of Mrs. Billington and Mr. Braham were specially displayed. The other performers at this festival were Messrs. Hawkins, Vaughan, Goss, and Elliott, Signor Naldi, Mrs. Vaughan, and a local musical prodigy, Master Simeon Buggins. The band and chorus were increased to two hundred performers, being the largest body ever previously assembled out of London; the increase in the latter department was chiefly due to the Birmingham Oratorio Choral Society, which had been organised that year by the exertions of Mr. Moore. The total receipts of this Festival were £5,411, and the profits accruing to the Hospital, £3,257. At the meeting of 1811 the committee once more came into collision with the manager of the Theatre Royal. The first week in October was again fixed for the Festivals, but Mr. Macready could not give up the theatre, that being the Fair week, and consequently the most profitable portion of his season. Mr. Macready, however, had been a good friend to the Hospital on many occasions, and the committee could not afford to treat him in the high-handed manner in which they had dealt with Mr. Yates, so the date of the Festival was altered to the last week

promise, and the Birmingham Festival was held as originally arranged, in the first week of October. The sermon, on this occasion, was preached by the Bishop of Worcester; the list of performers was unusually brilliant, including the names of Madame Catalani, Madame Bianchi, Miss Melville and Miss Jane Fletcher, and

BOTANICAL GARDENS, EDGBASTON

in September. Then a new difficulty arose; the Earl of Bradford (the President,) could not come during that week because he had engaged to go to Oswestry races. There was but one way out of the dilemma, and that was to get the date of the Fair altered, which was done, and so hereafter the Onion Fair was held on the three days ending with the last Saturday in September. Thus all parties were satisfied; Mr. Macready was able to gladden the hearts of country cousins at their annual visit to "the play," Lord Bradford went to Oswestry races according to

Messrs. Braham, William Knyvett, Vaughan, Harris, Bellamy, and Signor Tramezziani among the vocalists; and the instrumentalists included Cramer, Robert Lindley, Ashley, and Moralt, Mr. Wesley conducting this time, in place of Dr. Crotch. The principal attraction was again the "Messiah," the music for the other morning performances being selected from the "Redemption," the "Creation," "Judas Maccabæus," and "Israel in Egypt." The result of the liberal provision made by the committee was again shown by a continued increase in the proceeds.

56

which amounted to £6,680, and the profits to £3,629. At this meeting the prices were raised to 20s. in the morning and 10s. 6d. for the evening performances.

In 1814, the committee once more engaged Madame Catalani, and at this Festival Miss Stephens (afterwards the Countess of Essex) made her first appearance here, through the influence of the Marquis of Hertford with Mr. Harris, the Covent Garden manager, who, at his request, consented to allow Miss Stephens to appear at Birmingham; the other principal vocalists were Miss Smethurst, Miss Travis, Miss Stott, Mrs. Vaughan, and Miss Russell; and Messrs. Bartleman, Vaughan, Knyvett, Elliot, Denman, and S. Buggins. The band consisted of 84 performers—a larger number than on any previous occasion,—and the bâton was again wielded by Mr. Greatorex. The "Messiah," part of the "Creation," and a selection from the works of Mozart, Beethoven, and Pergolesi formed the principal attractions; the Earl of Plymouth was the President, and it was remarked by the newspapers that "the attendance of the nobility was much greater than at any former Festival." The proceeds amounted to £7,144, and the profits to £3,131.

The Festival of 1817 seemed likely at one time to be anything but successful, so far as the attendance of outsiders was concerned, at any rate, owing to a report which appeared in the London papers about the middle of September, to the effect that fever was making dreadful ravages in the town. Happily, however, the committee were able to contradict it on high medical authority, in good time to prevent it from damaging the prospects of the Festival.

In this year the patronage of members of the royal family was first extended to the Birmingham meetings, the Duke of Sussex having permitted the committee to use his name. The performances this year included the "Messiah" and portions of Haydn's "Seasons," Mozart's "Requiem," and Beethoven's "Mount of Olives." At one of the concerts in the theatre a scene from Mozart's opera of "Don Giovanni" was performed, and, on the same evening, concertos were played by Drouet on the flute, Weichsel on the violin, and Lindley on the violincello. Notwithstanding the fever scare, the receipts amounted to £8, 46, and the profits to £4,296.

For the Festival of 1820 the committee determined to devise even more liberal things than heretofore, and thus to place these celebrations in a much higher position than they had previously attained. This new policy was initiated, as may be expected, by Mr. Moore, on whose motion the committee resolved "that the next music meeting should be conducted on the grandest possible scale, in order to afford the highest musical treat which the present state of art in this kingdom will admit." In accordance with this laudable resolution the Festival was extended from three days to four, and instead of holding three balls, as they had done on previous occasions, they determined to hold only one, thus reserving all their resources for the more legitimate object of the meetings. The Earl of Dartmouth had consented to act as president, and the Bishop of Oxford to preach the sermon, but owing to the trial of Queen Caroline taking place during the week appointed for the Festival, their lordships were both detained in town, and were thus prevented from taking part in the Birmingham musical celebration. The Earl of Dartmouth, however, manifested his interest in it by sending a liberal donation, and by obtaining for the Festival the assistance of several members of the king's private band. Among the vocalists were Miss Stephens, Madame Vestris, Signora Corri, Mrs. Salmon, Miss D. Travis, Miss Fletcher, Messrs. Vaughan, Knyvett, Bellamy, Beale, King, Evans, and Goulding, and Signori Begrez and Ambrogetti. The instrumentalists, led by Cramer, Spagnoletti, and Mori, included almost every notable performer in the kingdom. The Festival commenced on Tuesday, October 3rd, with a full choral service at St. Philip's.

the entire choir of one hundred and thirty voices assisting therein; on Wednesday morning part of Haydn's "Seasons" was performed, with words newly arranged by Mr. Webb, a local clergyman; Thursday morning was, as usual, consecrated to the "Messiah;" on Friday, a selection of sacred music was given, including Mozart's "Requiem," which, it was stated, had "never yet been perfectly executed in this country, owing to the want of some wind instruments, of which, by the gracious permission of His Majesty, the Managers have been allowed to avail themselves from the Royal Household Band." On each of the evenings except Thursday (which was given up to the dress ball), a miscellaneous concert was given at the Theatre. The liberal provision thus made by the Committee for the enjoyment of their patrons resulted in an increase in the proceeds, which amounted to £9,483, being an increase of £1,000 over the receipts at any previous Festival; the profits were £5,000, "an amount," says Mr. Bunce, "which has been exceeded on five occasions only."

Encouraged by the success of 1820, the Committee entered upon the arrangements for the next Festival with the determination to "make the performances finer and more perfect than any that have taken place in the kingdom." Once more, and for the last time, we find the name of Madame Catalani among the principal performers, in company with Miss Stephens, Mrs. Salmon, and Miss Travis; and Messrs. Braham, Vaughan, Knyvett, Bellamy, Signor Placci, and other artists of note; the band and chorus together numbering 231 performers. The Festival commenced, as on the last occasion, with a full Choral Service, Tuesday October 7th, 1823; the other performances comprised "a new Sacred Drama entitled 'Gideon,'" part of the "Seasons," part of Mozart's "Requiem," the "Messiah,"and selections from the oratorios of "Judas Maccabæus" and "Israel in Egypt,"and from a Mass by Jomelli. Although the president (the Earl Talbot) was prevented by bereavement from being present at the Festival,

it is satisfactory to know that it was once more a great success, realising the unexampled amount of £11,115, of which the Hospital received £5,806.

At the Festival of 1826, which commenced on the 3rd of October, the list of patrons was for the first time headed by the name of the reigning Sovereign, an honour which has ever since been conferred upon the Birmingham Musical Festival. Among the principal vocalists appeared, for the first time, Madame Caradori; together with Miss Stephens, Miss Paton, Miss Bacon, the Misses Travis, Messrs. Braham, Vaughan, Knyvett, Phillips, and Signori Curioni and De Begnis. Among the instrumentalists were J. B. Cramer, De Beriot, Kiesewetter, R. Lindley, Nicholson, Moralt, Ashley, Distin, Puzzi, and others of note. The programme included selections from Mehul's "Joseph," Graun's "Tod Jesu," "Gideon," Haydn's "Seasons," and Handel's "Judas Maccabæus," besides other choice *morceaux*. The receipts were £10,104, of which the profits amounted to £4,592.

The last Festival held in St. Philip's Church commenced on the 6th of October, 1829. Within a few days of the celebration a circular appeared which seemed likely to damage its prospects somewhat, inasmuch as it appealed to the religious instincts of the people, calling on them to abstain from attending the performances, on the ground that they were inconsistent with, or opposed to, the spirit of Christianity. This circular was written by Thomas Swan, at the suggestion of that eminent and justly esteemed philanthropist, Joseph Sturge; and it naturally called forth considerable indignation on the part of the promoters and supporters of the Musical Festivals, the more especially from its ill-timed publication—which did not admit of a reply in time for the Meeting—and also from the fact that it was issued anonymously, and without even the name of the printer. To the former objection, however, Mr. Sturge replied, that the precise time of its appearance was accidental, the manuscript having been placed in his hands some time before, and his absence from home alone prevented its publication at an earlier period. " If, therefore, it was ill-timed," he adds frankly, " I am alone responsible." The name of the printer was, he further states, omitted inadvertently ; but that of the author designedly, as " it would give him unnecessary publicity to affix it."

Still, notwithstanding this undoubtedly well-meant opposition, the Festival proved a success. The novelties, which were but few, included a selection from the Service written by Cherubini for the Coronation of Charles X., of France ; also, at the evening concerts at the Theatre, a selection of operatic music (with the usual costumes and scenic accessories), " in which," says the historian of the Festivals, " the famous Malibran acquitted herself to the astonishment and admiration of a Birmingham audience, who now witnessed her performance for the first time." Among the vocalists on this occasion we meet with the name of Signor Costa, now better known as Sir Michael Costa—no longer as a vocalist, however, but as an eminent composer and conductor. The total amount produced by the Festival was £9,771, and the profits £5,964. During this Festival the Hospital celebrated its jubilee, having been established fifty years ; and during this period it had received from these musical gatherings no less a sum than £45,718.

We conclude the second period in the history of the Festivals, as we did the first, with a table showing the receipts and profits on each occasion :—

Year.	Total Proceeds. £	Net Profit. £
1802	3,329	2,080
1805	4,222	2,202
1808	5,411	3,257
1811	6,680	3,629
1814	7,144	3,131
1817	8,746	4,296
1820	9,483	5,000
1823	11,115	5,806
1826	10,104	4,592
1829	9,771	5,964
	£76,505	£40,257

CHAPTER LXIII.

EDUCATION IN BIRMINGHAM, 1801-1840.

The Sunday School Movement—The "Madras" and "Lancasterian" Schools—Education in Birmingham in 1827—The Free Grammar School—Increase of the Revenues—The Free Grammar School Bill of 1830—Opposition from the Dissenters—Defeat—The Act of 1831—Removal of the Old School—Mr. Barry's Design for the New Buildings—Description of the New Buildings—The Elementary Schools—The Birmingham and Edgbaston Proprietary School—St. Mary's National Schools.

IN our records, thus far, of the progress of Birmingham in the nineteenth century, we have purposely deferred the consideration of the educational history of the town until the period of the first real reform in the noble institution founded by King Edward the Sixth, and endowed, as we showed in an earlier chapter, out of the revenues confiscated by his royal father from our ancient Gild of the Holy Cross.

Having now reached that period, and before entering upon the further history of that institution, it will be well for us to take a glance at the provisions which had been made elsewhere for the education of the people. And among the most remarkable and interesting features in the educational progress of the town, as well as of the country in general, must be mentioned the Sunday School movement, which has been silently working a great reform in the manners and morals of the people, and which has, unnoticed by us in the course of our story, grown and flourished until it has become one of the most useful and valuable institutions in the country. We need not refer here to the origin of the Sunday School movement, but may mention that we owe its introduction, as far as Birmingham is concerned, to the Revds. C. Curtis, Rector of St. Martin's, 14,090 children receiving education in the various schools of the town (not including King Edward's) out of a population of 100,000 persons ; the table will enable the reader to form some idea of the work done by each of the schools mentioned :—

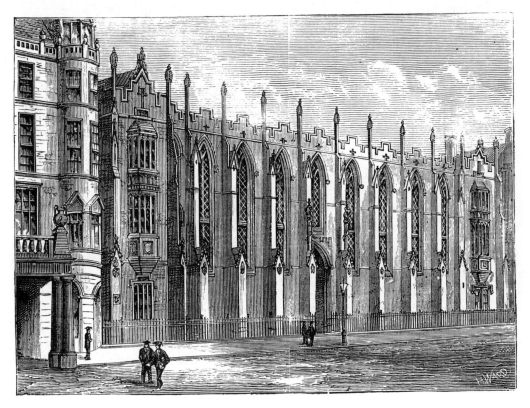

THE FREE GRAMMAR SCHOOL.

and J. Riland, of St. Mary's : the movement was speedily taken up by the dissenters, the Unitarians and the Methodists being among the most zealous in this good work. Secular instruction was also carefully looked after, and the provision made by the Free Grammar School, the Blue Coat School, and the Protestant Dissenting School, were supplemented by the establishment of a free school for the education of the poor on Dr. Bell's "Madras" system, in Pinfold Street, in 1812, and also of a school on the Lancasterian system. In 1827 there were, as appears from the following table printed in a late edition of Hutton,

	Boys.	Girls.	Total.
Blue Coat School	148 ...	46 ...	194
Infant School, Ann Street ...	80 ..	70 ...	150
Infant School, Islington ...	55 ...	50 ...	105
Asylum	130 ...	135 ..	265
National Schools	272 ...	170 ...	442
Schools of Industry	— ...	154 ...	154
St. Philip's	100 ...	100 ...	200
St. George's	140 ...	80	
St. Mary's	160 ...	190	
St. Martin's ...	112 ...	123	
St. Paul's	80 ...	20	
Christ Church	150 ...	187	
St. Bartholomew's, St. James's, St. John's, and Trinity, with the five above mentioned, making a total of	— ...	—	... 2,130

	Boys.	Girls.	Total.
Park Street	—	48	48
New Meeting	540	200	740
Old Meeting	441	109	550
Baptist and Sunday School Union	—	—	6,000
Cherry Street and Belmont Row (Wesleyan Old Schools) ...	—	—	1,600
Wesleyan, New	491	310	801
Bradford Street ...	160	200	360
Mount Zion	30	20	50
Islington	—	—	100
Thorpe Street	—	—	80
Inge Street	—	—	80
Roman Catholic ...	—	—	250
	3,089	2,212	14,099

While other educational institutions were thus growing and flourishing, the Free Grammar School appears, like the building in which it was held, to have fallen into decay. The instruction imparted therein was still circumscribed by the old barriers which regarded the acquisition of the learned languages as the be-all and end-all of education, and hence, inasmuch as the people of Birmingham were devoted to more practical pursuits, and desired for their sons an education befitting the calling they were destined to fulfil, the noble charity of our forefathers had ceased to benefit the town. But the progress of Time, which had crumbled the walls of the building, and had left the curriculum far behind the age, had also vastly increased the revenues of the institution—the simple £20 a year yielded by the lands which the inhabitants had so wisely preferred to the actual cash, the acorn which had been planted in the sixteenth century, having grown into a grand oak. The land originally lay outside the town, but by the growth of three centuries the town had encompassed it on every side, and it was now in a most central situation, yielding an annual return of £3,000; and with such ample means at their disposal, the governors determined to provide a school worthy of the town. Accordingly, a Bill was brought into Parliament during the session of 1830 to enable them "to pull down the present Master's houses, and School house, in New Street, in the town of Birmingham, and

to make and erect more suitable accommodations on a new site in the vicinity of the town, and to procure such new site, and to extend the objects of the charity, by erecting and making on the old site in New Street, accommodations suitable for a New School for teaching modern languages, the arts, and sciences; and to make certain additions to the estates of the said charity by purchase, and to raise money for the purposes aforesaid, by applying certain funds now belonging to the said charity, and by sale of part of the estates belonging thereto, and by mortgage, and for other purposes." There was however a weak clause in the proposed Act, which subjected it to the most determined opposition on the part of the dissenters; viz.: "that no person shall be elected a governor who is not a member of the Established Church of England." The opponents contended that it was not in accordance with the spirit of the endowment which provided only that the governors should be "of the more discreet and more trusty inhabitants of the town;" and "as the School was founded for the common benefit of the town, without exception, that eligibility to the situation of governors should continue to be the privilege of all; the rather, since the harmony and goodwill of the town and neighbourhood are disturbed by the introduction of the proposed enactment, and would be yet more seriously injured by its becoming a law."

The opposition thus raised was successful in overthrowing the Bill, which was lost on the motion for the third reading by a majority of six, twenty-two voting against, and sixteen for, the measure.

Early in 1831, however, the *Gazette* announced that "all the points of difference relating to the intended Free School Act have at length been arranged; and that, as now agreed to, the Bill will be introduced early in the next session of Parliament, and allowed to pass *pro forma* through all its stages." This welcome announcement proved to be true, and the Act passed almost unaltered, empowering the governors to expend

£50,000 in the erection of a suitable building for the reception of a select number of the "boys and youths" of the town, and further to lay out £4,000 on the school buildings for the children of the poorer inhabitants. Accordingly, the quaint old building of 1707 was removed in 1832 (the classes being held in the interim at the Shakespeare Rooms, New Street); and on the 18th of February, 1833, the *Gazette* published the following announcement relative to the intended new structure :—

"The Governors of the Free Grammar School have awarded their first premium of £100 for the best design for the New School Buildings and Masters' Houses to Mr. Charles Barry, of London ; the second premium of £70 to Mr. Hayward of Bath ; and the third of £40 to Mr. Godwin, of London. These three designs, we understand, were selected from among upwards of sixty others, the great majority of which were also Gothic. That sent in by Mr. Barry, and from which the new edifice will doubtless be erected, is a rich and beautiful specimen of the Florid style ; it is exceedingly appropriate, and is well adapted for the purposes for which it is intended, and while it serves to mark the era in which the school was founded, will prove highly ornamental to the town. Mr. Barry is an architect of well-known skill and experience, and has been employed in the erection of several Churches, under the Parliamentary Commissioners, his latest being the New Church at Brighton. The Royal Institution at Manchester, and the Travellers' Club House, in Pall Mall, were also built from his designs, and under his superintendence."

The felicitous choice made by the governors was approved not only by the inhabitants of Birmingham, but by people of taste throughout the country, and may really be said to have made the reputation of the architect. In Godwin's "State of Architecture in the Provinces," which was written while this structure was in course of erection, the author expresses his opinion that "it is not merely an ornament to Birmingham but to England," and that it "affords a fair evidence of the skill with which that gentleman [Mr. Barry] will carry out his beautiful designs for the Houses of Parliament, if permitted to act according to his own judgment."

The style adopted by the architect is very appropriately that which prevailed at the period of the foundation of the school—the Gothic of the Tudor era. The form of the building is quadrangular, the dimensions being 174 feet in front, 125 in flank, and 60 feet in height. The principal elevation, towards New Street, is composed of two stories, the upper series of windows being very lofty, and enriched with fine tracery, divided by eight buttresses, terminating above the embattled parapet, in a series of pinnacles, with the usual Tudor ornaments, consisting of the crown, rose, portcullis, etc. ; and the elevation terminates in two wings (ranging with the buttresses and their pinnacles, both in height and prominence), in each of which is a lofty oriel window, of two stories in height. The original plans contemplated the erection of a great central tower, but this has never been realized.

Entering the building through the spacious and richly ornamented porch, we find, on the ground floor, two large apartments, one on either side of the porch, each extending nearly half the length of the building, with oak panelled walls and ceilings ; these are the two subordinate schoolrooms. Ascending the handsome stone staircase, we reach the two principal rooms, which are connected by a corridor. One of these is the library, which is lighted by the noble series of windows of the front elevation, and is 102 feet long, 25 feet wide, and 31 feet high. It contains a valuable collection of books, and a fine bust of the founder, by Schumacher. The other room, which occupies a corresponding part of the rear of the building, is the grammar school ; the roof is carved and enriched with tracery, after the manner of those of Crosby, Eltham, and other halls of the Tudor period. At the end of the room, where the chair of the head master is placed, is a lofty and handsomely carved oak screen, behind which is a platform for visitors. "When peopled by the youthful votaries of learning, amongst whom the utmost order and discipline are maintained, it may be imagined that this fine collegiate hall, where—(it may be with no illusive finger)—

' Sagacious Foresight points to show
A little bench of heedless bishops here ;

Or here a chancellor in embryo,
Or bard sublime '——*

presents a most striking appearance."† The buildings in flank, together with the wings of the front and rear, form the residences of the masters, and apartments for private pupils.

The changes which had thus been brought about in the school buildings had also their counterpart in the school itself. The Greek and Latin, which had formed the whole of the instruction imparted, were now supplemented by more useful branches of learning, calculated to fit the scholar for business pursuits ; elementary schools were established in various parts of the town, and so the foundation which before the removal of the old building had provided for no more than a hundred children, now gave instruction to nearly fifteen hundred. The elementary schools, which are neat and even handsome buildings of brick, in the Elizabethan style, are four in number ; the first was erected in Gem Street, near Aston Street, in 1838, the second, in the same year, in Meriden Street, Digbeth, the third in Edward Street, Parade, a little later, and the fourth, in Pigott Street, Bath Row, in 1852.

The number provided for in these schools is as follows :—

	Boys.	Girls.
Gem Street	135 .	130
Meriden Street ...	240	
Edward Street ...	140 ...	140
Pigott Street	250 ...	250
	765	520

The extension of the course of instruction given in the Grammar School, which, in addition to the elegant attainments of classical learning, now provided also the more practical instruction in the arts and sciences, was highly eulogised by Dr. Buckland at the meeting of the British Associa-

tion, in 1839, of which one section was held in the rooms of this building. Such useful additions to the curriculum, he maintained, must have been the intent of the munificent founders of all colleges, though at the period they lived such studies may have been unknown.

In addition to the enlarged provision thus made for the education of the youth of all classes, an energetic and useful scholastic institution was established near the Five Ways, in 1838, by a body of Proprietors (and hence called the Birmingham and Edgbaston *Proprietary School*), in order to provide for their sons a school in which the advantages of a classical and commercial education should be combined, and from which corporal punishment, which at this time was regarded with growing disfavour among educationalists, should be excluded. Shares, entitling the holder to nominate one pupil, were offered at £20 each, and were made transferable.

The school building, which was completed in 1841, was designed by Mr. Hugh Smith, and is a handsome Elizabethan structure of red brick, with stone dressings. The frontage consists of the entrance to the school, surmounted by a handsome dwarf tower, lighted by an oriel window, flanked on each side by the masters' residences ; and there is an extensive play-ground in the rear.

We have not space to describe in detail the various national schools referred to in the table given at the beginning of this chapter ; the only building of this class having any pretension to architectural appearance, erected during the period under notice, is St. Mary's, in Bath Street, a neat little Gothic structure of stone, erected in 1846, at a cost of £2,187, of which £1,090 was raised by subscription, and the remainder received from the National Society, and the Privy Council Committee on Education.

---

* Shenstone.　† W. Bates, B.A., Pictorial Guide, p. 111.

CHAPTER LXIV.

THE BIRMINGHAM RAILWAYS

An unparalleled Coach-journey—Opposition to the Railway Movement— Early attempts of Murdoch and Trevithick—An affrighted Toll-gate Keeper—The London and Birmingham Railway—The Grand Junction Railway—Opening of the First Line in Birmingham—Completion of the London and Birmingham Line—The Midland Railway—Dr. Church's Steam Coach—Heaton's Steam Coach.

JUST a century had passed away since Nicholas Rothwell first performed his journey to London, in the Birmingham stage-coach, in the unusually short space of two days and a half; and the lapse of time had brought with it substantial improvements both in the speed and comfort of the stage-coach, which is well illustrated by the fact that on May-Day, 1830, the "Independent Tally-ho" performed a feat altogether unparalleled in the annals of coaching, by travelling the same distance (109 miles) in seven hours and ten minutes. But great as this speed must have appeared to the wondering inhabitants at that time, it was destined to be out-distanced before many years had elapsed; and already the minds of the people were exercised concerning a much-talked-of "puffing Billy" which had begun to run between Stockton and Darlington, the wonderful invention of "the engine-wright of Killingworth," as George Stephenson modestly called himself. Not that the people were much inclined to believe in the new wonder; for even an educated reviewer—one of the famous *Quarterly* writers—treated the whole matter with incredulity, stating that nothing could be more palpably absurd than the prospect held out of locomotives travelling twice as fast as stage coaches, and that people would as soon suffer themselves to be fired off upon one of Congreve's *ricochet* rockets as trust themselves to the mercy of a machine going at such a rate. They imagined all sorts of improbable difficulties; in some of the rural districts they were afraid lest the smoke of the iron horse should injure the fleeces of the sheep; others, as for instance

the now proverbial Member of Parliament, feared lest the straying of an occasional cow on to the line should prove an awkward obstacle to the train (to which, as everybody knows, the witty engineer replied that it *would* prove awkward,—"very awkward indeed—*for the coo!*"); others feared lest the sparks from the engine should set fire to the adjoining properties along the line; and all (the learned Lord Brougham, as we have recently heard, among the number) regarded the idea of travelling at more than eight miles an hour as a mere chimera.

There had been, twenty or thirty years earlier, among the old Soho circle, two men who implicitly believed in the ultimate success of steam locomotion. One of these was our townsman William Murdoch, who, as we know, had constructed a small locomotive during his residence in Cornwall, much to the astonishment of his neighbours; and an eccentric Cornishman named Richard Trevithick, who had seen Murdoch's engine, copied it, with some improvements, in 1802, and took out a patent for it. He afterwards exhibited it in London, on the very spot which was afterwards covered by the Euston terminus. An amusing story is told by Coleridge respecting Trevithick's engine. When the inventor was travelling with it to the port from whence it was shipped to London, he came in sight of a closed toll-gate, and immediately shut off steam, but the momentum was so great that the engine did not come to a stop until it reached the gate, which was opened with unaccustomed celerity by the gate-keeper.

"What have us got to pay here?" asked

Trevithick's companion and cousin, Andrew Vivian.

The poor toll-collector, who was trembling in every limb, while his teeth chattered in his head, after some moments of dumb fear, managed to cry out, "Na—na—na!"

"What have us got to pay, I say," repeated Vivian.

In 1832 the country was astonished by the proposal to construct a railway from London to Birmingham, for which a Bill was introduced into the House of Commons in the February of that year. The discussion on this stupendous undertaking was sustained with the utmost vigour, one pamphleteer "proving" (to his own satisfaction) "by facts, that it would never pay."

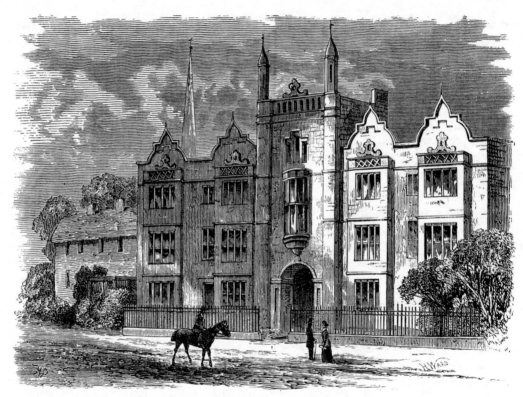

THE BIRMINGHAM AND EDGBASTON PROPRIETARY SCHOOL.

"No—noth—nothing to pay. *My dear Mr. De—Devil, d—do drive on as fast as you can!* Noth—nothing to pay!"

The other member of the Lunar Society at Soho who appears to have anticipated Stephenson's invention, was the erudite Dr. Darwin, who thus apostrophised the motor of the future, in his *Botanic Garden*, published in 1793 :

"Soon shall thy arm, unconquer'd Steam ! afar,
Drag the slow barge, or drive the rapid car ;
Or on the wide-waving wings expanded bear
The flying chariot thro' the fields of air !"

The Bill passed the Lower House successfully, but was rejected, in June, by the Lords. In the session of 1833 the application was renewed, and ultimately the Act was obtained, at a cost of £72,869.

In the following June the work of constructing the line was commenced, and was successfully completed in about four years,—a work involving, as has been shown, almost one-third greater amount of labour than did the construction of the Great Pyramid of Cheops, and which necessitated the removal of as much material as would encompass the earth more than three times with a band one foot high and three feet broad.

But while this great undertaking was in progress, another which fell but little short of it was set on foot. The first had already given promise of a successful line connecting our town with the metropolis, when the construction of a second line was projected, from Birmingham to Manchester, to be called the Grand Junction Railway. The royal assent was obtained for this line in 1833, and the work was completed in July, 1837, fourteen months earlier than the London and Birmingham line, and was therefore the first railway opened in the Midland Counties.

Early on Tuesday morning, July 4th, the town was in a state of commotion; before six o'clock the streets leading towards the railway terminus, were thronged with people, and from nearly every window hung flags and other decorations, while the strains of several bands of music gave evidence that even at that early hour the festivities of the day had already commenced. The *Birmingham Journal* of that day thus describes the scene :

At seven o'clock precisely in the morning, the bell rang, when the opening train, drawn by the 'Wildfire' engine, commenced moving. The train consisted of eight carriages, all of the first class, and bearing the following names :—the 'Greyhound,' tbe Swallow,' the 'Liverpool and Birmingham Mail,' the 'Celerity,' the 'Umpire,' the 'Statesman,' and the 'Birmingham and Manchester Mail.' The train started slowly ; but emerging from the yard [at Vauxhall] speedily burst off at a rapid rate. To those who for the first time witnessed such a scene it was peculiarly exciting, and the immense multitude, as far as the eye could reach, gave expression to their admiration by loud and long-continued huzzas, and the waving of hats and handkerchiefs.

Leaving the throng behind, the monster procession quickened its pace, and, instead of the ten or twelve miles an hour, soon began to afford the spectators a glimpse of the travelling of the future, running at a speed of not less than from thirty to thirty-five miles an hour. Later on in the morning a train of second-class carriages set out amidst similar demonstrations, and not long afterwards

the same attentions were bestowed upon the first train which arrived in Birmingham from Liverpool.

The people were not long in becoming accustomed to the new mode of travelling, and consequently when, in the following year, the London and Birmingham Railway was opened, there was considerably less excitement. The following paragraphs from the *Gazette* may serve to record the event :

August 27, 1838.—On Monday last the whole line of Railroad from this town to London was traversed by a train of four carriages, occupied by Directors and Shareholders. The party left the station, after partaking of breakfast, at half-past six o'clock in the morning, and arrived in London at about a quarter past one. An hour and a half was occupied in inspecting the tunnel at Kilsby and other interesting parts of the great work, so that the distance may be said to have been travelled in little more than five hours.

Sept. 17, 1838.—This morning the entire line of Railroad between this and London will be opened to the public. Birmingham will thus be brought within six if not five hours of the capital ; it remains only for those in this town, with whom is the power, to prepare such facilities of communication with the heart of the town as are requisite, and vast benefits cannot fail to result to all classes of the inhabitants.

A little later the Midland Railway was completed, connecting Birmingham and Derby; others of course soon followed, and of these we shall make record from time to time in our chronicle of local events. The two lines connecting Birmingham with London, Manchester, and Liverpool (and afterwards called the London and North Western Railway), and the Midland line, were centred in the terminus at Curzon Street, where a large and commodious block of buildings was erected to serve as a station and hotel. Meanwhile the public, who had at first looked upon the railway project with incredulity and fear, now veered completely round to the most unbounded exaggeration of the possibilities of steam locomotion. One of the most favourite hobbies of inventors and engineers, was to construct an engine which would run on common roads, and among the most successful projects of this description, was the steam coach constructed by the celebrated Dr. Church, who was at that time a resident in Birmingham. This vehicle, which carried forty persons, was used in the streets of Birmingham in 1833, and was doubtless one of the most practical attempts in that direction at that early period in the history of steam locomotion. In the same year the steam coach invented by Mr. Heaton also ran, and astonished the people by the speed and regularity of its movements, which were thus recorded in a local newspaper of the period :

The steam coach of Messrs. Heaton performed on Tuesday, August 7, with upwards of thirty passengers, the journey to Coventry and back with the same ease and expedition with which it last week travelled to Wolverhampton. Its average pace was eight miles an hour, including stoppages.

Experiments in this direction were not destined, however, to meet with general approval, being likely to prove dangerous to other traffic ; hence the attention of engineers and inventors was turned towards more practicable and profitable projects.

CHAPTER LXV.

POLITICAL HISTORY: 1833-1840.
Including the History of the Bull Ring Riots of 1839.

Re-action after the Reform Movement—The Irish Coercion Bill—Demonstration on Newhall Hill—Resuscitation of the Loyal and Constitutional Association—Conservative Activity—The Election of 1835—Conservative Banquet—Reform Banquet—Meeting on Newhall Hill—A "Woman's Political Union"—Death of the King, and consequent General Election—Riot in front of the Royal Hotel—Retreat of the Worcestershire Yeomanry—The Chartist Movement—The old policy of "Peace, Law, and Order" abandoned—Feargus O'Connor in Birmingham—The National Convention—Removal of the Convention to Birmingham—Turbulent Meetings—The Bull Ring Riots—Resignation of Mr. Attwood—Liberal Victory.

HAVING obtained the extension of the franchise, and the reform of electoral abuses, it may naturally be supposed that the people would now be contented and happy, and that the political historian of our town would have little to write concerning the few years that followed the excitement of 1832,—for it is during a period of unrest and dissatisfaction that political history is made ; political action is the outcome of oppression and abuses, and whenever oppression ceases and full liberty is granted, the book which records our political history may be closed. But political victory is not unfrequently followed by a reaction against the measure which has been obtained after so severe a struggle and such intense excitement ; and perhaps not unnaturally so. The public mind has been so completely concentrated upon the object for which the masses have been striving, that they had come almost to believe that, that object once achieved, all abuses will come to a speedy end,—that the measure for which they have striven will be a panacea for every ill.

So it was in the case of the Reform Bill. "Men had believed," says one writer, "that with the Reform Bill the influence of party would be subordinate to the public interest ; that legislation by the new House would make the country for ever prosperous ; that labour would be abundant, wages high, food cheaper than it ever had been before. There was no doubt great exaggeration in all this. The result of the elections showed that, much as democracy had gained, it had still more to obtain ; and the disappointment of the reality was proportioned to the extent of the anticipation. In Birmingham this was especially felt. The Ministers who had been glorified a few short months ago, became the objects of their distrust and anger."

The policy of the government on the Irish Coercion Bill first aroused the people on behalf of Irish liberty, and sent them once more into the field—the old battle ground of liberty, Newhall Hill,—on the 20th of May, 1833. It was surely the irony of events that, on that spot, the very people who had offered up thanksgiving for the return of Earl Grey, should, within a short twelve months, unanimously resolve to petition the king to dismiss the ministry they had themselves largely helped to place in power. It is said that more than 200,000 persons were present on this occasion; marching to the ground with flags and

The Petition to the Commons, from the same meeting, against all restrictions on the importation of animal and vegetable food, was presented, on Monday last, by Mr. Attwood; as also was one from the Council of the Union against the conduct of the police at the late Coldbath Fields Meeting."

This reaction against the ministers told with effect upon the Conservative party in Birmingham,

THE NEW ROYAL HOTEL NEW STREET.
Afterwards the Post Office and Inland Revenue Office.

banners, and a band of music. Amongst the members of the Political Council present, were Mr. Thomas Attwood, Mr. Muntz, and the Rev. T. M. McDonnell, accompanied by the liberator, Daniel O'Connell, Dr. Wade, and other friends of Ireland.

On the 1st of July we read, in *Aris's Gazette*, that :—

"Earl Fitzwilliam having declined presenting to his Majesty the Petition from the Newhall-hill Meeting, praying him to dismiss his Ministers, and his Lordship having returned it to the chairman, Mr. Muntz, accompanied with a letter of twelve pages, explaining his reasons for refusing, it has been determined to try Lord Melbourne.

which, during the heat of the reform movement, had hardly dared to show itself; a Tory could, indeed, scarcely avow himself in a public meeting without execration and insult; but the change in the public mind emboldened them to come out once more into the light, and to resuscitate the old Loyal and Constitutional Association, which had died a natural death in 1829. The Earl of Dartmouth was president, and the vice-presidents were the Earl of Bradford, Lord Calthorpe, the Hon. Frederick Calthorpe, Mr. W. S. Dugdale, M.P., and Mr. Gough; Mr. R. Spooner was chairman, and Mr. James Beswick, deputy chairman, and the Messrs. J. B. Hebbert, and George Whately, the secretaries. A "Declaration of Principle" was drawn up as follows, which every member was required to sign :

We, whose names are hereunto subscribed, declare our fixed determination to maintain the tried and antient principles on which the constitution of our country is established, and as members of this Association we hold ourselves pledged to resist all measures by which the connection between Church and State may be severed or relaxed—the dignity of the monarchy impaired, or its existence endangered—the efficiency of the House of Lords as an integral branch of the Legislature diminished, or the deliberative powers of the Commons' House of Parliament fettered or controlled ; as we are convinced that the independence of the established authorities is essential to the existence of social order, the security of property, and the interests of religion.

The association thus recalled to life, distinguished itself by considerable activity in various directions : in issuing addresses, inculcating their principles, organizing committees, attending to the registration of voters, advocating the church-rate question, and most especially preparing to contest the next election, resolving to attempt to wrest one, at least, of the seats for the borough from the Liberal party. At the end of the same year the opportunity arrived, and the Conservatives nominated as their candidate, Mr. R. Spooner. Everybody, except the parties concerned, regarded the attempt as hopeless, but they persisted in going to the poll, and did so, with the following result : Mr. Attwood, 1,718 ; Mr. Scholefield, 1,660 ; Mr. Spooner, 915. At the nomination, which took place on the 8th, of January, 1835, a somewhat serious accident occurred, which is thus recorded in the *Gazette* :

The greatest consternation was excited in consequence of a most alarming crash from the east end of the south gallery. In an instant persons were seen to be precipitated from the front of the gallery to the front of the hall, and, at the time, the general impression was that the gallery had given way. It appears, however, that owing to the number of persons who stood upon the uppermost bench, it gave way, and the natural consequence was that the occupiers of the bench were instantly thrown forward upon those in the front of them, and the effect extending to the seats in front of them, the weight became too powerful for the front of the gallery to withstand. The

panelling accordingly gave way, and several persons previously occupying seats in the front, were either precipitated or voluntarily jumped by way of safety, into the body of the hall and side galleries. Nothing could exceed the momentary alarm which the circumstance created ; and the confusion was so great that it was thought better, although Mr. Spooner had not concluded, that the Returning Officers should close the business by calling for a show of hands, which was declared to be in favour of Mr. Attwood and Mr. Scholefield. A poll was then demanded on behalf of Mr. Spooner, which was fixed to commence on the Friday morning. The meeting immediately separated.

The local political history of the year 1835, relates entirely to the Conservatives, who, notwithstanding their defeat at the election, still exhibited considerable activity. They held a great meeting to support Sir Robert Peel, and passed an address expressive of confidence in his government ; also a great meeting " of the friends of the Protestant Religion, and the Constitution in Church and State," on the 18th of November ; and on the 17th of December they celebrated their first anniversary, by dining together at the Town Hall, to the number of 848.

All the Conservative nobility, many of the clergy, and other influential inhabitants of the town and neighbourhood were present. " A few years before," said a writer in the *Birmingham Journal,* " such a gathering would have been impossible. Now they met in peace, in the very centre of the Reform agitation, and did not hesitate to denounce with boldness the principles and designs of their opponents."

At this meeting we meet with the first notice of " a new and most effective mode of cheering, called the Conservative or Kentish fire, which was quickly caught by the company, and all appeared to join in it with great glee." The Conservative reporter adds that—" it had a singular and pleasing effect from the galleries, and, we are told, was heard at a considerable distance from the hall."

But the Liberals did not mean to allow their opponents to have things entirely their own way, and on the 18th January, 1836, held a large meeting in the Town Hall, which was intended as "a demonstration which should overawe the House of Lords and perhaps the Throne itself." They adopted an address to the King, urging "an organic change in the constitution of the House of Lords," and a petition to the Commons in favour of "a more efficient measure of Corporation Reform." On the 28th of the same month a great Reform banquet was held in the Town Hall, at which no less that 900 persons sat down; amongst the guests were Joseph Hume, Sir William Molesworth, O'Connell, Sir J. Chetwynd, Sir Charles Wolseley, Mr. Attwood, Mr. Scholefield, the Hon. C. P. Villiers, and the Mayors of several of the surrounding towns. Among the toasts proposed were the following:

" *The People—and may they never forget to vindicate their rights and fulfil their duties.*"
" *The Reformers of the United Kingdom—and may they never forget that 'union is strength.'*"
" *The health of the Members for the borough.*"
" *Mr. Hume and the liberal and patriotic Members of the House of Commons, and the other distinguished Visitors who have honoured us with their presence.*"
" *The Borough of Birmingham, and may it speedily realise the benefit of a liberal and enlightened Corporation elected by the people.*"

On the following Monday, February 1st, about a thousand non-electors dined together at the same place, as a counter-demonstration to the recent gatherings of the Conservatives, who had claimed that *they* spoke the voice of the town.

The enthusiasm with which the Birmingham Liberals espoused the cause of the Irish, on all occasions, endeared the town and its people to the great liberator, who was a frequent visitor, and attended all the principal meetings of the party. On the 13th June, in this year, a public meeting was held in the Town Hall, under the presidency of the Low Bailiff, Mr. Tyndall—the High Bailiff, Mr. James, having declined to call it,—to take into consideration the position of the Irish Corporations Reform Bill, at which a petition, in favour of the Bill, was adopted, which received no fewer than 13,400 signatures in two days; and at the same time, in order to assist O'Connell in defending his seat for Dublin,

the sum of £100 was subscribed in five minutes!

The Conservatives were not idle during this period. They continued the issue of their gratuitous literature; they established a free library and news-room, the only qualification for readers being their adherence to the "Loyal and Constitutional Association"; they held frequent meetings, and, in fact, did everything within their power to arrest the progress of Liberal opinions.

In May, 1837, just before the death of William the Fourth, the Liberals formed themselves into a new Society, called the Reform Association, and on the 19th of June another great meeting was held on Newhall Hill, to inaugurate the movement. About fifty thousand persons were present, and considerable excitement prevailed; the dragoons were kept in readiness to mount, booted and saddled, and provided with ball cartridge. Happily, as on all previous occasions, military intervention was wholly unneeded; the proceedings were both loyal and orderly, commencing with a solemn prayer from the whole of the vast assembly, bareheaded, for the recovery of the King who lay dying. Mr. Attwood, Mr. Muntz, Mr. Salt, and Mr. Edmonds were present and addressed the meeting, and resolutions were passed in favour of household suffrage, the ballot, triennial Parliaments, payment of members, and the abolition of property qualifications. At the same time a "Woman's Political Union" was established, the business of which (as there is nothing new under the sun,—not even "woman's rights,") was entirely conducted by the softer sex, who held and addressed meetings, passed resolutions, raised subscriptions, and in other ways helped on the cause of political freedom.

The death of the King necessitated a general election, and the Conservatives again entered the field in order to win from the Liberals one of the seats for Birmingham. The Reform Association nominated the members who had served them faithfully ever since the enfranchisement of the town, Messrs. Attwood and Scholefield; and the

Conservatives selected as their candidate the Hon. A. G. Stapleton, and although the latter did not succeed he demonstrated that the party had somewhat improved its position. The polling took place on the 25th of July, with the following result:—Mr. Attwood, 2,165; Mr. Scholefield, 2,139; Mr. Stapleton, 1,049. The excitement on the polling-day was very great, and very nearly terminated in a riot. Large crowds of noisy and turbulent people met in front of the Royal Hotel, where Mr. Stapleton's Central Committee met, and ridiculed, in no measured terms, the defeated party. About half-past seven in the evening, some of the Conservatives attempted to drive away the people, who were probably not in the best humour to encounter opposition, after the drinking and general license which characterized election times in those days; and the crowd, becoming angry at the rather rough usage they received from their opponents, immediately hurled a shower of brickbats at the hotel windows, thereby doing considerable damage. Colonel Wallace, of the 5th Dragoons (then stationed at West Bromwich, in anticipation of a disturbance), seeing the state of affairs, went at once to Mr. Attwood's rooms, at the Clarendon Hotel, and requested him to use his influence to disperse the crowd. He went at once to the Royal Hotel, and taking his stand at one of the windows, addressed the excited throng, and ultimately persuaded them to desist from further disturbance and go to their homes in quietness. The Riot Act was then read in the presence of the few stragglers who remained, and the dragoons were drawn up in front of the hotel to preserve order.

The next morning the shattered windows of the hotel attracted a crowd of idle sight-seers, and among them a few mischievous lads, who, seeing a few windows which had escaped whole, and doubtless pained by the absence of uniformity of appearance, proceeded to smash them also. The Riot Act was therefore once more read, and Colonel Wallace again succeeded in appeasing

the crowd, when, at an inopportune moment, a troop of the Worcestershire Yeomanry appeared on the scene, and as they rode through the streets, attracted still larger crowds, hooting and pelting them with small pebbles, until they were compelled to take refuge in the Hen and Chickens yard; and at length, while Mr. Attwood attracted the attention of the crowd in New Street, the affrighted yeomanry managed to effect a retreat unscathed, down the back yard of the Hotel into Worcester Street. It was stated that they had been ordered to load with ball, and on the throwing of the first stone to fire upon the crowd; to which a Liberal paper boldly replied: "Yes, the crowd would have scampered. There would have been a ready victory; pistols to pebbles are a mighty odds. But the crowd would have re-assembled; *and they would have assembled in arms.* There are at least 100,000 muskets in Birmingham, and 40,000 men who know the use of them." Thanks, however, to the forbearance and tact of Colonel Wallace, and the influence of Thomas Attwood, such a catastrophe was averted, and the former well deserved the testimonial which the grateful people presented to him in acknowledgment of his gallant conduct.

Towards the close of this year, the Political Council of the Union issued an address to the Reformers throughout the kingdom, in which prominence was given to the chief points of "the Charter," viz.: Universal Suffrage, Voting by Ballot, and shorter Parliaments; adding that, with the general and hearty cooperation of Liberal, "the victory is won, even before the battle is joined. Are there any," they ask, "who will dare to stand against our united voices?" But alas! the cry was not taken up by the people in the old spirit of "peace, law, and order," this time! A few foolish leaders of the "Chartists" (as they called themselves from the "Charter" *

---

* The memorable 'five points' of this Charter were:—Universal Suffrage, Vote by Ballot, Annual Parliaments, Payment of Members and the Abolition of Property Qualifications.

FORWARD

RICHARD CHAMBERLAIN, ESQ.

PHOTOGRAPHED BY WHITLOCK.

BIRMINGHAM: HOUGHTON & CO., SCOTLAND PASSAGE.

which formed their programme), had affected to despise the old white "banner of strange device," and raised in its place the crimson folds of the force," in the presence of the peace-loving leaders of the Union, who denounced the scheme and condemned the doctrine. "No!" exclaimed

BISHOP RYDER'S CHURCH.

"physical force" flag, and "arms, arms, arms!" was now the cry of the dissatisfied and angry throng who met in the Town Hall of Birmingham, on Monday, January 15th, 1838. Again in November, the same cry was caught up, as Feargus O'Connor repeated the new formula of "physical

George Edmonds, in the heat of his righteous indignation,—"No, by the great God, the honest men of Birmingham will never stand it!"

But, unfortunately, the men of Birmingham had already been indoctrinated with the new principles; one hundred thousand of them had met at Holloway Head (one would imagine they had even yet some misgivings, and did not dare to desecrate the old meeting ground of Newhall Hill), on August 13th, and echoing the old Union cry of " the bill, the whole bill, and nothing but the bill," they demanded " the Charter, the whole Charter, and nothing but the Charter." It was in vain that any other reforms were suggested ; they did their utmost to stifle the Anti-Corn Law League at its very birth. The first great meeting held in Birmingham, on this question, on the 29th of January, 1839, was interrupted by the noisy cries of the Chartists, who would have "nothing less, nothing more," than their Charter. Ignoring the true remedy for the distress of that memorable year, they blindly followed the Chartist leaders, and soon succeeded, by their persistent advocacy of physical force, in repelling the really thoughtful and sensible amongst them. The Birmingham delegates to the National Convention (which was to supersede parliament),—Messrs. R. K. Douglas, Hadley, and Salt—withdrew therefrom in disgust at the violence of their colleagues ; and others, more violent but less known, were chosen in their stead. Sedition became the order of the day ; and torch-light meetings, and midnight drills, were as common as, ten or twelve years ago, they were among the Fenians in Ireland ; and at length the Government issued proclamations against them.

At length, the Metropolis being in a very exicited state, the Convention removed its sittings (or more properly speaking, *standings*) to Birmingham, where they attracted large crowds every evening, in the Bull Ring, during the last week in April, reading newspapers and delivering inflammatory addresses. Later on they met twice a day, during the dinner hour, and in the evening, impeding the traffic, causing most of the shop-keepers to close their places of business, and business itself to be completely suspended in that part of the town. Under these circumstances the magistrates did no more than their duty to the town, in issuing the following proclamation :—

" VICTORIA R.

" Whereas evil-disposed persons have of late held meetings, during the evening, in the Bull-ring, and then and there, by seditious harangues, have endeavoured to excite the people to violence and illegal proceedings ; and whereas such seditious speeches have, on several occasions, caused a large concourse of people, to the great alarm of her Majesty's subjects—we, the undersigned Magistrates, deem it our duty to command all persons to refrain from attending such meetings, as being contrary to law, and dangerous to the tranquillity of the borough ; and we further declare it to be our determination to prosecute all those who, after this notice, shall hold such meetings, or who, by inflammatory speeches, shall attempt to excite the people to any disturbance or breach of the peace.

William Scholefield, Mayor.

W. C. Alston	P. H. Muntz
S. Beale	C. C. Scholefield
T Bolton	C. Shaw
W. Chance	Joseph Webster
J. B. Davies	Joseph Walker

J. T. Lawrence.

Public Offices, May 10, 1839."

Several hundred special constables were sworn in, and a few of the leaders of the disturbance were arrested and escorted out of the town by a troop of dragoons ; but the meetings were continued with unabated vigour. "On Thursday night," says the *Journal* of June 27, " the Mayor addressed a few words to the people assembled, to induce them to disperse, and in the course of his address offered his influence to procure the Town Hall for one night in the week for popular meetings. The only result of this good-natured attempt, was the formation of a procession up New Street, along Colmore Row, and down Bull Street, and back to the Bull Ring, by which time it being the hour of ordinary breaking up, a breaking up took place."

And so matters continued until the beginning of July, the Chartists becoming bolder, and defying the magistrates, the police, and even the military. On the 4th of that month a body of London police was despatched to Birmingham, by railway, with orders to break up the meetings and arrest the leaders. A dense mass of people had gathered around Nelson's statue, and were just forming themselves into procession, to parade the town, when the police marched up Moor Street from the railway station with their staves in their hands, and rushed upon the crowd. What followed must be told by an eye-witness of the scene, the late Mr. James Jaffray :—

"The police," he says, "fought their way to the standard bearers and demolished the flags, whilst others knocked down all who opposed them. For the moment they partially cleared the Bull Ring, but the people rallied ; some tore down shutters of the shops in the neighbourhood ; others smashed them in pieces and supplied the crowd with bludgeons ; others again picked up heavy stones, and thus armed they returned to the charge. The police, who were by this time scattered, were surrounded and most of them overpowered. Some were knocked down, some kicked, some stabbed and stoned ; and had it not been for the arrival of the military the entire of them would have fallen a sacrifice to the fury of the people. Dr. Booth, however, accompanied by a troop of the 4th Royal Irish, and a company of the Rifle Brigade, having arrived on the spot at the moment, the Riot Act was read, and the struggle ceased. The crowd continued to increase, and many of them with arms of various kinds, seemed only anxious for an encounter. From fifteen to twenty of the London Police went into the Market Hall Tavern ; a large crowd followed, but the Riflemen soon dispersed them. Another body of the police went to the Grand Turk, the windows of which were demolished ; and the police would have been attacked there had not the soldiers arrived and once more dispersed the mob. Surgeons were speedily in attendance at the Public Office. The wounded police were brought in and dressed, and seven of the worst cases were removed to the Hospital. Two of the police had been stabbed, one in the abdomen and the other about the groin. Such of the police who were either only slightly or not at all hurt continued to patrol the Bull Ring along with the troops, and soon succeeded in taking into custody ten or twelve men, some of whom were armed with deadly weapons, while some of them had their pockets filled with stones. It was now

about eleven o'clock ; the crowd was still on the increase, and apparently determined on revenge. The troops, however, kept their temper admirably. The popular rage was, indeed, chiefly directed against the London police. The Magistrates rode up and down amongst the people, advising them to disperse, but without much effect. At length a cry of 'Holloway Head' was raised, and immediately some thousands marched off in that direction. They were addressed at Holloway Head by some person, who meant to appease the people and induce them to disperse quietly. It had but little effect, for, as if by one impulse, they moved off the ground, and proceeded to St. Thomas's Church. There they pulled down a range of about twenty yards of the iron railing which surrounded the building, broke the stones, and armed with the pieces of railings, and such other weapons as they could procure, they once more marched in divisions into the town. A large party proceeded to the Golden Lion, in Aston Street, from which house the members of the Convention, with the exception of Dr. Taylor, had just departed to their lodgings ; but no violence was done. Thus in comparative quiet passed the night of the 4th of July."

Early on the morning of the 15th, an injudicious placard was published, of which we give a copy, from a rare original in the possession of J. Lander, Esq. :—

RESOLUTIONS

Unanimously agreed to

BY THE

GENERAL

CONVENTION.

RESOLVED.—

"1st.—That this Convention is of opinion that a wanton, flagrant, and unjust outrage has been made upon the people of Birmingham, by a blood-thirsty and unconstitutional force from London, acting under the authority of men, who, when out of office, sanctioned and took part in the meetings of the people, and now when they share in the public plunder, seek to keep the people in social and political degradation.

"2nd.—That the people of Birmingham are the best judges of their own right to meet in the Bull Ring or elsewhere, have their own feelings to consult respecting the outrage given, and are the best judges of their own power and resources to obtain justice.

"3rd.—That the summary and despotic arrest of Dr. Taylor, our respected colleague, affords another convincing

Lovett, for signing this bill, and Collins for giving the order for printing it, were arrested and sentenced to twelve months imprisonment in Warwick Gaol.

INTERIOR OF ST. CHAD'S CATHEDRAL, BATH STREET.

proof of the absence of all justice in England, and clearly shows that there is no security for life, liberty, or property, till the people have some control over the laws they are called on to obey."

BY ORDER,

W. LOVETT,

Friday, July 5th, 1839.   Secretary,

The disturbances continued throughout Saturday, Sunday, and Monday, at intervals, but no serious damage was done, and when, at eight o'clock on Monday evening, the streets were cleared by the police, supported by the military, no further trouble was anticipated; the more especially as the remainder of the week was passed in tranquillity, except for the occasional political meetings which took place at Holloway Head. Three meetings were held on Sunday, the 14th, in the same locality, and it was rumoured that a fourth would be held at Smithfield in the evening; but this proved to be a false alarm, and the day ended, as had those of the foregoing week, without disturbance.

On the Monday morning, the neighbourhood of the Public Office was thronged by the Chartists and their supporters, anxious to learn the fate of the three prisoners, Harvey, Lovett, and Collins. The investigation was continued up to four o'clock, after which Lovett and Collins were liberated on bail, on learning which the throng dispersed quietly, and it seemed that once more order and confidence were restored. But this proved only to be the lull which preceded the storm. At seven o'clock the Bull Ring was once more crowded with persons, who seemed to have been brought together with the expectation of witnessing some pre-arranged event, but who nevertheless exhibited the utmost orderliness in their behaviour, insomuch that there seemed not the slightest necessity for interference on the part of the authorities. What they were evidently anticipating, however, may best be described in the following narrative, written by Mr. James Jaffray a few years after the events :—

"Shortly after eight o'clock," he says, "a mob of persons, to the number of about 500 were seen coming up Digbeth, armed with pieces of iron, wooden railings, and other weapons. On their arrival at Moor Street, they turned down to the Prison, and immediately commenced a furious attack upon the windows, almost all of which they demolished. The policemen who were inside closed the gates, having, it appears, orders not to act against the people without instructions from the Magistrates. The mob having demolished the office windows, and dared the police to an

encounter, retraced their steps, and immediately commenced an attack upon the windows in the long range of building, on the premises of Messrs. Bourne, grocers. After smashing every pain in the buildings which is five storeys high, with a frontage of about 40 feet, they divided themselves into parties, and commenced the work of destruction in good earnest. One party, at a quarter to nine o'clock, burst in the shop-door of Messrs. Bourne's house, and immediately commenced destroying the property. Tea, sugar, and every article they could lay their hands upon were thrown into the street, the canisters kicked out amongst the rioters, and the whole frontage battered in. The shopmates and inmates were paralysed, and fled out of the house by the side and other doors. Whilst this work of devastation was going on, another party effected their entrance into the shop of Mr. Leggett, feather dealer and upholsterer, and having got possession of a number of pieces of bed-ticking, some of them rushed into the street with them, and spread them like carpenting in all directions about the Bull Ring.

"Having placed the linen in this manner upon the pavement, one of the rioters deliberately went to a lamp at Nelson's Monument, and having lighted a piece of paper, he set fire to the ticking. When in flames it was rolled up into a heap, opposite the Monument, and from thence carried in different portions into the shops of Messrs. Bourne and Leggett. The fire almost instantaneously seized the counters and paper, and in a few minutes the buildings were in flames. The objects of the rioters were now so obvious that the concourse who had assembled in the Bull Ring became evidently alarmed, and dispersed, leaving the rioters in full possession of the leading streets.

"The attack was continued on the house of Mr. Arnold, pork butcher, nearly opposite the monument. They were, however, repulsed there, and did not succeed in firing the house. Other parties in the interim forced open the shops of

Mrs Martin, jeweller, next to Messrs. Bourne's, Mr. Banks, druggist, Mr. Savage, cheese factor, Mr. Arthur Dakin, grocer, Mr. Horton, silversmith, Mr. Gooden, Nelson Hotel, Mrs. Brinton, pork butcher, Mr. Allen, biscuit baker, Mr. Heath, cheese factor, and Mr. Scudamore, druggist. The front window of Mrs. Martin's house was completely smashed in, and all the property within reach, consisting of gold rings and jewellery, were thrown about, and a portion of them stolen. Mr. Banks's shop-window was broken in, and a great deal of property destroyed. The shop windows of the other above-named houses were stove in, and the windows in many of the rooms smashed. The attack upon Mr. Horton's shop was the most furious. The property, consisting of almost every species of manufactured silver and silver-plated goods, was thrown into the street, and scattered about, and even employed in smashing the windows of the adjoining houses. Some of the property was carried away, but a great portion of it was broken to pieces and kicked through the streets. The Nelson Hotel suffered greatly. The shutters of the coffee-room were completely destroyed, as well as the front of the liquor shop, and nearly all the windows in front of the house. A piece of burning timber was placed against one of the windows of the liquor shop, but it was removed before the wood of the building ignited. The work of devastation occupied until about twenty minutes to ten o'clock, when the police, and soon after the military, arrived, and the rioters fled in all directions. The Birmingham, District, and Norwich Fire Engines soon after arrived, some of them under the escort of the 4th Dragoons, and a good supply of water having been procured, they commenced playing with great effect, and happily confined the flames to the premises of Messrs. Bourne and Leggett.

" The confusion and alarm of the night were terrible. Many of the inhabitants in the Bull Ring and neighbourhood fled with their families, account books, and such portion of their valuable property as could be easily conveyed away. Mr. Belcher, who lived in the house adjoining Mr. Leggett's premises, and two ladies, escaped by means of a ladder. Detachments of the troops and rifle brigade were sent in all directions to clear the streets ; and the most fearful apprehensions were entertained that other parts of the town would be attacked in a similar manner. Nothing however of the kind occurred, and with the exception of the above outrage, which had been attended with the loss of many thousand pounds worth of property, the night passed over without further violence. By one o'clock the fire in Messrs. Bourne's premises was subdued, but not until the front building was a complete wreck, nothing being left standing except the walls. The fire in Mr. Leggett's house was extinguished about the same time, but the engines continued playing until three o'clock, when they returned to their respective offices. The whole of the men, assisted by a number of the inhabitants, worked with great skill and energy, and to their exertions may be attributed the fortunate termination of the fire. Several men and boys were arrested upon and after the arrival of the troops, and the prison in Moor Street was literally filled with them. Many of the parties were of course taken upon slight grounds, owing to the anxiety to apprehend the real offenders.

" The morning following—that of Tuesday—the town presented a most gloomy appearance. The shops in the principal streets were closed, and continued so during the day. Dragoons and riflemen were stationed at the top of High Street, leading down to the Bull Ring, in Digbeth, at the bottom of Spiceal Street, and at the end of Moor Street, leading into Dale End. The police and special constables patrolled the street, and the town had all the appearance of being under siege. The officers of the town were actively engaged in searching suspected houses for the property carried away the night before, but were unsuccessful. A search was also made in some of the lanes and courts for pikes, or such other weapons as might be in the possession of suspicious characters, and some few were found. At the close of the public business that day, the magistrates retired to their private room, where they and several others of the bench remained. As the evening advanced, fears were entertained that the night would not pass off quietly, and these apprehensions were enhanced by an announcement that a large body of Chartists were assembled at Holloway Head. The Magistrates issued a short but significant placard announcing that the Riot Act had been read, and another calling on the special constables to attend at their different wards The military were on duty in various parts of the town, and every precaution was taken to prevent a recurrence of the scenes of the previous night. Several manufacturers who were apprehensive of danger, had their premises guarded by men well armed, and had any further attempt been made on property, the assailants would not have escaped with impunity. By eight o'clock the shops were all closed, and the streets comparatively deserted, the peaceable inhabitants having remained in their dwellings. Shortly after eight o'clock Colonel Thorn and Colonel Chatterton, at the head of two troops of dragoons and a piece of ordnance, galloped at full speed from the barracks up Dale End, through High Street, up Paradise Street, and Broad Street to Holloway Head, where about 400 Chartists had been meeting. Before the arrival of the troops on the ground a detachment of riflemen had reached the field, and the Chartists had immediately scattered in all directions. The cavalry, under the direction of Mr. Alston, scoured the neighbourhood; and they and the foot soldiers took a number of men prisoners on and near the ground. Having conveyed them to prison, the troops proceeded to clear the streets and alleys, and arrested many persons found out of their houses. By nine o'clock the town was perfectly tranquil. The special constables and policemen still remained on duty, but the soldiers at an early hour were enabled to retire to their barracks. To guard against any attack in the suburbs the Yeomanry were stationed in various directions, and a large body of troops surrounded the town, ready to gallop in at any point, if required. These precautions had the desired effect. The town continued throughout the night in perfect repose; confidence to a considerable extent was restored, and the following morning numerous parties of all classes visited the Bull Ring, to see the ruins."

Many of the participators in the riots were apprehended and committed for trial at the Assizes, which were held in the following month. Four persons were condemned to death, viz., Howell, Roberts, Jones, and a boy named Aston, for the attack on Messrs. Bourne's; but all were reprieved and transported for life. Five were sentenced to imprisonment with hard labour for eighteen months; one to twelve months; one to nine months; three to six months; and one to one month's imprisonment. Lovett and Collins, as we have already stated, were each imprisoned for twelve months, for publishing the " inflammatory and seditious placard." Claims were allowed to the amount of £15,027, and the entire costs of the riots were not less than £20,000, to defray which two rates of £11,000 and £9,000 respectively were levied on the hundred.

At the close of the year 1839 Mr. Attwood resigned his seat, and accepted the Chiltern Hundreds, to the grief of all true liberals, who would have wished to see him retain a position he had earned so nobly and filled so well. The liberal party in Birmingham was divided in its choice on this occasion, and nominated two candidates to fill the vacant seat—Mr. Joseph Sturge and Mr. G. F. Muntz. Mr. Sturge, however, who had the support only of a minority of the party, wisely withdrew, and thus enabled Mr. Muntz to obtain an easy victory over his opponent, Sir Charles Wetherell; the numbers being—for Mr. Muntz 1454, for Sir Charles Wetherell, 915.

With this record of another successful election contest for the liberal party, we close the present chapter of our political history.

CHAPTER LXVI.

THE CHURCHES AND SECTS IN BIRMINGHAM, 1831—1840.

Church Building—All Saints'—Bishop Ryder's—St. James's, Edgbaston--St. Matthew's—Progress of Catholicism in Birmingham—Proposed New Cathedral- -Opening of St. Chad's—Description of the Building—New Presbyterian Chapel, Broad Street—Methodist Conference in Birmingham—Spring Hill College—Tercentenary of the Reformation.

In the last decade of the religious history of our town we had to record the erection of several large and commodious churches out of the fund provided for parliamentary grant for that purpose but in the present chapter we have to tell of no such assistance in making provision for the spiritual welfare of the people. Yet the work of the church-building was not impeded on this account : private enterprise stepped in, and made up for the lack of State aid, and we have the pleasure of recording, as the work of this decade, the erection of three new churches in the town.

The first of these was All Saints', erected on what was then known only as Birmingham Heath, although it was the centre of what was already becoming a very largely populated district, promising soon to connect the midland metropolis with the great " black country " beyond. As in the case of most of the churches erected subsequent to the Georgian era, All Saints' is built in the Gothic style. Although of plain materials —the main portion of the building is of brick, the pinnacles and cornices being of stone, at a cost of £3,817, exclusive of boundary wall ; and the church was consecrated September 28, 1833. It contains 1,200 sittings, of which 700 are free.

Our readers will remember that at the close of our last chronicle of public life and events, we recorded the formation of a new and important thoroughfare, Great Lister Street, rendered necessary by the rapid growth of the town on that side. Most of the inhabitants of this new locality were therefore, at this period, without church accommodation ; and this deficiency happily attracted the attention of the estimable Bishop of Lichfield, Dr. Ryder, and by his influence and example, other wealthy neighbours were stimulated to assist, with their subscriptions and by advocating the cause, in erecting a church for this large and poor neighbourhood. In grateful remembrance of the good bishop's kindly and disinterested help, the church was called after his name. It is a neat Gothic structure of brick and stone, relieved from the usual monotony of red-brick Gothic, however, by the handsome tower, which is to some extent a copy of that of the celebrated St. Botolph's, at Boston, Lincolnshire.

Dec. 24, 1838.—On Tuesday last the interesting ceremony of publicly dedicating this edifice to the service of Almighty God was performed, in the presence of a large and most respectable congregation, by the Lord Bishop of Rochester.

During the same month a new church was opened at Edgbaston, provided by the munificence of Lord Calthorpe :—

Dec. 3, 1838.—The elegant Chapel, [St. George's,] recently erected at Edgbaston by Lord Calthorpe, with a view to the supplying of the additional accommodation so much required for the purposes of public worship by the inhabitants of that parish, was consecrated by the Right Rev. the Lord Bishop of Worcester on Wednesday morning last. The site of this truly beautiful edifice was the gift of the Noble Lord, and the structure itself was erected by his Lordship at the expense of nearly £6,000, with the exception of £500 bequeathed by the late Mr. Wheeley. Lord Calthorpe, in addition, has very handsomely endowed the building, and provided the communion plate, service books, &c., &c. For the use of the poorer inhabitants two hundred free sittings are reserved ; and the remainder are to be rented, according to their various situations, at 20s., 16s., and 12s. per annum.

The patronage of the Chapel, we understand, is vested in the noble donor, Lord Calthorpe, the Ven. Archdeacon Spooner, and Mr. Thomson, of London; and the Rev. Isaac Spooner, son of Richard Spooner, Esq., has been appointed the first incumbent.

August 27, 1837.—On Wednesday last, during the assembling of the clergy and gentry who took part in the procession at the laying of the foundation stone of Bishop Ryder's Church, in this town, a very beautiful medallion of the size of life of the late Bishop, the work of our townsman, Mr. Peter Hollins, was exhibited at the Blue Coat School. Many of the Bishop's friends who were present, including the Rev. John Kempthorne, Chaplain

done, in building several churches in large districts unprovided for, and in indicating to others who were capable of completing the project, suitable fields of labour. The first church efforts of the society were directed towards the neighbourhood for which Bishop Ryder's had already made partial provision,—the new district called Duddeston, extending from Gosta Green to the outskirts of the town on the Saltley side. The great artery of this district, Great Lister

SPRING HILL COLLEGE.

to his Lordship when he presided over the See of Gloucester, pronounced the likeness, considering the circumstance under which it was produced (being altogether a posthumous work), a most extraordinary resemblance. It is a profile in low relief, and is intended to form part of the monument to be placed in the parish church of Lutterworth, where the pious and worthy successor of *Wickliffe* was for many years the affectionate and beloved minister.

During the year 1838 a new church-building association was formed,—chiefly through the exertions of the Rev. John Garbett, the Rural Dean—bearing the name of the Birmingham Church Society; its object being to aid in erecting ten new churches in the town. The entire programme of the society, however, was not carried out; but much good work was nevertheless

Street, was selected as the locality of the new church, of which the first stone was laid on the 12th of October, 1839, by the Bishop of Nova Scotia; and the building was consecrated October 20th, 1840. It is an exceedingly plain Gothic structure of red brick, with a neat stone spire, and has, we believe, a good organ, built by Halkshaw; the east window, of stained glass, was presented by the architect, Mr. Thomas, of Leamington. The church is dedicated to St. Matthew.

Passing to the history of other denominations during this decade, the first and most important addition to the church accommodation of our town, to be recorded in this chapter, is that of the long-talked-of Roman Catholic Cathedral. The building of this great central cathedral of the English Catholics was first proposed in 1834, and the earliest notice of the movement appeared in the local newspapers at the end of January in that year. The *Gazette* referred to the work in the following paragraph :—

January 27, 1834.—It will be seen by a notice in this page, that the practicability of erecting a Roman Catholic Cathedral in this town is under consideration. Dr. Walsh, Vicar Apostolic of the Midland district, presided at a meeting held in St. Peter's Chapel, yesterday week, and various resolutions to that end were entered into. Among those who took part in the proceedings were the Rev. Messrs. M'Donnell and Peach, Messrs. Hardman, Tidmarsh, Palmer, Hopkins, Brien, Green, Boultbee, Bridge, Chambers, and Hansom—the latter of whom stated that he was sure they might set up a building which would outvie any place of worship in the town. The Right Rev. Chairman expressed his intention of giving £200 to the fund, and a monthly contribution of one pound towards payment of the interest of money to be borrowed. Mr. M'Donnell said he should put down his name for £20, and for half a sovereign per month until the building is completed. Other persons present also promised pecuniary assistance toward the object.

The site selected for the building was that of the little chapel of St. Chad, in Shadwell Street, erected in 1813; an extended area being obtained, with a frontage to Bath Street, by the demolition of a number of the surrounding houses. The building was consecrated, with great pomp and solemnity, in the presence of the whole of the English Catholic hierarchy and nobility, and many of the most distinguished foreign bishops. These, in their mitres, with the rich dresses of their several orders, and youths bearing lights and lilies, preceded and followed the procession, forming one of the most magnificent ecclesiastical spectacles ever witnessed in England. We quote the following interesting description of the cathedral :—

"St. Chad's Cathedral stands at the meeting of Bath Street and Shadwell (Chad-well) Street. With the exception of the front towards Bath Street, St. Chad's is a very plain building externally. The material is red brick with stone dressings. The style throughout is Middle

Pointed. The front towards Bath Street is about seventy feet wide. A resemblance is traced by the Rev. W. Greaney, the historian of St. Chad's, between the west front of St. Chad's and the west front of the church of St. Elizabeth at Marburg in Hesse-Cassel. This front of St. Chad's is divided by buttresses into three compartments, the central division, containing the entrance doorways with a window of six lights over them, surmounted by a gable some eighty feet in height from the pavement ; the side compartments each containing a very lofty window, and carried upwards in the form of a tower with slender spire. The height to the summits of these spires is one hundred and fifty feet, eighty-five feet of which are occupied by the towers. From the fact that the buttresses die in the wall below the belfry stage, these towers have a somewhat meagre appearance : an effect from which Pugin does not appear to have shrunk, as he repeated it at St. Wilfrid's, Cotton Hall, near Cheadle. The western doorways are divided by a central pillar, which supports an image of our Lady and the Holy Child under a canopy, which occupies the apex of the tympanum of the containing arch, the side spaces of which are filled with adoring angels, one on either side. The doorways have 'shouldered' arches. The doors are of oak, with scroll hinges and other fittings carefully wrought. On a level with the height of the doors the mouldings of the first offset of the buttresses are carried along the basement of the towers, so that the canopied niches, with figures, that fill the lower spaces of the two narrow and lofty windows of the towers that range with the great western window of the nave, rest upon these mouldings. The great window is transomed, and its head is filled with tracery consisting chiefly of three large roses, with lesser circles and quatrefoils.

"The general plan of the church is cruciform, composed of nave with aisles, a transept, and an apsidally terminated choir, with two lateral chapels. Beneath the cathedral is an extensive crypt. The length of the church, including the porch, is 156 feet, the breadth 58 feet, the internal height 75 feet. The nave is divided from its aisles by six clustered columns on either side. There is no clerestory, and the roof is carried without break over nave and aisles. The braces are carved, and the principals, tie-beams, and other framing dressed and chamfered. The roof was painted and decorated at the expense of the congregation in 1844. The aisle windows, which, like those in the western faces of the towers, are lengthy, are of two lights with circles in the head. Against the great south-eastern pillar of the nave, at the junction of the nave with the transept, is the pulpit, a splendid specimen of oak carving, brought from the church of St. Gertrude, at Louvain, in Belgium, and presented to St. Chad's by the Earl of Shrewsbury. It is hexagonal, and has four of its sides adorned with foliage and tabernacle work, and seated figures of the four great doctors of the Latin Church. The gallery over the western porch was built for the organ and choir; but when a surpliced choir was established in 1854, the organ was removed to over the sacristy, and the west gallery became a tribune.

"The glass in the windows of the nave next demands attention. In the north aisle is the glassworkers' window, presented to St. Chad's by Mr. Hardman's workmen in 1854. The figure to the left of the spectator is St. Luke, the Evangelist, the patron of painters; that to the right, St. Andrew of Crete, another patron of this profession. Below, four workmen—all of whom are portraits—are represented. One is sketching, a second cutting glass, a third painting it, whilst a fourth is burning it.

"In the same aisle, in the bay immediately to the west of the baptistry, is a window erected in memory of Mr. T. Fitzherbert-Brockholes (son of Mr. W. Fitzherbert-Brockholes, of Claughton Hall, Lancashire), who died June 19th, 1851, aged 48 years. To the left of the spectator is St. Francis of Assisi, with the Fitzherbert arms

underneath. To the right is St. Thomas, Apostle, with the Brockholes arms below. In the sexfoiled circle over the lights is a figure of St. Cecilia, given to St. Chad's by Herr Benz, formerly organist of this cathedral, and now capellmeister at the Cathedral of Spires.

"In the south or St. Thomas's aisle, the second window westward of the transept is a stained-glass memorial one of Mr. and Mrs. Wareing, the former of whom died suddenly in St. Chad's, at High Mass on Passion Sunday, 1844. The principal figures are those of the Blessed Virgin and of St. George, under lofty canopies.

"The tower and spire over the crossing have never been built. Their design was in close conformity with that of the western steeples, although necessarily their dimensions were greater. The western towers have two windows of one light in each face of the belfry stage; the central tower was to have two of two lights in each face.

"The Flanagan window in the south transept was erected to the memory of the Very Rev. Thomas Canon Flanagan, who died at Kidderminster, July 21st, 1865. He was author of 'History of the Church of England,' 'Manual of English History,' and other works, and was at the time of his death one of the clergy attached to St. Chad's Cathedral. The window represents the life of St. Thomas of Canterbury, and miracles wrought at his shrine.

"The Walsh Monument is placed under the great window of the north transept. It was executed from the designs of Mr. E. W. Pugin. The material is Bath stone. The figure of Bishop Walsh, in pontificals, with crozier and mitre, is in a recumbent posture. In front of the tomb are shields with the arms of the bishop, the cathedral, Oscott College, St. Edward the Confessor, and of Bishop Walsh (repeated). The tomb is surmounted by an elaborate canopy. The dossal is diapered, and has a quatrefoil in the centre with a small figure of Bishop Walsh offering his Cathedral of St. Chad. The tomb is protected by an iron railing, with sconces for lights at the dirge on the bishop's anniversary. Bishop Walsh was Vicar Apostolic of the Central District for twenty-two years, and founder of St. Chad's; he died Vicar Apostolic of the London District, February 18th, 1849. His monument at St. Chad's was erected the year following by public subscription.

"Over Bishop Walsh's monument is the finest

head of the child, presented to St. Chad's by Dr. Moore in 1846. . . . . We now approach the most striking and solemn portion of St. Chad's—the chancel. This division of the cathedral is forty-five feet in length, and twenty-six feet in width. Formerly the choir extended only as far as the chancel-arch, but when the stalls were set apart exclusively for the cathedral canons,

INTERIOR OF THE MARKET HALL.

window in St. Chad's, presented by the Messrs. Hardman to the church. An elaborate account will be found in the work of the Rev. W. Greaney (pp. 56-62), to which we must needs refer the reader, as transcription of it would pass the fair bounds of literary obligation. The Hardman window was placed in St. Chad's in August, 1868.

"The baptistry opens from the north aisle. It has a large font for the baptismal water, and a smaller one to receive the water flowing from the

and a surpliced choir introduced, the choir was extended into the nave. The chancel is separated from the transept by a rich screen of open work, eighteen feet in height, formed by eight upright shafts enclosing seven open spaces, spanned by six cusped arches of equal, and one (the central) of greater, width, and forming a doorway closed with folding gates of eight open traceried panels above, and eight close beneath. The arches of the screen are surmounted by crocketed gablets, whilst the shafts are carried up as graceful finials.

Over all is a cornice crowned by a pierced parapet bearing standard for tapers. Upon a species of stage rising from the rood-gallery is the crucifix with attendant figures of St. Mary and St. John.

"The high altar and reredos are of stone. The baldachino or canopy over it is of wood, carved with flowers and angel cusps. Around the altar itself are four pillars, twelve feet in height, each composed of four large and four smaller shafts, with foliaged caps, the larger bearing figures of angels, each holding a standard and wax light ; the smaller surmounted by figures of bishops in pontificals coloured and gilded. The canopy is richly diapered and gilded. Beneath it, on the top of the stone reredos, is an enriched oaken case, painted and gilded, containing the remaining relics of St. Chad, Bishop of Lichfield (A.D. 669-672), and patron of this Cathedral Church. The three windows of the apse are divided into two lights, each containing two full length figures. The two figures on the upper part of the window on the Gospel side are St. John the Evangelist and St. Peter, and in the lower St. Michael and St. Edmund. In the centre window over the altar are the Blessed Virgin and St. Chad. The two figures in the upper part on the Epistle side are St. Paul and St. Joseph, and in the lower part St. Edward the Confessor and St. Edward, King and martyr. The stained glass of these windows was copied for the most part from ancient examples at Bristol Cathedral and Tewkesbury Abbey, and was a gift of the Earl of Shrewsbury. On either side of the chancel is a row of fifteenth-century stalls, with misereres of Flemish workmanship, formerly in the ancient church of Santa Maria, in Capitolio at Cologne. The canopy over the episcopal throne is from a design by Pugin. It is nearly thirty feet in height, and terminates in crocketed finials. Amongst its ornaments is a figure of St. Chad in pontificals. The bishop's choir stall is on the Epistle side, the lower part and priedieu correspond with the stalls, but the canopy is—as that of the throne—of Pugin's design. Round the walls, under the eastern win-

dows, runs the legend : 'Ecce tabernaculum Dei cum hominibus et habitabit cum eis, et ipsi populus ejus erunt.' On the walls of the chancel and of the body of the church may be seen the twelve 'consecration crosses,' to which lights are attached on the anniversary of the dedication of the church. The *lampadarium*, suspended from the ceiling by chains, is of carved wood, painted and gilt. It bears the legend : 'Adoremus in æternum sanctissimum sacramentum.' Three lamps hang from it. The *lectorium*, of solid brass, was a gift of the Earl of Shrewsbury. It formerly belonged to the collegiate church of St. Peter at Louvain.

"The Lady Chapel is on the Gospel side of the altar. It is separated from the transept by a carved oak screen, consisting of a central door-way and four compartments of open tracery, surmounted by crocketed pediments with pinnacles between them. There is a figure of the Blessed Virgin over the centre arch. The altar and reredos are of carved stone. In front of the altar are three groups, that in the centre representing the Nativity, with the Presentation on the north side, and the Adoration of the Magi on the south. Our Lady is in the centre of the reredos, with the Visitation on the south side, and the Annunciation on the north. Below these groups are four single figures, St. Mary Magdalene, St. Barbara, St. Cecilia, and St. Catherine. The tabernacle is of gilt metal-work, with the emblems of the four Evangelists in enamel. The floor of the Lady Chapel is laid with Minton's tiles. On a pedestal to the left of the Lady Chapel is an ancient carved oak figure of the Blessed Virgin, from Germany, presented to St. Chad's by the architect. . . In the north window of the Lady Chapel—which is of two lights—is depicted the Annunciation. Below each of these figures is a group of children, four in number, enclosed in a quatrefoil, those on the left of the spectator being boys, those on the right girls. The legends run : 'Per infantiam tuam, libera nos, Jesu ;' 'Sanca Virgo Virginum, ora pro nobis.' This window was the gift of the boys and girls of St. Chad's Poor Schools in 1844. As the windows in the chancel, these windows are by W. Warrington, from designs by Pugin.

"As St. Chad's stands upon a declivity, the east end in Shadwell Street being twenty feet lower than the entrance at the west end in Bath Street, the architect constructed a crypt or undercroft—dedicated to St. Peter—beneath the whole of the upper church. Only a part is as yet made use of. The solemn appearance of the crypt is much aided by all its windows being filled with stained glass. The crypt is divided into several chantries, four of them painted, and employed as oratories of the Hardman, Waring, Poncia, and Fletcher families. Previous to 1875, these and other lateral chapels were used for burials. There are memorials in the crypt—of Rev. Edward Peach, Rector of St. Chad's, who died in 1829; of the Rev. Charles McDonnell, Provincial of the Franciscan Order in England, who died in 1843, aged 72; of the Rev. Joseph Carpue, of the chapel of the Spanish Embassy, London, who died in April, 1849; of the Rev. Joseph Lycett, who died at Solihull, March 15, 1853; and of Very Rev. Canon Moore, who died in June, 1856."

Near St. Chad's is the Bishop's house, erected by the same architect, as the residence of the bishop and the officiating clergy. . . . . . "A residence (says Pugin) which, both in its ecclesiastical character and extent of accommodation, is in all respects suited for the occupation of the bishops and clergy, and also for transacting the increased business of the district, has been erected for a sum which does not involve a greater annual outlay than would have been required for two large modern houses, which must have been destitute of every requisite for this important purpose."

While the churches of the Establishment were thus flourishing and increasing in number, and the Church of Rome had made the greatest stride since their establishment in the town, the protest-ant dissenters do not seem to have made any great progress during this decade.

In May, 1839, the foundation stone was laid of an Independent Chapel in Wheeler Street, Lozells; and in the same month the Unitarian chapel and school buildings on Newhall Hill were commenced.

A small Presbyterian chapel was erected in 1834, on the site afterwards occupied by a larger building of the same character in Broad Street.

While the dissenters were thus inactive, for a time, in the work of chapel building, however, two of the more prominent sects were busy in other ways. The Independents during this period established a college for the training of young men for their ministry, and the Methodists, in 1836, held their annual general Conference in the town.

The Independent College was, we believe, suggested in the first instance by the Rev. Timothy East, of Ebenezer Chapel, Steelhouse Lane, to George Storer Mansfield, Esq., who gave some landed estates for that purpose; to which he and his sisters, Miss Glover and Miss Mansfield (who resided on Spring Hill), set aside a considerable sum of money for the support of the institution. Being anxious that it should be established during their lifetime, the ladies, with the most praiseworthy self-sacrifice, resigned their own dwelling-house for that purpose, and "Spring Hill College" was opened in 1838, for the reception of students, and thirteen young men at once entered the institution and commenced their studies. The college was afterwards affiliated with the University of London and is empowered to send students there to take their degrees. A good library was provided for their use, and, besides the theological tutor, two others were engaged, the one for philosophy, and the other for biblical and classical philology. But the full development of the college, placing it on a level with the best institutions of the kind in the kingdom, did not take place until after its removal to Moseley; this part of its history we shall have to leave to be recorded in a future chapter, at its proper date.

We close this chapter of the religious history of our town with a notice of an interesting celebration ; that of the Tercentenary of the Reformation :

September 28, 1835.—At a General Meeting of the Clergy of this town, held on Wednesday last, the following resolutions on the subject of solemnising the Third Centenary of the Reformation were unanimously adopted :—

1st. That as there is manifested throughout the kingdom an intention of solemnising the 4th of October next (falling on the Sabbath) as the day in the year 1535, when the first entire English version and publication of the Bible were accomplished, by Miles Coverdale, Bishop of Exeter, it is their duty to observe that day as a day of Thanksgiving to Almighty God for the blessings of the Reformation, and of prayer for the continuance of them.

2nd. That in case no prescribed form be issued by authority for the purpose, the Clergy feel it to be their duty to call upon their respective congregations and parishioners to observe it privately, and that they should make the blessings of the Reformed Religion a prominent feature of their Sermons in the ministration of the day, determined, however, to keep the question entirely clear of every political bias ; and lastly,—

That suitable hymns be selected and printed for the occasion, and a cheap medal be struck to commemorate the celebration, to be presented to the Sunday School Children and Teachers. In accordance with the latter part of this recommendation, medals, we understand, have been struck, and hymns prepared to assist in a devout and grateful celebration of the day. There appears now to be no doubt but that the event will be generally celebrated throughout the country, and in many places collections will be made for the relief of the distressed Irish Clergy.

October 12, 1835.—The third Centenary of the Reformation, on Sunday, the 4th inst., was generally observed in this town. Sermons appropriate to the day were delivered in the various Churches and Chapels of the Establishment, and in several of the Dissenting Meeting Houses. Congregations so large and attentive have seldom been simultaneously assembled, and the occasion was rendered memorable to the Children of the Sunday Schools by the distribution of medals struck in commemoration of the event.

CHAPTER LXVII.

PUBLIC LIFE AND EVENTS, 1831-1840.

Building of the Town Hall—Descriptions of the Building—The Market Hall—Visit of Lord Brougham—Joseph Sturge and the Slave Trade—Death of William IV.—The Young Queen—Local Celebration of Coronation Day—The Incorporation Movement—The Last of the Old Government of the Town—Obituary Notices—The British Association and the First Exhibition—More Loyal Celebrations, etc.

At the close of the last chapter of the chronicle of public events we took note of the projected erection of a new Town Hall, and we have now to record its erection. A design for this building was supplied by Mr. Barry, and exhibited at the Royal Academy, but was not adopted by the Commissioners. A description of this design (which possessed certain points of resemblance to the building subsequently erected, and was by no means devoid of beauty, although somewhat flat and heavy,) appeared in the *Gazette*, and will doubtless interest our readers :—

It is not of a description to strike at first view, except as being an admirably executed drawing, it seeming to consist of little more than an hexastyle portico of a very plain character ; when we come, however, to examine it, we discover it to be replete with beauties, and to afford evidence of study, of original thought, and more than ordinary feeling. The order is a Doric, or rather what is usually denominated Tuscan, the columns having bases and unfluted shafts, and the frieze being without triglyphs ; still Tuscan would very ill designate the general character, which is treated more in the spirit of the Grecian Doric than any other style. The columns are raised on a basement or stylobate, pierced only by three doors of narrow proportions, and with exceedingly deep plain lintels and architraves. These doors correspond with the centre and two extreme intercolumns of the portico above, so that the distance of solid unbroken wall between them is very considerable, and conveys the idea of very great strength. Still, this arrangement would have been attended with a disagreeable appearance of weakness, as the lateral doors would have been too near the angles, had not the architect most felicitously overcome this inconvenience by extending the basement at each end beyond the portico itself, by the addition of a very bold pedestal, carried up as high as the bases of the columns. Another circumstance that contributes materially to enhance the rich picturesque effect of the whole, yet which is apt to escape notice in a drawing, is that he has introduced columns within the portico behind those in front, thereby producing not only a fine degree of *chiar' oscuro*, but great perspective variety and force. The building is insulated, and the columns are continued along the sides; yet from want of a plan, and owing to the point from which the edifice is viewed, we cannot say whether there is a regular intercolumn between the column and the wall. We should apprehend that their bases are close to the wall, even if no part of the shafts is engaged in it, otherwise, as the building is only hexastyle in front, the interior space would be too confined, except formed into a single large apartment. Rarely have we seen a design possessing so much originality, with apparently no pretension to novelty; or so true to the spirit of classical architecture, without at all reminding us of any individual model.

The Commissioners decided to accept the design, however, of Messrs. Hansom and Welch, in preference to that of Mr. Barry, and the building was commenced on the 27th of April, 1832. Many hindrances occurred, partly owing to the fact that the contractors (who were also the architects) had under-estimated the cost of the work, having contracted for its completion for the sum of £17,000, with about £1,700 for extras, whereas the total cost was about £25,000, although the Anglesey marble, with which it is faced, was presented to the architects by Sir Richard Bulkley, Bart., the owner of the Penmon Quarries, from which it was obtained. A report was published shortly after the completion of the building, by the Securities, showing the losses sustained thereby, as follows:—

BIRMINGHAM TOWN HALL.

January 26, 1835.—We, the undersigned Securities for erecting this magnificent building, beg to lay before the public the following statement of monies lost by us, in consequence of our connection with the Birmingham Town Hall, and to invite the respectable inhabitants of the town and borough to institute an inquiry into the fair value of the building, with a view of determining whether something ought not to be done for our relief.

We feel convinced that the inhabitants of the borough do not desire to possess the building at a less cost than, under all circumstances considered, was absolutely necessary for its erection, nor would they wish to leave us, the Securities, exposed to those ruinous consequences which must ensue unless we are protected by the generous interference of the town.

Money advanced by Mr. Welch, sen., at the commencement of the work, to enable the Architects and Builders to proceed	£1,310	0 0
Money ditto by Mr. Tench	500	0 0
Money advanced by Mr. Welch, sen.	1,300	0 0
Money ditto by Mr. Lloyd	1,300	0 0
Money ditto by Mr. Welch, sen., in September, 1834	1,000	0 0
Money ditto by Mr. Lloyd	1,000	0 0
	£6,410	0 0

W. P. LLOYD,
JOHN WELCH,
EDWARD TENCH,
Jan., 1835. Securities for erecting the Birmingham Town Hall.

An admirable description of the building was given by Mr. Bates, in his interesting *Guide*, which we give entire, in preference to entering upon a new description of what has already been so frequently described before:

"The hall," he says,—"as to the architectural merits of which criticism has been most minute and diverse, but which popular opinion, after all, the true test, has long ago decided to be an ornament to the town, and a credit to the public taste and spirit of its inhabitants—may be instanced as a remarkable attempt to apply to modern purposes a style of structure which belonged essentially to the Greek temples. Upon a rusticated basement or arcade, rising to the height of about twenty feet, and pierced with doorways and windows, for the convenience of the interior, is placed a splendid series of Corinthian columns, about forty feet high, supporting entablatures above. Of these there are, at present, thirteen along each side, and eight in the principal front, where they are surmounted by a lofty pediment. The columnar ordinance employed is in imitation of the Roman foliated, or Corinthian, example of the Temple of Jupiter Stator, at Rome; the columns are fluted, and the entablature greatly enriched, though not to the full and elaborate extent of the original. The basement forms a promenade, and can afford standing room for more columns and their accessories are composed. The bricks were made on the spot, of the earth taken from the foundation. A new species of machinery

OLD VIEW OF THE TOWN HALL, FROM HILL STREET.
From an original drawing.

than 1,500 persons. The projection of the arcade in front, over the causeway, is a departure from the original design, which consisted of a *single* arched piazza. The structure is of brick, faced with Anglesea marble, of which latter material the was also constructed to raise the framed tie-beams and principals of the roof to the top of the building, a height of seventy feet. In this operation an accident occurred, through the hook of a pulley block breaking, by which two workmen were killed. They were interred in St. Philip's Churchyard, and a monument, consisting appropriately of the base of a pillar which had been wrought by one of the sufferers, was erected to their memory by their employers and fellow workmen.

"The main part of the interior consists of one large hall—the object of the building being the accommodation of public meetings and other large assemblies. This hall can accommodate about 4,000 persons *sitting*, but more than double that number when standing up. It is 145 feet long, 65 wide, and 65 high, being somewhat smaller than Exeter Hall, and ten feet higher from the floor to the roof than the Opera House. Light is received from windows behind the columns in the body of the building—one to each intercolumniation. There are corridors of communication running along on each side of it, on its own level, and staircases leading to upper corridors to give access to galleries. Rooms for committees, the accommodation of performers, etc., are formed at the upper end of the building, and under the orchestra. The ceiling is chastely and appropriately decorated, and the spaces between the windows ornamented with fluted Corinthian pilasters. The admirable marble bust of Mendelssohn is from the studio of our townsman, Mr. Peter Hollins, and has but recently [1848] been placed in its present appropriate situation.

"In a recess at the end is the magnificent organ, constructed by Hill of London—one of whose best productions it is considered to be—at a cost of between from £3,000 to £4,000. Though the mechanical details are uninteresting, and inconclusive as to the character of the instrument, we subjoin a few particulars. The outer case (from a design by Mr. Mackenzie, in harmony with the architectural style of the building) is 40 feet wide, 45 feet high, and 17 feet deep. There are 71 draw stops, 4 sets of keys, and above 4,000 pipes; the largest wooden pipe has an interior capacity of 224 cubic feet. It is calculated that the timber alone employed in the construction of this organ must weigh between 20 and 30 tons, while the metal and other materials used in the structure raise the weight of the whole to at least 40 tons. The bellows are necessarily of great size, containing about 300 square feet of surface. This organ is distinguished by many peculiarities in the arrangement of the keys, etc., by which the performer is enabled to produce an almost endless variety of tone and power. Of these our limited space forbids a detail—which would, indeed, be uninteresting to the merely general reader. A visit to the *interior* of the instrument, cannot fail to be productive of much pleasure to a scientific person. It is composed of three stories, to which corresponding staircases lead; there is ample room to walk, and the various compartments of this immense piece of mechanism, with their forests of pipes, may be surveyed. Looked into from the gallery over it, the largest wooden pipe, which is 3 feet square and 32 feet deep, will appear like the shaft of a mine; and if the full powers of the instrument are developed while the visitor is still in the recesses of the machinery, he will be deafened by the awful roar, and may well imagine that the building is about to be rent asunder by a terrific explosion.

"But though this wonderful instrument is thus capable of simulating the most awful voices of nature, or the most terrific blasts of the ear-splitting trumpet, it is equally well adapted to produce, under the hands of the talented organist, Mr. Stimpson, the finest and most complete strains of the octave flute. Had we not already exceeded our limits we should have had much pleasure in instituting a comparison between this and the principal organs in our own country and on the continent; we can, however, but add that looking to the number of *pipes* as a more accurate criterion of the power of an instrument, than the number of *stops*, on which it is customary to dilate when describing an organ, it may be affirmed that the Birmingham organ and the new one at York, are the largest and most powerful in the world."

Thus much as to the description of the hall; but our readers will also read with interest, we think, the impressions produced by this noble structure upon the mind of a true poet, and one whom all Birmingham men must love and admire —Charles Reece Pemberton.* He says :—

" The Birmingham Town Hall is a noble edifice —look at it from any of the five lines of approach, when you will. Seen under a very clear sky, it is silent glory and beauty ; under the bright light of the moon—but more so when the clear moon is now *dark'd*, now flashed out again suddenly, by the rapidly-scudding black storm-clouds,—it is, of all the buildings I remember in this kingdom, the most thought-suggestive. And, probably, much of this power is ascribable to those very matters of objection, which tastes, that I must consider superior to mine, have taken to its site and neighbourhood. I like it for standing near to those humble brick dwelling-houses. Knowing and feeling, as I do, the purpose and spirit which urged its erection, it looks to me like their magnificent, not insolently condescending, friend—not their haughty lord. Had its site been more elevated ground, and its whole more isolated, I think it would not have possessed that look of the kindly grand, that countenance of the benevolently beautiful, which, to my sense at least, it now possesses. The pro-

jection beyond the street line in the south front, which a skilful and scientific architect pointed out to me as a great defect, I like ; this must be my bad taste. It steps out with a generous and complacent bravery, as if it would say, ' I belong to you all, and will protect and befriend you all. I am here with you ; come to me all as fellows and friends :' not as an insolent blusterer, with one leg thrust out like a bully, because he happens to be strong and a big fellow, as who should say, ' Keep off, you rabble, you vagabonds ! or come on if you dare, and I'll smash you !' I believe there is not any building in England that can exhibit such a glorious range of columns. Afar off they attract, near they fascinate the gaze. Get into an angle with the eastern line of them, and they become countless, calling up a fancy of ' there are thousands more,' only your vision is too weak to trace and follow the line. Stand at a distance, and look to the roof; the sky and it are associated; they are mighty and graceful dwellers together. The fabric is a splendid poem.

" It has, besides, recommendations to the ' practical man,' *par excellence*. Had Government done the town the honour of patronizing the building, contrivance would have been successful in making the same thing a subject of taxation to the amount of a hundred thousand pounds. The men of Birmingham know how these matters are managed well enough; and so, by escaping from the aid of royal, ministerial, and aristocratic patronage, they saved their fellow-townsmen some seventy thousand pounds.

" But the imposing grandeur and gratifying beauty vanishes when you have entered the building. The poetry is gone. Imposing effect is utterly sacrificed to the sheerest utility, *i.e.*, the anti utilitarian's utility. Yet do I opine that even more utility might have been maintained if attention to poetical effect had not been so entirely superseded. Those galleries appear like hasty excrescences—a defect which, certainly, is diminished when they are occupied by some

---

* Charles Reece Pemberton, of whom, had space permitted, we had intended to have spoken more fully in a future chapter, was born at Pontypool, South Wales, on the 23rd of January, 1790, and was educated at the Protestant Dissenting Charity Sch ol, Park Street, Birmingham. He was apprenticed to his uncle, a brassfounder, in Livery Street; but, disliking his employment, he ran away at the age of seventeen, and went to sea. In the West Indies, whither he went, he indulged his long cherished desire to become an actor, and became successful and prosperous; but an unhappy marriage with an actress who proved untrue to him, led him once more to return to England, alone, to seek histrionic fame among his own countrymen. His "Shylock" was universally admired, and es ecially by Serjeant Talfourd, (afterwards Mr. Justice Talfourd,) the dramatist. In 1833 he published in the *Monthly Repository* "The Autobiography of Pel Verjuice," in which, under a thin disguise, he pourtrays his own life. Subsequently he took to the lecturing platform, and delight.. large audiences at the Mechanics' Institute of his own town, and elsewhere throughout the kingdom. In 1838 his health unfortunately gave way, and he was compelled to try a milder climate, visiting Gibraltar, Malta, Egypt, etc., and returned only to die, at the house of his brother, Mr. W. D. Pemberton, Ludgate Hill, Birmingham, March 3rd, 1840. Our quotation, which serves as an admirable example of his style, is taken from his " Life and Literary Remains," edited by John Fowler.

eight hundred or a thousand persons: but then they have a look of unsafeness, capable, and strong as a close inspection convinces us they are. There is about them a character of heavy fragility; it is ponderousness resting on filagree. The *coup-d'œil*, perhaps, would have been much more satisfactory and grand, if, instead of the

at present; though, in respect of egress from the ground floor, I know no public building for popular assemblages that surpasses it; the alarm on the nomination day tried the case thoroughly.

"Good people of Birmingham, let all strangers see the inside of your noble building (that building of which you justly may be proud), when

INTERIOR OF THE TOWN HALL.

ugly excrescences and projections, which now constitute the galleries, gradations of seats had risen directly from the floor, exactly at the lines from which the front seats of the galleries are perpendicular with the base. Such a construction would not only have given a reality, but, what is almost equally necessary, also an appearance of satisfactory strength and stability, besides an increase of accommodation, as to the number of sitters, for all seek to avoid the spaces under the galleries. Ingress and egress, too, would have been no less, perhaps more, easy than

it is crammed full of your fellow-townsmen on some great and stirring occasion   .   .   . Let the spaces which allow of two thousand people to arrange unruffled their gala dresses, to stretch out legs and take good elbow-room, be quintuply packed, showing a sea of faces and heads as closely piled and wedged as if they have been rammed together by paviours' rods, just as they were crowded, and crammed, and rammed, and wedged on Wednesday, January 7th, 1835 and the eye will sweep over a spectacle which is equalled by nothing but old Niagara—a spectacle at once awful, sublime, and heart-throbbing. Then all excrescence, all incongruity, littleness, and disappointed expectation are swept away.

"On that day there were ten or perhaps twelve thousand people packed together. The seats being removed, left the great floor clear; and every avenue, aisle, and accessible window place was filled with bodies crushed up into the smallest dimensions; thousands of arms were literally wedged to the sides by the pressure. The organ-loft, from which my view is taken, was occupied by the committees and friends, who were admitted by ticket. From this station the eye ran over the whole plain and mountains of hats and faces; up from which rose, on every occasion of circumstantial or verbal appeal to their approving senses, cheers that would have made silent the loudest thunder; rattling, and ringing, and reverberating with such passionate sublimity, that one actually, for a moment, felt a dread that the roof and walls would split under that mighty burst of voices; while hats and arms shook and shivered like the crossed and splintering billows of the sea, in a black night, when opposite and furiously sharp blasts are battling o'er its surface　And, look there—I am supposing the reader has eyes—imagination would scarcely have helped me to the conception of such a scene and effect, if I had not witnessed them *de facto*. There were many dashings, rushings of those who were outside the building, in bodies of some hundreds at once, attempting to force themselves into that solid mass; they seemed to drive into the compact body a huge inky billow—it swept on as if an ocean from without had made a tremendous SEND of its waters into the land-locked haven, which it caused to heave, and sway, and swell as though it would burst every barrier, and overwhelm all in its course. Another *send*—and another—and then I had the similitude of a dark pine forest, swinging its clinging and intertwisted branches, at one instant with one motion, as the rattling tempest rolled over them, unfearing and un-

scathing. I have seen many strange and stirring things in my time, but that is, perhaps, one of the most extraordinary."

We have already recorded, in the last chapter of our chronicle of local events, the steps taken by the Town Commissioners for the provision of a convenient Market Hall. Early in this decade the work of erection was commenced, and in the *Gazette* of February 16th, 1835, we read that "The new Market Hall was thrown open to the public on Thursday last (February 12th), and during the day it was crowded with persons, a considerable portion of whom were no doubt attracted by curiosity. On Saturday it was again visited by great numbers, and in the evening was lighted up with gas for the accommodation of buyers and sellers."

The site selected for this building was that portion of the old town lying between Bell Street and Philip Street, and extending from the Bull Ring back into Worcester Street. The length of the hall is three hundred and sixty-five feet; its width, one hundred and eight feet; and its height, sixty feet. There are two principal entrances, facing into the Bull Ring and Worcester Street, the arches being supported by massive Doric columns; and on either side of the building are smaller entrances. Accommodation is provided for six hundred stalls, fitted up for the sale of fruit, game and poultry, fish, butchers' meat, fancy articles, live pets, poultry, etc. The total cost of the building was about £67,261.

In 1851 a handsome fountain of bronze was erected in the centre of the hall, adorned with well designed figures representing the various manufactures, groups of fish, fruit, flowers, etc. It was designed and executed by Messenger and Sons, and was inaugurated December 24th, 1851.

Birmingham, after having taken so prominent a position in the great political movement of 1830-32, grew considerably in importance and dignity, and attracted many distinguished visitors. On February 18th, 1835, the Turkish Ambassador and suite visited the town, and spent a day or two in going the round of the most interesting manufactories. In July of the same year Lord Brougham came, in order to inspect the still famous establishment at Soho ; and was the guest of the junior partner of the firm, James Watt, Esq., at Aston Hall. On the 23rd of July, 1838, His Royal Highness the Duke of Cambridge called at Birmingham, staying for a few hours at Dee's Hotel. After inspecting the celebrated establishment of Mr. George Richmond Collis, he proceeded to the Town Hall, where the powers of the great organ were displayed by Mr. Hollins. The Duke then returned to Dee's Hotel and shortly afterwards continued his journey to London. A week later, July 30th, Marshal Soult, attended by the Marquis of Dalmatia, the Marquis de Mornay, the Duc de Vicenza, the Duc de Bassana, the Comte de Praslin, M. de Francqueville and others, arrived at the same hotel ; where a guard of honour of the 14th Light Dragoons were stationed, and offered him a salute. " The visitors," we read " were received by the High and Low Bailiffs, F. Lloyd, Esq., and Mr. G. R. Collis,—visiting first the splendid establishment of the latter gentleman, thence to Messrs. Sarjeant's Gun and Sword Manufactory, which appeared to afford extreme interest to the whole party, and, as a kindred subject to them, led to many enquiries. The Papier Mâché Manufactory of Messrs. Jennens and Betteridge ; the Britannia Nail Works of Mr. T. M. Jones ; the Proof-house ; and the extensive Button Manufactory of Messrs. Hammond, Turner and Sons, were subsequently visited, and each of the processes led to various expressions of astonishment and of high gratification.

" His excellency was then conducted to the Town Hall, which had been previously and for some hours filled to an overflow by anxious but orderly inmates, who waited with extreme interest the arrival of the veteran visitor, but very judiciously Mr. Hollins entertained the

assemblage with an occasional performance on the organ. On the arrival of the Marshal in the Town Hall he was warmly greeted by those assembled. Mr. Hollins performed some pieces on the organ, and after spending some time in this scene, the Marshal returned to Dee's Royal Hotel, where dinner had been provided in the large room."

On the 16th of April, 1833, an agitation was commenced, upon which all who took part therein may look back with commendable pride and satisfaction ; an agitation which did honour to Birmingham, and in which one of our townsmen acquitted himself like a true hero, and reflected credit and renown upon the town which had produced a Joseph Sturge. A meeting was held on that date at Dee's Hotel Assembly Room, Mr. John Simcox, the High Bailiff, presiding ; the object was to support a petition for the " immediate and complete " abolition of the iniquitous Slave Trade. But as in the case of other reforms, there were " vested interests " in the way, and the friends of liberty were not permitted to have matters all their own way at the meeting ; an opposition, headed by Mr. G. F. Muntz and other members of the Political Union, raised the cry of " spoliation of property !" The result was a scene of disorder, the room being densely crowded, and the parties pretty equally divided. On behalf of the opposition Mr. G. F. Muntz moved, " that anxious as we are for the early but gradual abolition of Negro Slavery, we cannot admit that, in the peculiar crisis of the country, it is a subject which calls for the attention of His Majesty's Government, in preference to the measures necessary to be carried into effect for promoting the commercial and manufacturing interests of the country, nor can we sanction any proposition for the abolition of Negro Slavery, unaccompanied by an offer of granting to the owners of West India Estates such compensation as Parliament may think proper." A resident in the West Indies,—the Rev. P. Duncan—detailed many incidents illustrative of the horrors of the Slave Trade, and supported the petition, and at the conclusion of his speech, owing to the continued interruption the High Bailiff was compelled to dissolve the meeting.

On the 22nd of the same month another meeting was held, for the same object, at the Public Office ; Thomas Lowe, Esq., in the chair. On this occasion the expression of opinion was unanimously in favour of immediate abolition of the Slave Trade ; and it was resolved, " that petitions to both Houses of Parliament for the immediate Abolition of Slavery, to be entitled the Petition of the undersigned Magistrates, Clergy, Ministers, Bankers, Merchants, Manufacturers, and other Inhabitants of the Town and Neighbourhood of Birmingham, be forthwith prepared and circulated for signature."

On October 17th, 1836, Joseph Sturge set out on his long-contemplated journey to the West Indies, with the view of making personal inquiries as to the state of the Negro population, in the hope of obtaining an amelioration of their condition. Previous to his leaving home, a complimentary address, signed by the leading inhabitants, of all parties, was presented to him. The following communication was received from him early in the following year, and published in the *Birmingham Journal* of January 28 :—

" As we shall not be able to send our document home in a suitable state by this packet, our friends will be glad to know what has been the general result of our enquiries during a residence of nearly a month, from personal investigation in different parts of the island, and from information derived from members of the legislature, magistrates, legal and medical practitioners, ministers of the Church of England, and of the Methodist and Moravian persuasions, schoolmasters, merchants, planters, attorneys, overseers, managers, and the negroes themselves.

" We think we may safely say, that the great experiment of conferring at once immediate freedom on 36,000 slaves, has, after two years' trial, succeeded beyond the expectations of those in the colony who were most favourable to the measure. The universal testimony both of the employer and negro is, that the state of things is immeasurably improved. It is true that all the sanguine hopes of those are not fully realised who did not take it sufficiently into account that, in the immediate change from slavery to freedom, the new state of things would have to contend with the prejudices of the planter on the one hand and of the labourer on the other, against the introduction of those changes which are needful to ensure its complete success.

" The remaining evils (which do not exist where the principles of freedom have been more fully understood, and have been more completely acted upon for a long period) might, we believe, be remedied by a temperate, firm, and judicious exercise of authority of the Government at home. One of the most pressing evils is the want of proper provision for the aged and infirm, especially those who have become so since the 1st of August, 1834, for whom there is no legal provision. We hope to speak more particularly upon the principal points embraced in our enquiry when we have leisure to do so.

" 12 Month, 14, 1836."

On May 27th, in the same year, we read :—

Mr. Joseph Sturge arrived safely at home, *via* New York, on Wednesday last, in good health. He left his friends, Dr. Lloyd and Mr. Harvey, in Jamaica, quite well, on the 7th ult. It is stated that Mr. Sturge's friends, and the friends of emancipation, contemplate inviting him to a public breakfast on as early a day as can be arranged.

On the 6th of June a public breakfast was given to this noble hearted philanthropist, in the Town Hall, " for the purpose of congratulating him on his safe return from the West Indies, and to express the high sense of his unwearied and philanthropic exertions in the cause of negro emancipation ;" when upwards of five hundred persons assembled to do him honour.

We have already briefly referred, in the Political History of this period, to the death of William IV. and the accession of Victoria. On the 26th of June, 1837, the new Queen was proclaimed in Birmingham, and the event was celebrated with enthusiasm by the people. Twelve months later—on the 28th of June, 1838, the Queen was crowned, and once more the people of Birmingham testified their loyalty to the youthful sovereign in a manner suitable to the occasion. The celebration commenced with divine service at all the churches of the Establishment, and appropriate sermons were preached. Then the children of the schools connected therewith were " regaled with good English fare ;" the children of the Wesleyan Methodist Schools, four thousand in number, walked in procession to an open space at Holloway Head, and, after hearing an address from their ministers, joined in singing a hymn and "God Save the Queen;" the other Sunday Schools also assembled, and all were 'regaled.'

"At one o'clock," says the *Gazette,* "the doors of the Market Hall were thrown open, and an interesting sight presented itself of tables most judiciously arranged, and abundantly provided for dining four thousand of the industrious classes, of both sexes, who were admitted by the tickets of subscribers to the fund raised for the purpose. The fare consisted of roast beef and plum pudding and a quart of ale to each guest. The hall was most beautifully decorated, and too much commendation cannot be bestowed on the zeal and judgment manifested in the arrangements made by the gentlemen of the Committee. The offices of Stewards were most effectually sustained by respectable inhabitants of the town, in the proportion of one to fifty guests. A Band of Musicians played before and in the intervals of the festive scene. At each end of the hall a booth was erected, in which the Chairman and Vice-Chairman were stationed ; that in the direction of Worcester Street being occupied by the High Bailiff, supported by J. T. Lawrence, and W. Chance, Esqrs. Mr. Geach, and Mr. Phillips the Chairman of the Committee of Management, and several ladies were accommodated in this booth. Above the High Bailiff a gallery was erected for the reception of ladies, which was soon filled, as were the various passages between the tables, by spectators of the cheering scene."

The day closed with a ball at the Town Hall, dinners at several of the hotels and inns, bell-ringing, fireworks, illuminations, and other tokens of joy.

Although the people of Birmingham were now represented in Parliament, and thus had a share in the government of the nation, they were as yet without a suitable governing body in their own town. The old form of local government by the High and Low Bailiff, Headborough, and Consta-

bles, was now, it is true, supplemented by the Commissioners appointed under the several Street Acts ; but neither of these bodies were elected by the voice of the people. The Court Leet of the Lord of the Manor was an irresponsible body, and the Commissioners were almost as far removed from popular influence as the Justices of the Peace. It was not to be supposed, therefore, that a large community which had already exerted so powerful an influence upon the destinies of the country should rest satisfied with an irresponsible local government ; and accordingly we find that, before the end of the year 1833, the initiative step had been taken towards obtaining a municipal corporation for the town. On the 16th of December in that year we read in the *Gazette* that "two of the commissioners appointed by Government to make enquiries as to the suitable division of towns into districts, and other matters connected with the granting of Charters of Incorporation to the new [parliamentary] Boroughs, were last week in the town, pursuing the objects of their appointment." Among the provisions recommended by these commissioners were, the division of the town into twelve districts, each of which should choose its own alderman ; the appointment of a stipendiary magistrate ; the holding of a Quarter Session in Birmingham ; and the erection of a Borough Gaol. But these fair promises seem for a time to have been forgotten, and we hear nothing more respecting the incorporation of the town until June, 1835, when the Municipal Corporation Reform Bill was introduced. In August the Bill was rejected by the Lords, and on the 18th, an indignation meeting was held in Birmingham, addressed by Mr. P. M. James, (High Bailiff.) Mr. T. Tyndall, (Low Bailiff,) the Rev. T. M. McDonnell, Thomas Attwood, M.P., George Edmonds, Wm. Beale, and other leading inhabitants.

After expressing their "grief and indignation" at "the arbitrary interference of a powerful

FORWARD

T. C. S. KYNNERSLEY, ESQ.

PHOTOGRAPHED BY WHITLOCK.

BIRMINGHAM: HOUGHTON & CO. SCOTLAND PASSAGE.

MONUMENT TO JOSEPH STURGE.
Erected at the Five Ways, Edgbaston

majority in the House of Lords with the measure of Corporate Reform, which especially interests the people," they resolved "that the earnest thanks of the meeting be presented to that glorious and patriotic minority in the House of Lords, who have nobly vindicated those principles which they have professed, and now stand as inflexibly by the cause of the people as they did in the memorable passing of the Reform Bill;" and finally, "that a memorial be adopted, and that it be presented to Lord Melbourne by the Members for the Borough." But once more the necessary reform was delayed, until, on the 30th of October, 1837, a meeting was held in the Town Hall, and a petition was adopted, praying the Queen in Council to grant a Charter of Incorporation for the borough. The matter was taken up this time in a party spirit, and a strong opposition was organized by the Conservatives, who held a meeting at Dee's Hotel on the 3rd of January, 1838, and passed resolutions in favour of remaining " as they were ;" being of opinion " that a Charter of Incorporation would be highly detrimental to the interests and prosperity of the borough of Birmingham." On the 13th of July the adjourned question as to the Incorporation of the borough came before the Privy Council, and memorials were put in both by the advocates and the opponents of Incorporation ; deputations were also received from both parties by the President of the Council, and every effort was put forth on both sides to influence the decision of their Lordships. But all opposition happily proved useless ; the Privy Council agreed to the grant of Incorporation, and on the 5th of November the new Charter was publicly read in the Town Hall It was addressed by the Council to the ex-High Bailiff, Mr. William Scholefield, and empowered him to make out the first burgess list, and to act as Returning Officer at the first election of Town Councillors. The district incorporated included the town and manor of Birmingham, the parish of Edgbaston, the hamlets of Deritend and Bordesley, and Duddeston and

Nechells ; and was divided into thirteen wards. The corporation was to consist of a Mayor, sixteen Aldermen, and forty-eight Councillors ; and the first election of Councillors was fixed to take place on the 26th of December, 1838, and of Aldermen and Mayor on the 27th of the same month.

The elections took place as appointed, Mr. William Scholefield being unanimously elected the first Mayor; Mr. William Redfern was appointed Town Clerk, and Mr. R. K. Douglas was unanimously elected to the office of Registrar of the Mayor's Court.

On the 7th of May, 1839, the Mayor announced that the petition of the Council for a separate Court of Quarter Sessions, had been granted. Matthew Davenport Hill, Esq., was appointed by the crown to the office of Recorder ; and, at the next meeting of the Council, Mr. George Edmonds was unanimously elected Clerk of the Peace, and Dr. Birt Davies to the office of Coroner. On the 7th of April, 1840, Mr. Redfern resigned the office of Town Clerk, and Mr. Soloman Bray was elected in his stead. A complete list of Mayors from 1838 to the present time, will be printed in the appendix to the present volume.

A few worthy townsmen of the period we are leaving behind us, passed away during this decade. First among them, in point of time, was James Armitage, a chemist, who for nearly twenty-seven years acted as Treasurer to the Birmingham Old Library. In the pursuit of his favourite study, the science of Botany, he rendered valuable assistance to the Botanical and Horticultural Society of Birmingham, and his extensive correspondence with several of the most eminent botanists of the day, obtained for the Society considerable advantages. He died at his residence in the Aston Road, in May, 1833, in the 75th year of his age.

On the 28th of December, 1836, Dr. John Johnstone, who had practised as a physician in Birmingham for upwards of forty years, passed away from our midst, to the great grief of many who had been indebted to him for renewed life and vigour.

"The confidential friend and biographer of Dr. Parr," says the *Gazette*, "was himself a scholar of no ordinary acquirements, and his biographical memoirs of that celebrated man, display sound judgment, refined taste, and classical learning."

Our old friend James Dobbs, the comedian, of whom we have previously made mention on several occasions, died, after an illness of fourteen days, at his brother's house in Newton Street, November 1st, 1837, at the age of 56; and on the 12th of the same month died an old Birmingham worthy, M.. Thomas Blakemore, at the patriarchal age of 105. He had formerly kept the old *Bird-in-Hand* public house, in Dale End, where he took in the *Gazette* in the days of its original proprietor, Thomas Aris, who died in 1761, seventy-six years before his subscriber!

In 1839, the *Gazette* had to mourn the loss of its editor, Mr. Thomas Knott, who had held that honourable position for a quarter of a century, being at the same time one of the proprietors of that journal. He had taken the utmost interest in everything which concerned the welfare of the town,— the General Hospital, King Edward's School, the Public Library, the Botanical Gardens, the Society of Arts, and the Church Building Society, all benefited by his judicious counsel and effective support. He died at his residence, Camp Hill, on the 9th of July, 1839, at the comparatively early age of forty-nine.

In August 1839 the ninth Annual Meeting of the British Association for the Advancement of Science was held in Birmingham. The Inaugural Address was delivered in the Town Hall, August 29th, by the Rev. W. Vernon Harcourt; and Reports of Researches in the various Sciences were read by the Rev. Baden Powell, Sir David Brewster, Richard Owen, Edward Forbes, and other eminent scientific writers, upwards of fourteen hundred members of the Association attending the meetings of the various sections. During the visit of the Association a happy idea was carried into execution by the people of Birmingham, of showing their distinguished

visitors what our artisans and mechanics were capable of accomplishing in the various arts and manufactures, by means of an Industrial Exhibition—the first of the kind ever attempted, and the forerunner of those great international shows which have since been held in almost every capital throughout the civilized world. The objects of this exhibition were :—

1st. To present, in one view, the various stages through which the principal articles manufactured in this district have to pass, commencing with the raw material.

2nd. To make known the value of any recent improvements in the arts and manufactures.

3rd. To collect together any curious specimen occurring in practice, whether in mechanics or chemistry, which may lead to the suggestion of further improvements in the application of science to practical purposes.

In some one of these objects we presume that most manufacturers must feel an individual interest, and will therefore contribute as far as they can to the success of the exhibition.

This little exhibition was held in the principal rooms of the Free Grammar School, and subsequently, in consequence of the great success which attended it, at the Shakspeare Rooms, where it was visited by a large number of the inhabitants. Several of the pupils of the Mechanics' Institute* were deputed to explain the various objects of interest to the visitors, and probably from their connection in this manner with the undertaking, the members of the Institute resolved themselves to hold a similar exhibition of objects illustrative of the fine arts, experimental philosophy, manufactures, etc., which was opened on the 17th of December in the same year, and proved equally successful. Another exhibition was organised by the Mechanics' Institute in the following year, but did not meet with success, and consequently involved the society in financial difficulties which ultimately proved its ruin.

In 1840, we find our townsmen again testifying their loyalty to the young Queen, on the occasion of her marriage, which took place on the 10th of February, in that year. From some cause

---

* It was while in this exhibition that Mr. Daniel Wright, formerly master of the Protestant Dissenting School, and at that time conductor of the classes in the Mechanics' Institute, was seized with a fit of apoplexy, and died on the spot.

it appears that no organised plan was adopted for the celebration of the auspicious event ; but the spontaneous loyalty of the people expressed itself in spite of indifference on the part of the authorities, and the day was celebrated with all the usual tokens of joy.   In the June following the inhabitants of Birmingham joined with all classes of the Queen's loyal subjects throughout the kingdom in thanksgivings and congratulations for the happy escape of Her Majesty and the Prince Consort from the hand of the would-be assassin, Oxford.

And with these gratifying tokens of the continued loyalty of the people of Birmingham, we close another decade of the public life of our town.

CHAPTER LXVIII.

AMUSEMENTS OF THE PEOPLE :
Including the History of the Theatre Royal, from 1831 to 1840.

Paganini in Birmingham—Sheridan Knowles—Charles Matthews—The Young American Roscius—Alteration of Prices—Taglioni—A Disappointment—"Irregular" Performances—New Management—Charles Reece Pemberton—Mr. Armistead's Failure—A Theatrical Riot—The *Lady of Lyons*—First Christmas Pantomime—Lectures—Other Amusements.

At a time when the popular mind was exercised to the utmost in political strife, those institutions which exist to provide amusement and recreation were not in the most flourishing condition ; and consequently the history of the Theatre and kindred institutions has but little to record during the first two years of this decade, occupied, as they were, with the great agitation chronicled in a foregoing chapter.   Only two events need be recorded previous to the year 1833, viz., the appearance of the world-famous Paganini, in February, 1832, and the performance of Sheridan Knowles's fine play, *The Hunchback*, in which the author sustained the character of Master Walter.   Both these artistes again appeared in the season of 1833, the latter, with Miss Ellen Tree, playing in *The Wife* and other of his dramatic works.   This season opened with Mr. Macready's appearance in *Virginius;* and during the year Mr. and Mrs. Wood, appeared in the Opera of *The Barber of Seville.* Mr. Charles Matthews presented, " at home "—at his Birmingham home, the Theatre Royal,—" the fourth volume of his Comic Annual."   The " American Young Roscius," Mr. Mangeon appeared, with Miss Inverarity, and, on the 21st of October, Paganini gave a farewell performance, " previous to his final departure for the Continent."   An entertainment entitled " Dramatic Recollections " was also given in November of the same year, at Dee's Royal Hotel, by Miss Kelly.

The theatre was opened for the season of 1834, under new management, Messrs. Fitzgibbon and Wightman having succeeded Mr. Watson, as lessees.   A change was made in the prices by the new managers ; there had hitherto been only one price for boxes,—four shillings—but these were now divided into upper and lower, and the former reduced to three shillings, the pit being also reduced from half-a-crown to two shillings.   Mr. Charles Kean appeared during the opening week of the season, in the round of characters formerly sustained by his father ; and he was succeeded by Mr. Balls and Miss Ellen Tree, who appeared in the *School for Scandal.*   For the first week in August, " the two first dancers in

Europe," Madame Taglioni and Mons. Silvain, were engaged, but at the date announced for their appearance, a notice was inserted in the newspapers, informing the public that the engage- been entered into," the prices would be as formerly, four shillings for both upper and lower boxes, two shillings and sixpence for the pit, and one shilling and sixpence for the gallery. Further

ST. PHILIP'S CHURCH, FROM THE EAST END.

ment of the former with Mons. Laporte, of the King's Opera, would necessitate the postponement of her visit to Birmingham until the 11th and 13th of the month, adding that in consequence of the " enormous and tremendous engagement of ' one hundred pounds per night,' which has advertisements were also issued announcing the positive appearance of Madame Taglioni, Madame Giubelei, and Mons. Silvain, but after all the announcements and puffs preliminary, the public were disappointed ; " severe indisposition " preventing the great *danseuse* from appearing in Birmingham.

The "irregular" season, which intervened between the autumn of 1834, and the spring of 1835, was marked by the appearance of Mr. West's Equestrian Troupe at the Theatre Royal, recorded in the following extract from the *Gazette:*—

February 16, 1835.—The splendid Dramatic Spectacle of Mazeppa attracted numerous and respectable audiences to the Theatre during the past week, and the flattering reception it has met with on each successive night must be highly gratifying to the Manager, to whom much credit is due for the admirable manner in which the entire piece is got up. Mr. West's fine Equestrian Troop are seen to great advantage in the Tournament, in which there is introduced a combination of gorgeous scenery and dresses, investing the pageant with a vivid and dazzling appearance, and rendering the scenic display peculiarly effective. It will be seen that Mazeppa, together with the novel entertainment of "Raphael's Dream," is announced for repetition this evening.

The history of the season of 1835 is full of the names of artists whose performances have caused old-fashioned playgoers to regard the days of their youth as the golden age of the drama—Macready and Charles Kean, Charles Kemble and T. P. Cooke, Madame Vestris and Mrs. Stirling, and others equally well-known. At the beginning of the following season the management passed into the hands of Mr. Armistead; and early in April "a splendid Oriental Spectacle," called *Sadak and Kalasrade, or the Waters of Oblivion*, (taken from the beautiful *Tales of the Genii*), was produced, which, we are told, "drew crowded audiences at Liverpool for two hundred nights." The *Wandering Minstrel* was also played during the same month, for the first time in Birmingham, with Mr. Wright as Jem Bags. Later on in the season, Birmingham playgoers had the rare treat of witnessing the performance of their brilliant townsman, Charles Reece Pemberton, in his most celebrated parts, Shylock and Macbeth, in aid of the building fund of the Mechanics' Institute.

The most noteworthy event in the season of 1837 was the engagement for three nights of one of the most remarkable combinations of theatrical "stars" which have ever graced the boards of a Birmingham theatre, comprising Mr. and Mrs. Yates, Mrs. Honey, Mrs. Fitzwilliam, Mr. O. B. Smith, Mr. Buckstone, and Mr. John Reeve, who appeared on the 13th, 14th, and 15th of July. Previous to this engagement, Mr. Templeton, a famous tenor in those days, appeared with Miss Sherriff in a series of operas; and, later on in the season, Mr. Vandenhoff, Madame Vestris, and Mr. Charles Matthews again appeared before Birmingham playgoers. Still, notwithstanding the ample provision made by the manager for the delectation of his patrons, the theatre did not pay, and Mr. Armistead added one more to the already long list of managers who had failed to make the Birmingham Theatre Royal a financial success. The following paragraph from the *Gazette* records Mr. Armistead's failure :—

August 28, 1837.—In consequence of non-fulfilment of the terms of the lease, and of non-payment of the rent by the manager, the Trustees of the Theatre, on the part of the Proprietors, took possession of the premises last week. This act was resisted on behalf of Mr. Armistead, and five persons were taken into custody while attempting to regain possession during the night of Sunday. The parties were charged with forcibly entering the theatre, and the circumstances were investigated at the Public Office on the following morning. The sitting magistrate, Mr. Lloyd, decided that the proprietors had obtained legal possession; and on the understanding that the manager would consent to give up all further claim, the defendants, upon entering into their own recognizances, were ordered to be discharged. At the close of the proceedings, application was made to Mr. Barker, the Solicitor to the Proprietors, for the use of the Theatre for a performance in aid of "the distressed workmen," on the evening of Friday. The request was subsequently granted, and the performance took place. The house was pretty well filled; and a correspondent writes us, that by way of acknowledgment "three groans were given for the tories."

This was the year of the Musical Festival, and as the theatre offered a chance of remuneration to anyone who cared to risk the undertaking, a short season was commenced under the management of Mr. Clarke, and during the autumn many of the old favourites appeared, including Madame Vestris and Mr. Charles Matthews, Mr. Phillips, Mr. Charles Kean, and others.

On the 4th of March, 1838, an amateur performance was given at the theatre by Mr. Joseph Smith (at that time an amateur actor of some note), assisted by Mr. J. C. Onions and the well-known "Ned Farmer," in aid of the suffering poor. Early in April the Theatre was re-opened by Mr. Munroe, with Mr. M. H. Simpson as stage-manager, the first piece being an adaptation of the immortal *Pickwick Papers*, with which "Boz" had convulsed the whole reading world only two years before. The piece was entitled "Sam Weller ; or, The Pickwickians," and the title *rôle* was sustained by Mr. Hall.

One of the first measures taken by the new management to ensure popularity was a further reduction in the prices of admission—the boxes being lowered to 3s. and 2s., the pit 1s., and the gallery 6d. One of the curiosities of this season's engagements was the once famous "Gnome Fly," Hervio H. Nano, who visited the town in June, and again in September ; and, during his second engagement, was the cause of a disgraceful theatrical riot—happily almost the only one in connection with the Birmingham stage. It is thus recorded in the *Gazette* :—

October 8, 1838.—A disgraceful riot took place at the Theatre in this town, on Monday night last. It appears that a dispute had arisen between the Manager and Signor Hervio Nano, with reference to a pecuniary demand of the latter in a settlement which took place on Saturday. Hervio Nano at the time when his presence was required for his part on the stage, was seated in one of the boxes of the Theatre, and on being applied to, in an audible voice refused to take his part unless a settlement was made to his satisfaction. The Stage Manager explained that there was no claim existing on the part of the complainant, as a full settlement had been made with Mr. Yates, of the Adelphi, to whose company the Signor was attached. An attempt was made to remove Nano forcibly from the box, and in the scuffle the latter passed over into the pit and on to the stage, and in the course of the struggle was aided by some of the audience. From the stage he proceeded again to the boxes. After another attempt on the part of the Manager to proceed with a different piece, Signor Nano addressed the audience, and being so advised, proceeded to the green-room, soon after which a scuffle was heard on the stage, and Nano, having raised the curtain, was seen struggling with several persons. A

rush was made by some of the audience from the pit and boxes, but to no avail, as the subject of sympathy did not re-appear. Hereupon the occupants of the gallery, having given notice of their intention to those assembled in the pit to clear away, began to tear up the benches of the gallery, and to throw them into the pit, breaking the chandeliers and whatever came in the way of the missiles, the havoc and confusion continuing until the lights were extinguished.

During this season was presented, for the first time before a Birmingham audience, the ever-popular *Lady of Lyons*, the part of "Claude Melnotte" being sustained by Mr. Balls. The music-loving portion of the audience at the theatre was not forgotten by the enterprising managers ; in October Mr. Braham appeared for two nights, and Mr. Templeton followed, in the ensuing week, in the opera of *La Sonnambula*. On the 9th of November, on the occasion of his benefit, Mr. Thompson delighted the audience by "introducing the Statue of Nelson, a copy from the one in the Bull Ring, but in white, to resemble marble," which, we are told, "was a beautiful fac-simile, and drew forth continued applause from all parts of the house." On December 7th, Mr. Munroe appeared for the first time, in the part of "Falstaff," in *King Henry the Fourth*, for the benefit of his stage manager, Mr. Simpson.

The season of 1839 presents but few matters calling for special notice ; mention should be made, however, of the production, for the first time in Birmingham, of "an entirely new drama, written and arranged from the celebrated work of 'Boz,' and prepared for dramatic representation by Edward Stirling, Esq., entitled *Nicholas Nickleby*." This was presented on the 5th of March ; and for the following evening was announced :

A Burletta, to conclude with Gustavus, or the masked Ball, in the last scene of which will be given a Grand Masquerade. Parties taking Lower Box tickets are entitled to admission to the Stage or Lobby doors. Masks, Dresses, or Dominoes to be had, on application to Mr. Simpson, or Mr. Wadds, at the Box Office.

This ingenious device of combining a theatrical performance with a masked ball, (the play being evidently written to introduce the ball), reminds us of the "little piece" which Douglas Jerrold "wrote up to" an old Admiral's coat, in the early days of his career as "stock author" to a metropolitan theatre; and it is not surprising to find so questionable a device for drawing a good house followed by the invasion of the boards by a circus company, that of the famous Ducrow. At the commencement of the regular season, however, more intellectual fare was provided. *Virginius, Hamlet,* (in which Mr. Cowle made his first appearance on the local stage,) and the *School for Scandal,* (with Charles Matthews as Charles Surface, and Madame Vestris as Lady Teazle,) occupied the place which had been usurped by clap-trap pieces, Ducrow's horses, and Van Amburgh's wild beasts. On the 23rd of July, Taglioni appeared, for one night only; and she was followed by a troupe of "Bedouin Arab Vaulters." On this occasion, we read, the stage represented "the great Desert of Sahara! with Tableaux Vivans of the evolutions, dances and exercises peculiar to the Bedevi, or sons of the Desert, which will be given in the representation of an Arabian Festival, by the native Bedouins."

The Autumn season opened with the "Grand Romantic Operatic Spectacle of Blue Beard," in which, by arrangement with the proprietor of the Zoological Gardens, Liverpool, "*a stupendous elephant*" was introduced. After this interregnum of spectacle and realism, Mrs. Honey commenced a five nights' engagement in *Blue Jackets;* and in November Mr. Buckstone appeared in his new comedy, *Single Life,* performed for the first time in Birmingham, on the 8th of that month.

The list of engagements for the season of 1840 was a very brilliant one, including the names of Mr. Templeton, Mr. Buckstone, Mr. Yates, Paul Bedford, Mr. Braham, Mrs. Honey, Miss Ellen Tree, Mr. and Mrs. Wood, and other eminent artistes. Among the attractions provided for less critical tastes were Ducrow's famous stud of horses, Van Amburgh's lions and tigers, and a grand Christmas Pantomime, (the first of a long

series of successes during the Messrs. Simpson's management) entitled "Harlequin and the Knight of the Silver Shield; or the Goblin Mill," "written and produced by Mr. De Hayes, under the immediate direction of Mr. Simpson;" and with this "Christmas Annual," the theatrical history of the decade under notice comes to a close.

The other amusements of this period exhibit a gradual improvement in the manners and tastes of the people. We have not to chronicle any of the brutal and demoralising sports, which have of necessity found a place in all previous chapters of our history of the amusements of the people; but in their place we have the pleasure of recording a meeting of "gentlemen friendly to the project of providing ground 'for the encouragement of cricket, racket, and other games,'" which was held at the Public Office, June 10th, 1834, the High Bailiff presiding. It was proposed to rent a piece of land, about six acres in extent, in the neighbourhood of Holloway Head, which had been offered by the proprietor for that purpose, at a rental of £150 per annum, although estimated by him at double the amount asked; and it was further proposed that about £1,200 be expended in the formation of the projected recreation ground. It does not appear, however, that this laudable project was ever carried into execution, and the lovers of athletic exercises were yet to wait twenty years before any provision should be made for their enjoyment by the public authorities of the town.

It is with pleasure that we transcribe the last reference in the local journals to the cruel pastime of

BULL-BAITING.
To the Editor of Aris's Gazette.

October 12, 1835.—SIR,—It must be gratifying to every friend of humanity, that, during the last Session of Parliament, a bill, the provisions of which, if strictly enforced, will have the effect of abolishing the horrid and demoralising practice of Bull-baiting, was introduced and received the Royal assent. It therefore behoves the Ministers and Churchwardens of those parishes where the cruel system has been pursued, to avail themselves of the power now placed in their hands, and zealously to carry into effect the humane intentions of the framers and supporters of the bill, while every sincere friend to humanity will cheerfully lend his assistance. As an individual deeply interested in promoting the happiness of the brute creation, I shall devote my time and labour in this good cause, and exert myself to render the bill effectual to the end designed. For want of such exertion, Bull-baiting was carried on to a horrible extent during the last wake at Brierley Hill, and thousands of people from distant

letters and science; and among others James Montgomery, the poet, delivered a course of lectures on the English Poets, at the Philosophical Institution, in the winter of 1838; and their own Charles Reece Pemberton, in the fading years of his life, lectured on several occasions,— now discoursing grandly on Shakespeare's

INTERIOR OF THE THEATRE ROYAL.

parishes congregated together to enjoy this feast of blood. Three bulls were then baited on the Saturday evening previous to the wake Sabbath, and for four successive days they were torn and lacerated for their amusement in a manner too shocking to relate. Trusting that the diabolical sport will be speedily abolished, I remain, Sir, your obliged servant,　　　　　　　A. SMITH.
　Brierley Hill, Oct. 3, 1835.

Many who had, in days gone by, found their chief recreation in the public house, the wake-feast, and the fair, now sought enjoyment in more intellectual pursuits, at the Mechanics' Institute and kindred societies. Lectures were delivered, from time to time, by eminent men of

character of Brutus, and now describing, with a rich glow, the scenes and sights he had looked upon in the far East, on the dusky Nile, or the sunny banks of the Mediterranean. The following graphic description of the lecturer and his theme, on the occasion of his lecture on "Brutus," which he also delivered at Sheffield, is quoted by Dr. Langford from the *Sheffield Independent*:

　"When he stepped upon the platform there was a tremendous outburst of cheering, which speedily sunk into a more subdued manifestation of welcome.   What a change had come upon him ! He was but the shadow of himself ; his manly bearing and his free action were gone, and in their place were come the stooping gait and the feeble walk.   But oh ! what a tale of suffering was told when he opened his mouth and spoke.   His voice, which had been sweet as the lute and loud as the trumpet, had become weak, cracked, and discordant !   And there was the dreadful cough that appeared to be everlastingly tearing at his heartstrings ! Well, but he did speak ; and, wonderful to behold, as he gradually advanced he got the mastery of his infirmities. The subject of the evening's lecture was Brutus, in Julius Cæsar.   He brought out, one by one, the beauties of the character, and when he made it appear, as it really is, a glorious specimen of the best qualities of human nature, he held it up for admiration and instruction.   Pemberton was no longer the man he had been some short time before—he had left all his own weaknesses and entered fully into the loveliness and truth of Brutus. The illustrative passages were given with the delicacy and power of former times.   It was life in death ; and showed how the vigorous soul can impart energy to the wasted body."

In June 1832, the art-loving public of Birmingham had provided for them a free treat of no common order, in the exhibition of Lodge's famous Gallery of Historical Portraits, which was opened "for gratuitous inspection" in the large room of the Society of Artists, in order to display the richness of that collection of engraved portraits, which was then about to be published in monthly parts.

Among the other exhibitions and amusements of this period, may be mentioned Signor Bertolotto's Industrious Fleas, which were here in January, 1837 ; Ryan's Amphitheatre ; Waxworks ; Professor Anderson ; and the miscellaneous entertainments which, from time to time, were given at Vauxhall Gardens, which were during this decade at the height of their splendour and success.   Variegated lamps and fireworks, comic singing, galas, and occasional performances by he 'stars' of its metropolitan namesake, formed the chief attractions at this favourite resort of the people.

We have now completed our story of the rise of Birmingham from the little village held of William Fitz-Ausculf, in the days of William the Conqueror, to the parliamentary and municipal borough of 1840, with its miles of streets, its hundred and fifty thousand inhabitants, and its manifold industries. We have noted the gradual improvement in its appearance, in the style of its public buildings, the number of its churches and schools, the refined character of its amusements, and the increased attention given to its sanitary condition.   The town which in Leland's day had but one street and "one paroch church." has now an abundance of both ; and has moreover a noble town hall, a commodious public office, a large and handsome market hall, several good hotels, an elegant and comfortable theatre, a new grammar school, botanical gardens, public library, and many other requirements of public and social life   But between the new borough of 1840 and the Birmingham of 1879 there is still a great contrast ; and it will be our task in the few succeeding chapters, to record the growth of the town during the intervening period ; to present, in fact, an adequate picture, so far as we are enabled, of *New Birmingham*.   To do this in detail, on the same scale as we have endeavoured to depict the life of Old Birmingham would require several large volumes, and would moreover make this portion of our work a mere newspaper chronicle of modern events, well remembered, doubtless, by most of our readers. We propose, therefore, in the remaining portion of our narrative, to present a continuous history of each section of the public and social life of our town, rather than to divide it into periods, either of a single decade or longer, as in the foregoing chapters.

OLD AND NEW BIRMINGHAM.

PART II.

FROM THE GRANTING OF THE CHARTER OF INCORPORATION TO THE PRESENT TIME.

IN entering upon the history of what may fairly be termed the "New Birmingham" period,—dating from the commencement of the first decade of the existence of the Corporation, and consequently of the municipal life of the town,—it will be necessary, as we have previously intimated, to adopt a somewhat different order in the course of our narrative. In each division of our subject,—municipal, political, religious, educational and literary, commercial, and general, as well as in noting the changes in the appearance of the town, and the amusements of the people,—we propose to deal with the history of the entire remaining period, from 1841 to 1879. For the guidance, therefore, of the reader who may be disposed to accompany us through this lengthy period, in which we shall find greater activity than we have hitherto met with in the course of our local records, we subjoin a sketch of the proposed order of the succeeding chapters of our history.

1841—1879.

I. Municipal History.
II. Political History.
III. General History: Public Life and Events.
IV. Churches and Sects.
V. Education and Literature, Literary Institutions, etc.
VI. Charitable Institutions.
VII. The Triennial Musical Festivals.
VIII. Amusements of the People.
IX. Trade and Commerce.
X. Public Buildings, and appearance of the Town.

CHAPTER I.

MUNICIPAL HISTORY OF THE BOROUGH.

The Borough Incorporated—Celebration of the Event—Conflicting Authorities—Attempt to close St. Philip's Churchyard—Proposal to adopt the Public Health Act—Mr. Rawlinson's Report—A Surveyor of the Old Type—The Birmingham Improvement Act—The Borough Goal—The Lunatic Asylum—Public Baths and Washhouses—The New Workhouse—The Free Libraries Movement—Defeat of the Proposal to adopt the Act in Birmingham—Cruelties at the Borough Goal Proposed New Improvement Bill defeated by the Ratepayers—The First Stipendiary Magistrate- The First Public Park—The Queen's Visit to Birmingham—Woodcock Street Baths

—The Free Libraries Act adopted—Street Tramways—Town Improvement Bill sanctioned—A Borough Analyst appointed—The New Borough Cemetery—The Purchase of Aston Park—Street Improvements—Sir Josiah Mason's Orphanage—New Fish Market—A New Street Tramway Scheme—Visit of Prince Arthur—New Division of the Borough into Wards—Proposed New Corporation Buildings—A new experiment in Street Paving—Presentation of a Diamond for the Mayor's Chain—Cannon Hill Park—Construction of the First Tramway—The Sewage Difficulty—Proposed Increase of the Borough Rate—Purchase of the Gas-works—The New Corporate Buildings Commenced—Purchase of Land for a New Park at Highgate—Purchase of the Waterworks—Small Heath Park—New Chief of Police—The Improvement Scheme.

IT is not proposed, in the present outline of the Municipal history of Birmingham, to record in detail the work of our local legislature, or to take note of all its enactments; and happily this is not needed, since the invaluable *History of the Corporation* by Mr. Bunce, of which the first volume is already issued, will supply the student who seeks to know more of that great governing body with all the information he may require. All we propose to do in these pages is to point out and make record of those special acts of the Town Council which have raised Birmingham to its present position, and have placed the Corporation of Birmingham in the front rank among the local governing bodies of England.

We have already referred to the incorporation of the borough, and have placed on record the names of our first Corporate Officers; as we stated, the new borough was divided into thirteen wards, returning forty-eight councillors, and these were apportioned to the several wards as follows:—

Ward.	No. of Representatives.	Ward.	No. of Representatives.
Ladywood	... 3	St. Peter's	... 6
All Saints'	... 3	St. Martin's	... 3
Hampton	... 3	St. Thomas's	... 3
St. George's	... 3	Edgbaston	... 3
St. Mary's	3	Deritend & Bordesley	6
St. Paul's	... 3	Duddeston & Nechells	6
Market Hall	... 3		
		Total	48

Sixteen aldermen were also appointed, thus bringing up the total number of the Council to sixty-four.

We may here, however, make reference to the celebration of the event by a public dinner, which took place on Thursday, February 21st, 1839, at which the Mayor presided. The scene is well described in the *Journal* of that week:—

"Immediately above the Mayor's chair there was suspended, in the way of canopy, a large and very hand-some Crown, festooned with laurel, and having a union jack waving over it. Over the vice-president's chair there was a splendid silk banner, with the Birmingham arms painted on it, and resting on the rail of the great gallery was placed the well-known symbol, the bundle of sticks, surmounted by a cap of liberty, to indicate that freedom can only be upheld by union, and accompanied by a pair of scales, as emblematic of equal justice to all, the great purpose why liberty ought to be vindicated and maintained. In the organ gallery were two very handsome transparencies, and in the great gallery was a third transparency, of very large dimensions. Banners of blue, purple, and white, were suspended from the candelabra, two from each, and the entire front of the galleries was festooned with laurel branches and artificial flowers and rosettes, the number of the rosettes being not less than fifteen hundred. When to the effect of these very tasteful decorations, we add the attractions of the hall itself, with the blaze of light running along its extensive walls, the cheerful faces of not less than five hundred gentlemen at the tables below, and above all the blooming cheeks and bright eyes of nearly twice that number of elegantly dressed ladies in the galleries, the rich tones of the magnificent organ, and the pealing anthem swelling the note of praise, we shall not be accused of exaggeration when we say that the *coup d'œil* at the moment that 'Non nobis' was being solemnly chanted, was one of very great and rare beauty."

It was necessary that the new Council should possess a Corporate Seal; and a report was presented by the Committee appointed to consider the matter, on the 19th of January, together with five suggested designs; which are fully described in Mr. Bunce's History. It may suffice, therefore, to say here that the design wisely chosen by the Council as the arms of the Borough, (in preference to the vaguely symbolical lions and lambs, locomotive engines, union banner, cap of liberty, and other similar insignia suggested,) was the Arms of the ancient and honourable family of Bermingham, (engraved on our first page,) with the simple and appropriate motto, "Forward."

Although the government of the town was now invested in the representative body thus incorporated, the jurisdictions of the authorities which were previously in existence, still continued, and hence a great portion of the rightful work of the Council still remained in the hands of the Commissioners; and it must be remembered that the several districts—the older

Town Council for some years almost in the position of a mere debating society, discussing subjects over which they exercised no control whatever; and not unfrequently, the several

PORTRAIT OF G. F. MUNTZ, M.P.
From an old Caricature print, "The Great Brummagem Organ."

portion of Birmingham, Deritend and Bordesley, Duddeston and Nechells—had each their own distinct Boards of Commissioners, who had the control of the lighting of the town, the markets and fairs, the cleaning and repairing of the streets, and other important local affairs. This left the

bodies came into collision with each other. One of the earliest instances of this occurred in the attempt of the Commissioners to close the walks around St. Philip's Churchyard. It would seem that at that time the walks—which not only crossed the churchyard, but surrounded it on all sides—were much frequented by the idlers who most religiously observed "Saint Monday," and found the sacred enclosure a convenient place for pedestrian matches, twice round the churchyard being roughly estimated as one mile. These races and walking matches were occasionally followed by the most unseemly "rows," and had become almost a public scandal ; * and hence the proposed action of the Commissioners. At a meeting of the Town Council, however, during the first week of January 1839, Mr. Alderman P. H. Muntz moved : "That it is the opinion of the Town Council that the walks of St. Philip's Church- yard are an ornament to the Borough, and should be kept in proper condition, and that they give this their decided opinion, that it would be injurious to the town if they were closed up." Shortly afterwards the Town Clerk gave an opinion, at the request of the Mayor, as to the legality of the proposal of the Commissioners to obtain an Act for this purpose, as follows :—

"On the whole I am of opinion that it is not competent for the Street Commissioners to carry into effect their proposed arrangement respecting St. Philip's Church- yard, and that if they should do so they will exceed their authority—will misappropriate the funds entrusted to their care—and will furnish good grounds for an appeal against the rate."

Mr. Muntz then moved—"That in the opinion of this Council the proposed arrangement of the Street Commissioners with respect to St. Philip's Churchyard is illegal—involves a mis- application of public moneys, and would permit a good ground of appeal against the rate ; nor, in the judgment of this Council, is the illegality of this transaction at all redeemed by its utility, or by its consonancy with the public wishes ; that this Council, therefore, still hopes that the Commissioners will see fit to abandon a measure which cannot be persevered in without producing a strong resistance on the part of the town." This proposition was seconded by Mr. Alderman

* For this fact we are indebted to an old Birmingham reformer, Mr. F. Appleby, who was one of the earlier members of the Political Union, and now (1879) resides at Onchan, Isle of Man, being still hale and hearty, and deeply interested in the welfare of *new* Birming- ham.—R.K.D.

Hutton, and carried unanimously. Thus the Corporation successfully resisted an attempt to close almost the only green spot in the heart of the town, and preserved for future generations a most invaluable "lung," close to our busiest thoroughfares. The "races" were stopped by closing the walk round the boundaries of the churchyard, and opening new thoroughfares across it in every direction instead. But could not a strip be spared in 1879, when such scandals would be impossible, to form a path from the Blue Coat School to Temple Row West, running parallel with Colmore Row ?

During the year 1844, the Mayoral chair was filled by Mr. Thomas Weston, and at the close of his year a tea party was held at the Town Hall, November 11th, in testimony of the able and impartial manner in which he had discharged the duties of his office, and an address was presented to him on this occasion. In acknowledging the honour thus conferred upon him, he gave some interesting particulars as to his early life, viz :—

That thirty-seven years ago he came to Birmingham a poor boy. Through kind patronage, he had gained ex- perience, he had gained importance, he had prospered, and he felt proud of the community in which he resided. He was the son of a working man, and was sent from a rural district, like many other boys, to take his chance in this town. His parents were working people, unable to pro- vide for themselves in their old age, but they transmitted to their children a name unsullied and untarnished ; and he hoped, too, so to transmit his name to his children. Although his parents were totally unable to give him a fortune, they gave him what was better—they taught him the rudiments of reading, writing, and arithmetic, and laid the foundation of his future success.

On the passing of the Public Health Act of 1848, an unsuccessful attempt was made by the Council to avail themselves of its provisions, in order to bring about the desired consolidation of the governing bodies of the town ; and in accordance with a memorial of the ratepayers, an enquiry was conducted by Mr. Robert Rawlinson, C.E., one result of which was the publication of a most valuable and interesting pamph- let respecting the natural history — if we may so describe it—of the town. We would gladly transfer much of this report into our pages did not the exigencies of space forbid ; but we cannot forbear quoting one or two paragraphs, and gathering together some of the most interesting particulars, for the benefit of those of our readers who may not have met with this now

lias. The Alps were yet below the salt wave, although the Grampians of Scotland had existed countless centuries, and the hills of Cumberland had passed their state as glaciered mountains. Wales was dry land, and the Cotteswold Hills, in Gloucestershire, and some few parts of central England, were above water. The rocks of Dudley had subsided even before the deposit of the sand-rock began ; huge ice-floes and bergs came floating up

INSANITARY HOUSES : A COURT IN JOHN STREET.
About to be removed under the Artisans' Dwellings Act.

scarce pamphlet. The formation of the "new red sandstone" upon which Birmingham is built, is thus picturesquely described by Mr. Rawlinson :—

 "Could we have seen the form of country when the diluvium on which Birmingham now stands was being deposited, we should have found the sea-shore forming a boundary probably not unlike the curve of the outcropping

from some northern continent long since drowned, grinding the imbedded fragments torn from their parent rock, wearing banks and shoals, and ultimately depositing their stony burden in scattered groups over vast areas hereafter to become dry land. The whole site on which Birmingham stands has been subjected to this wearing action, and the present valleys of the rivers Rea and Tame are but the indentations of the old sea-shore ; the sand and gravel now dug from beneath the streets was washed and rolled by comparatively shallow water into its present bed ; the alternations of clay and marl speak of deeper water, or a more quiet shore."

It is this sand and gravel which preserves the foundations of the buildings dry; while the undulating surface of the land assists in keeping the town clean and well ventilated, and the streets comparatively dry. The report further states that there is a marked dryness in the air, the average rainfall in Birmingham being about one-third less than in Liverpool or Manchester; and whereas the damp atmosphere of Lancashire is necessary to the profitable spinning of cotton-yarn, the drier atmosphere of Warwickshire is, we are told, equally advantageous to the iron manufacture, to the production of polished steel implements, and the metal-plated wares in general of Birmingham.

The trades of Birmingham are not forgotton by Mr. Rawlinson, and some of his remarks on this subject are worth quoting :—

"There are," he says, "about 520 distinctly classified manufacturers, traders, or dealers, and about twenty separate professions in Birmingham, and each trade may certainly be divided into five branches, which will give 2,600 varieties of occupation; but I have no doubt this is understated, as there are fourteen distinct branches named in the Directory as engaged in the manufacture of guns. The trades carried on in the town are not only numerous, but they are also, in a great measure, distinct and independent of each other in their manufacture and after use. To the knives, swords, and spears of the ancient Britons has been added a splendour of finish and polish unknown to the magical blades of Damascus; and there is a small instrument of skill manufactured in millions, the pen, more powerful in the world at this day than all the swords, spears, and scythe-armed chariots of past ages. The black and dingy 'nayler' of Leland has for his town companion the electro-plate and papier-mâché manufacturer, by the latter of which the lustre and polish of the precious metals is outshone by the iris-dyes of the pearl."

One peculiar feature in the commercial aspect of Birmingham is noted by Mr. Rawlinson which should not be overlooked, as it supplies the stranger who may be interested in the history of our town with an explanation of the independent, self-reliant character of the Birmingham artisan. "The variety of trades and occupations exercised," he says, "tends to a more equal and general diffusion of wealth amongst the master manu-facturers, and the means of acquiring it in moderation among the workpeople; there are few 'millionaires,' connected with trade in or near Birmingham, if we except the Staffordshire iron-masters; there are few who occupy the position of the 'cotton lords' of Manchester, or the 'merchant princes' of Liverpool; but there is a numerous class of master tradesmen whose wealth tends to comfort rather than ostentatious show, and there is a race of workpeople comparatively independent and self-relying. Some observant and intelligent writers have considered the prosperity of the town has arisen from its perfect freedom from the corporate trammels of past ages, or the blind, exclusive guild, which affects to give privileges to the few, by the Chinese plan of stereotyping the initiated." From Mr. Rawlinson's further remarks on the local trades we learn the following facts respecting the increase of steam power. From 1780 to 1836 there were 169 steam engines erected in Birmingham with a total of 2,700 horse-power. In 1839 the horse-power was 3,436, consuming 240 tons of coal daily; and in 1849—the date of the report—the horse-power was about 5,400, with a daily consumption of about 377 tons of coal, and an equivalent of labour to that of 86,400 men.

The allotment gardens, which still lingered at Edgbaston, Bordesley, Handsworth, Moseley, and along the valley of the Rea, are noted with commendation by Mr. Rawlinson, and the large number of public houses—1,363 in all, including beerhouses, wholesale stores, etc.—with disfavour and concern; and he then passes on to the important subjects of gas and water, to which we shall refer more particularly later on. The crowded and neglected condition of the church-yards are next commented on, and contrasted with the clean and neat condition of the two recently opened cemeteries,—the General Cemetery at Key Hill, and the adjacent Church of England Cemetery; and then the Inspector deals with the main subject of enquiry, the government and sanitary condition of the town; adverting to the absence of a general system of sewerage, the imperfect condition of the streets and roads, the high rates and inefficient service which resulted from the multiplicity of conflicting authorities, and to the hindrance to good government, and wasteful multiplication of officers which such a condition of affairs entailed.

He sums up the result of his enquiries in the following recommendations :—

"Having fully examined the town and suburbs of Birmingham, I beg respectfully to recommend that the Public Health Act be put in force ; that the local power so necessary to cheap and efficient government may be consolidated, and that the whole sanitary work of the borough may be placed under one establishment.

"I beg respectfully to lay the following summary before the General Board of Health for their consideration :

"1. That the borough of Birmingham is not so healthy as it may be, on account of unpaved streets, confined courts, open middens and cesspools, and stagnant ditches.

"2. That excess of disease may be distinctly traced to crowded lodging-houses and want of ventilation in confined courts, and to the want of drains generally.

"3. That the present church and chapel yards within the town which are used as burial grounds should be closed.

"4. That a better supply of water should be provided, and that a perfect system of sewers and drains should be laid down.

"5. That public parks and pleasure grounds would be very beneficial to the working classes and their families.

"6. That a consolidation of the conflicting powers exercised within the borough would produce great economy.

"7. That the health of the inhabitants would be improved, their comforts increased, and their moral condition raised—1. By a perfect system of street, court, yard, and house drainage. 2. By a constant and cheap supply of pure water under pressure, laid on to every house and yard, to the entire superseding of all local wells and pumps, the water of which is impure. 3. By the substitution of water-closets or soil-pan apparatus (for the more expensive existing privies and cesspools), with proper drains to carry away all surface-water and refuse from the roofs, streets, yards, and water-closets. 4. By properly paved courts and passages, and by a regular system of washing and cleansing all courts, passages, footpaths, and surface channels.

"8. That these improvements may be realised independently of any advantage to be derived from the application of town refuse to agricultural purposes, at the rates per week for each house and labourer's cottage here stated :—1. A full and complete system of house and yard drains, with a water-closet and soil-pan, and yard drain to each house, three half-pence per week. 2. A constant high-pressure supply of pure water laid on in each house with a water-tap and waste-water sink to each house com-plete, for three-half pence a week. 3. Complete and perfect pavement to all yards and courts, with proper surface channels and grates, at one farthing a week each house. 4. Washing, cleansing, and watering streets, courts, foot-walks, and surface channels, at one farthing a week each house.

"9. That from the character of the soil in the neighbourhood of the town, sewage manure may be applied to the agricultural land by irrigation, with singular advantage, so as to increase its value to the farmer, and yield an income for the benefit and improvement of the town.

"10. That these improvements will increase the health and comfort of all classes, and reduce the amount of poor's rates.

"11. That the direct charges stated will be the means of a direct and indirect saving to the inhabitants generally, but to the labouring man especially, of many times the amount to be paid.

"12. That the outlay will not be burdensome or oppressive to any class of the community, as the capital required may be raised by loan, and the interest upon it reduced to an annual or weekly rent-charge."

In consequence of the rivalry and bitter hostility which prevailed in the town, between the various governing bodies, the enquiry was unproductive of any immediate reform. Although the Government of their own motion included Birmingham in the schedule of a bill, to apply the Public Health Act to several towns, the Commissioners, by their determined opposition, were successful in defeating the proposal so far as it related to the mis-governed midland metropolis.

Mr. Bunce gives a curious illustration of the way in which public work was performed under the regimé of the Commissioners. The acting surveyor of the hamlets of Duddeston and Nechells was, he tells us, "a saddler and beer-seller by trade," and "had received no training of any kind as a surveyor, but, for a salary of £30 a year, he boldly undertook the management of the drainage of his district, his qualification for this function being, to use his own phrase, that he was a kind of 'universal genius.'" When giving evidence before the Parliamentary Committee, in 1845, he declared, amid roars of laughter, that "he never could see that there was any art in laying down sewers," that "he never had no instruction," that he knew nothing of the use of a spirit level, and that he "took levels (for sewers and roads) by three sticks : crow-sticks." How satisfactory this method proved may be read in Mr. Rawlinson's report, from which we learn that in the district presided over by this natural genius, "an expensive culvert of little or no use to the hamlets had

House of Commons in the following March, and although threatened with a formidable opposition on the part of the numerous local 'interests,' it was happily brought to a successful issue, and became law on the 24th of July, 1851.

INSANITARY HOUSES: NO. 2 COURT, JOHN STREET.
About to be removed under the Artisans' Dwellings Act.

been made, as one part is too low and other parts are too high, and that no side or cross street drains had been laid in."

In August, 1850, however, the Council resolved to make another vigorous effort to remove the stigma of misgovernment, and to make an end of the chaotic mob of conflicting authorities, by preparing a bill to consolidate the governing bodies of the town, which was introduced in the

The Act transferred to the Council all the powers previously exercised by the Boards of Commissioners and Surveyors ; and, in addition, empowered the Council to undertake street improvements, to remove all turnpikes within the Borough, and to purchase the Waterworks ; and the rating for the purposes of the Act was fixed at two shillings and sixpence in the pound—an Improvement Rate of two shillings, and a

Street Improvement Rate (for the purchase of scheduled properties) of sixpence.

On the 1st of January 1852 the new Act came into operation, and the whole of the non-representative bodies, with the old system of divided responsibilities, were swept

borough, all prisoners were sent to the county gaol at Warwick, and all except petty sessions cases had to be tried at the county sessions; the lock-up at Moor Street was used only for the detention of prisoners waiting the decision of the magistrates; and the entire constabulary force in

INSANITARY HOUSES: NO. 1 COURT, STEELHOUSE LANE.
About to be removed under the Artisans' Dwellings Act.

away; and on the 3rd of January the Council met for the first time under their new powers, having entire control over the municipal work of the town.

In one department, however, the new authorities had already worked a great reform, before the passing of the Improvement Act,—namely, in the administration of justice and the preservation of the peace. Previous to the incorporation of the

the town, previous to 1838, consisted only of nineteen men, to protect the lives and property of more than 150,000 inhabitants! But after the creation of the representative municipal government, the new police system was introduced in Birmingham, and something like an adequate force organised, consisting of a superintendent, 8 inspectors, 8 sub-inspectors, 26 sergeants, and 293 men,—making a total of 336. For a time, however, the Government retained the management of the force ; but, after continued remonstrance and opposition on the part of the inhabitants, resigned its control into the hands of the Council.

We have already recorded, in the last chapter of our chronicle of local events, the establishment of a separate Sessions for the Borough, at the requisition of the Town Council ; there needed now, therefore, only a suitable House of Correction to complete the machinery of justice, and to render the Borough independent of the county town, except for the more important cases committed for trial at the Assizes. It was therefore resolved by the Council, in 1844, to erect a Borough Gaol on Birmingham Heath ; and the first stone of the building was laid by the Mayor, Mr. Thomas Phillips, on the 29th of October, 1845. The Gaol was completed in 1849, the first prisoner being received within its walls on the 17th of October in that year.

It was built from the designs of Mr. D. R. Hill, and arranged upon the system of Pentonville. The building is of brick with stone dressings, the style adopted being a kind of Romanesque ; the warders' turrets, on the walls, give to the place a castellated appearance quite in keeping with the purpose for which it was erected. It was originally built to contain three hundred and thirty-six cells ; but the additions which have since been made have increased the number to about four hundred.

The next undertaking of the Corporation was the erection of a Borough Lunatic Asylum, on a site in the neighbourhood of the Gaol. The first stone was laid September, 29th, 1847, by the Mayor, Mr. R. Martineau ; and the building, which was erected from designs by Mr. D. R. Hill, was completed in June, 1850. It contains accommodation for nearly 400 patients, and is admirably adapted with a view to the cure of the unfortunate inmates ; being provided with books, newspapers and periodicals, and other means of diverting the patients during their temporary

exile, and surrounded by well-kept grounds and gardens.

Meanwhile, although the Council had not as yet made any provision for the healthful enjoyment of the people, the public mind was awake to the necessity of such provision being made, and a public meeting was held on the 19th of November, 1844, to promote the establishment of Public Baths, and the formation of Public Parks in the town, and upwards of £4,400 was subscribed for the purpose in one week. The matter was, however, allowed to drop for a time, and it was not until June, 1846, (by which time £6,000 had been subscribed), that the Public Baths Association chose a site, in Kent Street, for their first experiment. At a meeting of the Council on the 7th of October in the same year, on a motion of Mr. Alderman Cutler, the Buildings Committee were empowered to take the necessary steps for adopting the Public Baths Act in Birmingham, and in the following month a meeting of the Association was held, at which it was resolved that as the Council had the matter in hand, the land acquired should be transferred to that body. On the 2nd of October, 1848, the Council gave their final consent for the erection of the first set of Public Baths on the site selected by the Association, at an estimated cost of £10,000 ; but it was not until October 29, 1849, that the first stone was laid,—that ceremony being performed by Mr. S. Thornton, Mayor,—and the building was not opened until the 12th of May, 1851. The designs selected were those of Mr. D. R. Hill, the architect of the Borough Gaol and the Lunatic Asylum ; the exterior is in the Elizabethan style, and the establishment comprises sixty-nine private baths, two swimming baths, and three plunging baths. The washhouse department contains twenty-five washing stalls, and thirty-two drying horses, and is abundantly supplied with hot and cold water, every convenience being provided in the large laundry adjoining.

Although not the work of the corporation, it is

fitting that we should record in this chapter the erection of the new Workhouse. The old building in Lichfield Street had begun to fall into a dilapidated condition, and the growth of the town around it had rendered its site entirely unfit for such an institution. It was no longer possible to see from its windows (as its earlier inmates might have done) the beautiful undulating sweep of country from Aston to Barr Beacon, and from Erdington to Sutton Park; the view was now shut out by the wilderness of dingy brick and mortar on every side, which rendered it close and unwholesome; and at length it was resolved by the ratepayers that a new building should be erected on the land belonging to the Parish at Birmingham Heath, in the neighbourhood of the Gaol and the Lunatic Asylum. It was built from the designs of Mr. Bateman, but has since been enlarged under the superintendence of Messrs. Martin and Chamberlain. The first stone was laid September 9th, 1850, and the building was opened on the 29th of March, 1852, when upwards of 8,000 persons visited it. It is planned with considerable care and thoughtfulness for the comfort and welfare of the inmates; all the apartments used by the aged poor being on the ground floor, and every room in the building having the benefit of sunshine during some portion of the day, whereby both the health and cheerfulness of the inmates is enhanced. The chapel, which faces the road, is very tastefully fitted up, and is capable of accommodating 1,000 worshippers. It is a neat structure in the perpendicular style of architecture, surmounted by a light and elegant bell-turret. The aisles, nave, and chancel, are paved with encaustic tiles, presented by the architect, Mr. Bateman, and Mr. Minton; and several of the windows are filled with stained glass, by Messrs. Chance. The total cost of erection, including land, furniture etc., was £44,476.

In 1850, as most of our readers are aware, the first Free Libraries Act was passed, mainly through the exertions of Mr. Ewart; and by this Act town councils were authorised to establish public libraries and museums in their towns, providing a majority of two-thirds could be obtained on a poll of the burgesses, favourable to the adoption of the Act. This Act had not been on the Statute Book much more than twelve months, when an attempt was made to apply its provisions to Birmingham. At a meeting of the Town Council, on the 6th of February, 1852, Councillor J. R. Boyce moved that at their next meeting the Council should take the subject into consideration, and then decide as to the advisability of introducing the Act into the Borough. The next meeting was held March 19th, and thereat the Council resolved that the Mayor be requested to take the necessary steps to determine, in accordance with the Act, whether or not the Public Libraries Act should be adopted. The Mayor, Mr. Henry Hawkes, thereupon appointed April 7th as the day on which the town should decide the question. The cry taken up by the opponents of the measure was that it would violate the principle of voluntaryism, and would prove another "state endowment;" they were not all believers in voluntaryism—many were quite otherwise—but in their love of darkness and ignorance they willingly joined the party which seemed to have the most plausible ground of opposition to the movement. The opposition was led by a somewhat erratic independent minister, the Rev. Brewin Grant, who, *mirabile dictu!* has since become one of the staunchest advocates of state endowment, and a clergyman of the Church of England. The supporters of the movement were fully as active, however, as their opponents. A meeting was held on the 31st of March, at the Public Office, presided over by Mr. T. Weston; and a sub-committee (consisting of Messrs. J R. Boyce, E. C. Osborne, George Dawson, M.A., Samuel Timmins, J. A. Langford, and W. Harris,) was appointed to canvass the town, with a view of setting before the inhabitants the true issues of the decision, and to endeavour to obtain the necessary majority of votes. The polling took place, as appointed, on April 7th; 534 votes being recorded in favour of adopting the Act, and only 363 against it; but as by the obnoxious clause introduced by Mr. R. Spooner, M.P., a majority of two-thirds of the votes recorded was necessary for the adoption of the Act, the proposition was lost, and the intellectual advancement of the people was retarded for almost a whole decade.

Only two years after the defeat of the Free Library Movement, however, the Town Council were successful in obtaining an Act enabling them to render invaluable assistance in the erection of the Birmingham and Midland Institute, and thus some atonement was made for the temporary loss of Free Libraries in the town. Of the action of the Council in the matter of the Institute, we shall have to speak further in our history of that institution.

During the spring of 1853 the humanity of the town was shocked by reports which were current of the most inhuman cruelties practised at the Borough Gaol, the truth of which was borne out by several suicides committed by prisoners confined therein. A public meeting was held, and a deputation, consisting of Messrs. Joseph Allday, G. Turner, W. Hale, and J. H. Cutler, was appointed to wait upon Lord Palmerston, to present a memorial adopted at the meeting, praying for a public enquiry into the discipline at the gaol. On the 29th of June, the report of the visiting justices, in reference to these charges, was presented to the magistrates at their usual session, together with the report of the government inspector, Mr. Perry. The former reported that they had ever "found Mr. Austin (the governor of the gaol) faithful, energetic, and painstaking in the discharge of his difficult and laborious duties; and that since his appointment as governor, he has maintained good order, both among officers and prisoners, with that consideration for the officers which ought to have received not only the obedience, but the support, of all; and as regards the prisoners,

although occasionally using some severity and discipline, yet always with a sense of their position, and a desire to avoid the necessity of recurrence to harsh measures." Such was the model governor of the gaol, as painted by the hand of those who, as representatives both of the law and of the people, were entrusted with the duty of visiting the gaol on behalf of the outer world; and who should have insisted in all cases that the merciful words of the law, "not exceeding," should never be disregarded. How this duty was fulfilled, the report of the inspector, presented on the same occasion, shall say.

"In the course of this enquiry," he says, "facts have been brought to my knowledge which warrant me in stating that the governor is in the habit of inflicting on the prisoners, especially those of the juvenile class, punishments not sanctioned by law, which, while they are not even effectual in repressing disorder, are in their nature repugnant to the feelings of humanity, and likely to drive the prisoners to desperation." *

One of the favourite instruments of torture used by this "considerate" governor was the crank, which one poor prisoner was condemned to turn ten thousand times in one day, in an almost nude condition. Two thousand times had the poor wretch to turn this hideous crank before breakfast, four thousand times between breakfast and dinner, and four thousand between dinner and supper. Several others were punished in even a more barbarous manner, bringing to mind rather the regimé of the Inquisition than the prison discipline of one of the most liberal and enlightened communities in England, during the latter half of the nineteenth century. They were kept for several days without food, fastened to the wall by a collar which almost strangled them, and made to wear a strait jacket of the most ingeniously cruel contrivance. When the miserable victims fainted from exhaustion,

---

* "Not only likely," adds Dr. Langford, "but which actually did drive, in less than four years, seventeen persons to desperation,'

FORWARD

J. A. LANGFORD, L.L.D.

PHOTOGRAPHED BY WHITLOCK

BIRMINGHAM: HOUGHTON & CO., SCOTLAND PASSAGE.

buckets of cold water were thrown over them, by order of the humane and considerate governor; and other tortures were devised, which made death seem to the wretched prisoners a happy release. It is pitiful to read of even "mere youths being driven to suicide under this monstrous treatment."

It is not to be wondered at that the report of the visiting justices aroused the indignation of the people, and the Government enquiry promised by Lord Palmerston was looked forward to with great anxiety. On the 15th of August, the governor of the gaol tendered his resignatio n, and the enquiry was commenced, at the Queen's Hotel, on the 30th of the same month. The Commissioners were, Mr. Welsby, Recorder of Chichester; Capt. Williams, Inspector of Prisons for the Home District; and Dr. Bailey, Medical Inspector of Millbank Penitentiary. The enquiry occupied twelve days, and every case of alleged cruelty was investigated, confirming the report of the inspector in every particular. The Commissioners' report was published in July, 1854, and forms a contribution to the history of Birmingham which may well cause the cheek to burn and the head to hang down, as we remember that the cruelties recorded therein were perpetrated in our midst only five and twenty years ago; that, as the *Times* said, " Birmingham Gaol was in secret the scene of doings which literally filled the public with horror," and that stories " which would have been thought exaggerations if found in one of Mr. Dickens's books," should have been true of our borough gaol in 1853.

In 1855, we have to record another step towards the establishment of a Free Library in the town, in the presentation to the town of about 200 volumes of the Patent Office Publications, on condition that they should be deposited in a library to which the inhabitants could have free access. This gift from the Commissioners of Patents was reported to the Town Council on the 5th of June, 1855; and it was resolved that the Midland Institute be requested

to accept the books, and place them in their rooms, where they might be used free of charge ; and that when a Free Library should be established, the works should be transferred thereto.

During the closing weeks of the year 1855, the Council was occupied in the preparation of a new Improvement Bill, and a meeting of the ratepayers was held December 18th respecting the project. Amid great confusion the following resolution was moved, almost in dumb-show, by Mr. Lucy :

That the Council of this Borough be authorised and empowered to make application to Parliament in the ensuing session, for an Act to amend the Birmingham Improvement Act of 1851, and for other purposes, in accordance with the published parliamentary notice now read by the Town Clerk ; and that among such other purposes the said Committee be authorised and empowered to obtain powers to raise and borrow for the purpose of the said intended Act, the sum of £80,000, upon the credit of the rates authorised to be levied by the said intended Act, and to consolidate the rates called respectively, the Borough Improvement Rate and the Street Improvement Rate, authorised to be levied by the said Birmingham Improvement Act, 1851.

A poll was demanded, which the Mayor appointed to take place on the three following days, and the poll resulted in an overwhelming majority against the proposed bill, only 170 votes being recorded in favour of it, and the large number of 3,402 against. The result of this apparent want of confidence in the Town Council was, that the directors of the Birmingham Banking Company declined to increase the account against the local authorities, and the two committees concerned— the Finance Committee and the Public Works' Committee—tendered their resignations at the next meeting of the Council.

On the first of April, 1856, the Council appointed a Stipendiary Magistrate for the Borough. Four candidates were nominated : Mr. Kynnersley, Mr. Adams, Mr. Bevan, and Mr. Simons; and the first-named gentleman was elected, 50 votes being recorded in his favour, only 33 being given for the highest unsuccessful candidate. Mr. Kynnersley's appointment having been confirmed by the Queen, he was introduced to the Council on the 19th of the same month, and took his seat on the Bench the same day.

We have now to record the establishment of our first public parks.

In 1855, Mr. C. B. Adderley, M.P. (now Lord Norton), offered to the Council ten acres of land at Saltley, for a public park, the conditions being that the Council should pay a nominal rent of £5 per annum for the land; that they should lay out the park in a proper manner; and that the donor should share in the control of the same and have a voice in the regulations relating thereto. These conditions being considered objectionable, the General Purposes Committee recommended that the offer be declined, and the Council ratified their decision. This elicited from Mr. Adderley the following letter:

Hams, 23rd of August, 1855.

Dear Sir,

I have received from you a copy of the resolution of the General Purposes Committee declining my offer of ten acres of land at Saltley for a public park.

It appears that they have throughout misunderstood my offer to have amounted to a free gift to them of the land, though from time to time I have endeavoured to correct such a misapprehension, and to state it clearly to be an offer to give the land for the purpose of a Park on certain conditions, being the same conditions as land might be offered upon for the same purpose by other landowners.

There occurring a delay in any other offer being made, they asked that the conditions might be reduced to writing. I requested you to state them on my part, which I meant to amount to a very reduced rent, a voice in the regulations of the park, and a guarantee of a proper laying out of the ground.

Objections appear to have been raised to all these, although the rent which you proposed was at least one-sixth of the real value, and being intended more as an acknowledgment than a rent, I would willingly have reduced lower still; and the stipulation for proper fencing was not on my own account, but part of a set of park regulations, which they requested me to obtain from Manchester.

I should regret that the public should now be deprived of an expected place for recreation, by the offer having failed; I will, therefore, myself, set apart the same space of ground in the proposed quarter for the public; and as it appears (objections having been made to a fence) that the Committee had no intention of ornamenting the proposed park, such a piece of ground will serve as well all the purposes of a play-ground for all classes of people.

Yours, truly,

C. Couchman, Esq.   C. B. ADDERLEY.

The Corporation did, however, subsequently accept Mr. Adderley's generous provision for the recreation of the toiling artisans of Birmingham, but in a modified form; the land was leased to them for 999 years at a peppercorn rent of 5s. per annum. This, our first public park, the forerunner of a goodly series of such institutions—was opened on the 30th of August, 1856. The event was celebrated by a dinner, at which 400 guests sat down, in a marquee erected in the park; and a concert was afterwards given, which included an ode, written for the occasion by R. Monckton Milnes (now Lord Houghton), and set to music by Dr. Belcher.

In commemoration of Mr. Adderley's generosity the Council resolved, December 9, 1862, to "erect a suitable and imperishable monument," which took the form of a portrait, painted by Weigall, and was deposited in the Corporation Art Gallery.

In the meantime another small park was offered to the town, on somewhat similar terms, by Lord Calthorpe. On the first of April, 1856, the General Purposes Committee presented the following report to the Council in reference to his lordship's proposal:

That they had received from Mr. Whateley Lord Calthorpe's proposals for letting to the Corporation, for purposes of public recreation, between twenty and thirty acres of land in the Pershore Road, by way of experiment, for one year, at a rental of £3 per acre. The land appears in every respect suitable, being in a pleasant and comparatively rural situation, and at the same time contiguous to the centre of the town. The following is a copy of the proposal:—"Lord Calthorpe proposes to let to the Corporation for *one year*, about thirty acres of land, at a pasture rent, for the purpose of recreation for the working classes, in *order to try the effect of it*, on the following conditions:—1.—That the working classes shall have free admittance at all hours of the day during the six working days. 2.—That no person shall be admitted on the ground on a Sunday. 3.—That all gambling, indecent language, and disorderly conduct be strictly prohibited. 4.—That no wine, malt liquor, or spirituous liquors be sold or consumed on the ground. 5.—That no smoking be allowed. 6.—That no horses and carriages be permitted to enter the grounds, except chairs on wheels with invalids and children. 7.—That no Dogs be allowed to enter. 8.—That no games be allowed, except cricket, rounders, trap-

ball, battledore, quoits, gymnastics, and archery. 9.—
That bathing be prohibited. 10.—That Sunday and
day school children be admitted on the days of their
respective anniversaries. 11.—That a proper number of
police officers be in attendance strictly to enforce the above
regulations. 12.—That the fences be preserved from
injury."

The regulation as to the closing of the park on
Sundays having been withdrawn, at the request
of the Council, the offer was accepted and at
the conclusion of the trial year the land was
handed over to the town on a lease similar to
that of Adderley Park. As in the previous case
the new park was called by the name of the
donor, and was formally opened on the 1st of
June, 1857, by the Duke of Cambridge.

The possession of these two small parks or
recreation grounds only whetted the public
appetite for still more accommodation of a like
character, and attention was now turned to the
noble fragment which still remained of the park
enclosed by Sir Thomas Holte at Aston. The
greater part had been cut up into streets and laid
out for building land, but was as yet to a great
extent unbuilt-upon.

The first reference to the purchase of Aston
Park by the Council occurs in the Minutes of the
Quarterly Meeting of the Council, August, 6th,
1850, where we read that "the Mayor informed the
Council that he had received an offer of the Aston
Park Estate, and brought under the consideration
of the Council the propriety of entering into a
treaty for the purchase of the estate as a place of
public recreation and amusement for the Burgesses." On this information a committee was
appointed "to open a communication with the
proprietors of the estate with the view of obtaining
the refuse of purchase until the end of the next
Session of Parliament." On the 29th October the
Committee reported to the Council; they had
applied to Mr. E. Robins (who was acting for the
proprietors in the sale of the estate) in accordance
with the resolution; but, as the Council had not
as yet obtained their Improvement Act, and
consequently were without legal power to purchase, Mr. Robins declined to enter into any

treaty lest it should inadvertently involve both
parties in litigation and difficulty. The matter
was therefore shelved for a time, and we hear no
more respecting the purchase of the park until
August 22nd, 1856, when the question was once
more raised, and the following resolution
adopted :—

That the General Purposes Committee be authorised
and instructed to communicate with the Proprietors of
the Aston Park Estate, and ascertain upon what terms
the estate may be acquired as a Public Park and place of
recreation for the inhabitants of the Borough.

In pursuance of these instructions the Committee, with the Borough Surveyor, viewed the
estate, and on the 28th October reported to the
Council on the subject. They had instructed
Mr. John Lewis Hornblower "to select from
Aston Park, for a place of public recreation, such
an eligible portion thereof, comprising the Hall,
as might be purchased for a sum not exceeding
£30,000, and to submit a plan of the portion
selected, and to report thereon not only the particulars before referred to, but his opinion upon
the general capability and value of Aston Park and
Hall, as it lies within the park pale, as a whole."
In reply Mr. Hornblower selected eighty-two acres
of the land immediately surrounding the hall, as
being specially suited to the requirements of a
public park, and valued the same at about £23,000.
There was at that time, enclosed within the park
palings, the whole of the land now bounded by
Victoria Road, Birchfield Road, Aston Brook,
Trinity Road, and Park Road, about 160 or 170
acres in all—and this Mr. Hornblower valued at
£50,000. The proprietors of the estate, however,
had set a higher value upon the land; estimating
the selected eighty-two acres at £60,900, and a
narrower circle of land surrounding the hall—
about thirty acres—at £24,500. To this the
Council demurred, and instructed the Committee
to ascertain from the proprietors whether any
reduction of the price could be made, and to
report thereon, "with such recommendations as
they think fit to make as to the extent of land
which they deem it desirable to purchase, and the

price which should be given by the Council for the same." The proprietors of the estate, however, declined to make any reduction or abatement whatever in the price asked, as they considered the land alone to be worth the money, and that the hall would be given into the bargain. At the meeting of the Council at which this decision of the proprietors was reported, the General Purposes

While the Council were thus hesitating and chaffering over the price, a limited liability company was being formed for the purchase of a portion of the Aston estate, including the hall, with a view to the conversion of the same into a place of public recreation, on the model of the Crystal Palace, which had been opened a few years earlier at Sydenham. The objects of the

JOSEPH CHAMBERLAIN, ESQ., M.P.

Committee were instructed to ascertain and report to the Council the original and subsequent cost of the several public parks in other large towns, and from their report we learn that at that time, while Birmingham was as yet without a public park, Nottingham had two, one of which was eighty acres in extent, and the other fifty acres ; Leeds and Bradford each had one of sixty-two acres in extent ; Glasgow had three, (including Glasgow Green) covering in all upwards of three hundred acres ; and Derby had one of sixteen acres.

Company, as stated in their Memorandum of Association, was :—

1. To purchase Park, etc., with a view to derive a profit from such purchase, and thereby compensate the Company for outlay.

2. With ultimate intention, *after* providing such compensation, to appropriate Hall and premises to the use of the Public ; *so far* as to admit the public thereto, and to apply all profits that may be made to maintenance and improvement of Hall and premises, and not for any pecuniary benefit of Company or Shareholders.

The purchase money amounted to £35,000 ; and the company having been established, and the transfer of the estate completed, there was an universal desire that the Queen should be asked to open the park in person, and that desire was conveyed by the Mayor, Mr. John Ratcliff, to the Earl of Shaftesbury, in the following letter:

Birmingham, March 6th, 1858.

MY LORD,—I have the honour to inform your Lordship that an Association, formed for the purchase of Aston Hall and Park,—an Estate lying closely adjacent to this Borough,—have just entered into possession of the same.

Your Lordship is perhaps aware, that the property has been acquired for the purpose of providing a convenient place of recreation for the inhabitants generally, but especially for the Working Classes of this important and rapidly increasing Borough.

For such a purpose a more desirable place could not be easily imagined; the means of access are numerous and easy, and its proximity to that part of the Borough which abounds with manufactories and works, renders it extremely eligible and convenient as a place of healthful resort for the large number of artizans employed therein. Its situation commands the finest views of which the neighbourhood can boast. It lies open on one side to the fresh and invigorating breezes which blow from the highest table land in the kingdom. Its undulating surface presents to the eye alternately the wood-fringed lake, the beautiful lawn, and the noble avenue; and last, but not least, the picturesque and ancient mansion of its former possessors, the Holtes, with whose history and sufferings in the Royal Cause, in the time of the Rebellion, almost every inhabitant of the Borough is acquainted.

The acquisition of this property, the value of which is daily increasing, not only intrinsically, but for the purpose for which it is intended, is being mainly effected by the issue of shares of twenty shillings value to the Working Classes, aided by the voluntary subscriptions of the wealthier inhabitants.

Having thus imperfectly brought under your Lordship's notice this subject, it remains only for me to communicate to you the one anxious hope of those who are labouring to effect their most commendable purpose. That hope is, that by means of some proper representations made to the Queen, Her Majesty may be induced graciously to consent to open the Park in person, some time in the months of May or June next, as may best accord with Her Majesty's convenience.

If Her Majesty would consent to this, success would be certain, and the toil-worn, smoke-inhaling artizans of our teeming population would receive as from the free grace of their beloved Queen, the greatest boon which could be collectively conferred upon them.

I need hardly remind your Lordship that Her Majesty performed a similar gracious act at Manchester to that she is humbly desired to perform here; and I can safely assure your Lordship, that the high esteem and affectionate regard in which Her Majesty's royal person is here held, by all classes of her subjects, will ensure for Her Majesty a most loyal and enthusiastic reception.

I have the honour to be, my Lord,

Your Lordship's humble Servant,

JOHN RATCLIFF, *Mayor*.

The Right Honourable the Earl of Shrftesbury, &c., &c.

At a meeting of the Town Council, on the 15th of April, the following welcome letter was read:

Windsor Castle, April 8th, 1858.

SIR,—I am now authorised to inform you, that the visit of Her Majesty the Queen to Birmingham, will take place upon some day in the week beginning the 13th of June.

All further details must be matter for future arrangement.

I have the honour to be, Sir,

Your obedient humble Servant,

C. B. PHIPPS

J. Ratcliff, Esq., *Mayor*.

As soon as the news became known the utmost joy prevailed. It was the first time any English Sovereign had thus honoured the town, and the people resolved to give Her Majesty a hearty Birmingham welcome. A special meeting of the Council was held April 27th, to receive a report from the General Purposes Committee as to the arrangements for the reception of Her Majesty in a proper and becoming manner. Briefly, these were as follows: That, as Her Majesty had signified her intention of receiving an address from the Council, the Town Hall and its various committee rooms should be adorned and fitted up; that the members of the Council should wait the arrival of Her Majesty in the hall, and that the Mayor and Town Clerk alone should attend upon her at the station and accompany her to the hall; that the route from the Town Hall to Aston be through New Street, High Street, Dale End, Stafford Street, Aston Street, and Church Road to the Park; that three triumphal arches should be erected by the Council, one at the junction of Dale End with High Street, another at Gosta Green, and a third at the borough boundary, in Aston Road; and that certain of the apartments in Aston Hall should be suitably furnished with a view to Her Majesty's comfort and entertainment. Other suggestions and arrangements were made which need not be detailed here; and, as the story of the Queen's visit has been frequently told and is well-known to all our readers, it may suffice here to place the event on record in the official report presented to the Council on the 13th of July, 1858, by the General Purposes Committee:

"The General Purposes Committee have now the gratification to report, in order that it may be recorded on the Minutes of the Council, that on the 15th day of June last, the inhabitants of this loyal Borough were honoured by the presence of their Sovereign, and her Illustrious Consort, who arrived at the Station of the London and North Western Railway a few minutes after twelve o'clock, when the Mayor and the Town Clerk, attired in full official Municipal Costume, were in attendance to receive and conduct the Royal Visitors to the Town Hall. Her Majesty and Suite having taken their seats in their carriages, escorted by a detachment of the 10th Hussars, and preceded by the carriage containing the Mayor, the Town Clerk, and the Mayor's Chaplain, proceeded by way of Great Queen-street, Worcester-street, High-street, Bull-street, Colmore-row, and Ann-street, to the Town Hall, alighting at the principal entrance in Paradise-street. Her Majesty and Her Royal Consort passed into the Reception Rooms prepared for them, and in a few minutes afterwards were conducted by the Mayor and Town Clerk into the body of the Hall, when Her Majesty ascended the daïs, the Prince Consort standing on her left, and the Ladies of Her Suite taking their places behind the Throne. The National Anthem having been sung by the choir, the Mayor advanced to the daïs and said:—May it please your Majesty, I have a loyal Address of the Corporation of this Borough, which on their behalf I desire to present to your Majesty; the Town Clerk will now read it. Her Majesty having graciously signified her assent, the Address adopted by the Council at its Meeting on the 7th day of June last, was read by the Town Clerk, and the Mayor having formally presented it, Her Majesty read the following gracious reply:—

"I have received with pleasure your loyal and dutiful Address, expressing your sincere and devoted affection to my Person and my Throne.

"It is most gratifying to me to have the opportunity of visiting this ancient and enterprising town, the centre of so much of our manufacturing industry; and I trust you may long remain in the full enjoyment of that liberty and security, without which even industry itself must fail to reap its appropriate reward.

"I desire you will convey to the vast community which you represent, my sincere thanks for their cordial welcome, assuring them at the same time of the pleasure I have derived from witnessing the great and increasing prosperity of Birmingham and its neighbourhood.

The Queen having handed this gracious reply to the Mayor, His Worship then said:—"I have also the honour, your Majesty, of presenting an Address to your Royal Consort from the Town Council, which I will request the Town Clerk to read." The Town Clerk then again advanced and read the Address to His Royal Highness, adopted by this Council at its Meeting on the 7th day of June last. To this Address the Prince Consort read the following reply:—

"MR. MAYOR AND GENTLEMEN,

"I thank you very sincerely for your kind and flattering address

"It is most gratifying to me to find that the views which I expressed on the occasion of my last visit to Birmingham coincide with those of its industrious and enlightened citizens, and to hear that the Institution I was then called upon to inaugurate bids fair to answer the expectations of its enterprising founders.

"It is with unmixed pleasure that I have witnessed this day your cordial and loyal reception of your Queen; and when I reflect that each visit which it has been my good fortune to pay this town has been occasioned by some fresh effort, on your part, to promote either the social happiness or the moral and intellectual improvement of your fellow citizens, I can only express my hope and confident trust that the blessing of Almighty God may continue to attend your exertions in so noble a cause."

At the conclusion of the Prince's reply, the Secretary of State communicated to the Mayor Her Majesty's commands to him to approach the Throne. The Mayor having obeyed, Her Majesty, receiving the Sword of Her Equerry, conferred the honour of Knighthood upon His Worship. Mr. Alderman Hodgson and Mr. Alderman Palmer, the mover and seconder of the Address to Her Majesty, and Mr. Alderman Phillips and Mr. Alderman Carter, the mover and seconder of the Address to the Prince Consort, were severally presented to Her Majesty and had the honour of kissing hands. The other Members of the Council were then individually introduced to the Queen. Her Majesty and the Prince Consort then retired and were re-conducted to their carriages by the Mayor and the Town Clerk, accompanied by the Members of the Council. Her Majesty's procession, preceded by the Mayor and Town Clerk, was then formed and proceeded by way of New-street, High-street, Dale End, Stafford-street, and Aston-street, to the Boundary of the Borough, from whence the Royal cortege (joined by the carriages of several of the County Magistracy) passed onward to Aston Hall, where Her Majesty, after having partaken of Luncheon, (provided by your Committee,) received the Address of the Interim Managers, and formally inaugurated the Hall and Park. Her Majesty, the Prince Consort, and Suite, accompanied by the Mayor, the Town Clerk, and several Members of the Corporation, then proceeded to the temporary Railway Station at Aston, from whence the Queen and the Royal Party took their departure. Previously to leaving, Her Majesty beckoned the Mayor to Her, and was graciously pleased to express to His Worship her high gratification at the reception she had received.

The hall and park thus opened, became one of most popular resorts in the midland counties, and we shall notice some of the entertainments provided by the Company, in our chapter on the Amusements of the People. We may here digress, however, in this respect, to record briefly an event connected therewith, which, to a certain extent, comes within the scope of the present chapter. A woman, named Powell, who styled herself "the Female Blondin," was engaged to perform at Aston Park on the high rope, on—— 1863; and during the performance the rope broke and the poor woman was killed instantaneously. Considerable excitement prevailed, and not a little indignation at the action of the Company in thus pandering to the taste for such demoralising exhibitions; and this was heightened by the receipt of a letter addressed to the Mayor by command of the Queen, expressing "her personal feelings of horror that one of her subjects,—a female,—should have been sacrificed to the gratification of the demoralising taste "for such exhibitions, and trusting that the Mayor, in common with the rest of the townspeople of Birmingham, would use his influence" to prevent in future the degradation to such exhibitions of the park which was gladly opened by Her Majesty and the Prince Consort, in the hope that it would be made serviceable for the healthy exercise and rational recreation of the people."

This unfortunate occurrence was partly instrumental in bringing about the acquirement of the hall and park by the Town Council. At the same meeting at which the Queen's letter to the Mayor was read, another communication was also laid before the Council, viz., a copy of two resolutions passed at a meeting of the Managers of Aston Park, which were as follows:

" That the Managers consider that the recent calamity at the Park, on the occasion of the Foresters' Fête, resulting in the death of Mrs. Powell, will increase the difficulties of the Managers in securing the Hall and Park on the original Plan of the Limited Liability Act; and therefore they are desirous that steps should be taken to arrange with the Corporation for the completion of the purchase."

" That a copy of the above Resolution be forwarded to the Mayor, and that he be respectfully requested to take such measures on the occasion as may appear to him advisable."

As a result of this communication from the Aston Hall Company, a letter was addressed by the Mayor to the Lord Lieutenant of the County (Lord Leigh), as follows:

" Borough of Birmingham, Mayor's Office,
Oct. 8th, 1863.

MY LORD,—I am informed, and I believe correctly, that the Aston Hall and Park Company will be unable to hold much longer the possession of their establishment; and unless means are used, without delay, to secure the property in perpetuity for the rational recreation of the people, possession will be resumed by its former owners.

To prevent this catastrophe it will be necessary to vest the property in a responsible public body, and possibly your Lordship may agree with me that the Corporation of Birmingham would be the most proper public body to whom it could be conveyed.

To effect this desirable object no less a sum than £28,000 will be required to discharge existing liabilities, and a considerable additional outlay must be incurred in fencing, restoration, and otherwise, to render the Hall and Park suitable for the contemplated purpose.

Notwithstanding this heavy burden on the Park, I believe that redemption is even now not impossible, if prompt and energetic measures be adopted.

That belief rests partly on the Corporation, and partly on your Lordship, and the Justices and Gentlemen of the County.

The former have the power and I believe the will to render aid in the shape of a round sum of money; and I am satisfied from the loyal, emphatic, and spirited language of the Resolution adopted at their Meeting at Warwick, over which your Lordship presided, those Gentlemen will not be far behind the Corporation of Birmingham in their efforts to prevent an occurrence which will be stigmatized as a disgrace to all parties concerned.

Under these circumstances I venture to ask your Lordship's advice and assistance.

Will your Lordship immediately convene another Meeting of those Justices and Gentlemen who so recently and earnestly expressed their sympathy with the common object we have in view, and lay the facts before them?

If your Lordship will adopt this course, help will come to us, and such help I am satisfied as with our own means will accomplish our wishes.

In short, if the County will move in the matter promptly and energetically, as they will I am sure on your Lordship's call, I will move the Council for a vote of £20,000, and I am satisfied I shall not move in vain.

I am, my Lord,
Your Lordship's faithful Servant,
CHARLES STURGE,
Mayor of Birmingham.
The Right Honourable
THE LORD LIEUTENANT OF WARWICKSHIRE
Stoneleigh."

In reply to this appeal the following resolution was passed at a meeting of the County Magistrates, on the 20th of the same month :

"Judge's House, Warwick, October 20th, 1863. The Lord Lieutenant having taken the opportunity of

Magistracy of the County for the purpose suggested by the Mayor of Birmingham ; namely, to raise a sum, by contribution, of about £8,000, in aid of the funds of the Corporation for securing the possession of Aston Hall and Park to the Inhabitants of Birmingham."

This decision of the County Magistrates was

THE RIGHT HON. JOHN BRIGHT, M.P.

the Quarter Sessions, when a large number of the County Magistrates are assembled at Warwick, to lay before them two Letters of the respective dates of the 8th and 12th instant, addressed to his Lordship by the Mayor of Birmingham, on the subject of Aston Hall and Park, and the same having been taken into consideration, and the suggestion contained in them having been considered, We, the Magistrates of the County of Warwick now present, express our opinion, that it is not advisable that the Lord Lieutenant should convene any Meeting of the

communicated by the Mayor to Colonel Sir Charles Phipps, for the information of the Queen, who, in reply, expressed through Colonel Phipps, her regret that there existed " a possibility of the people of Birmingham losing the enjoyment of Aston Park as a place of healthy exercise and recreation." " In such a hive of industry "—continues Her Majesty—" an open area for relaxation and amusement after toil must be invaluable. Her Majesty had hoped that this requirement had been permanently provided for; and Her Majesty is still unwilling to believe that, in a locality in which so much wealth is found in proximity to the hard labour by which

Corporation amounted only to £19,000. On the 22nd of September, 1864 the hall and park were opened to the public free, for their use and enjoyment " for ever." The facts relative to the purchase of the estate are set forth on a Memorial Tablet of brass, which is placed in the large

THE EXCHANGE.

it is produced, funds can be wanting to secure to the population an enjoyment the value of which they have been taught to estimate by the temporary use of Aston Park, and of which it would be very injudicious and undesirable now to deprive them."

Ultimately the sum of £7,000 was contributed by several of the wealthier inhabitants of the town and neighbourhood, and as by this time the amount subscribed by the company had reached £9,000, the balance remaining to be paid by the

65

Entrance Hall, and bears the following inscription :

Be it remembered that on the Twenty-second day of September, A.D. 1864, and in the Mayoralty of the Rt. Worshipful William Holliday, Esqre., this hall and Forty-three acres of land surrounding it, having been purchased by the Corporation of the Borough of Birmingham, were formally dedicated to the use of the people for their recreation, as a Free Hall and Park for ever.

And be it also remembered that of the sum of Twenty-six Thousand Pounds paid by the Corporation, as the purchase money, the sum of £7000 was contributed by the benevolent Lady and Gentlemen whose names and donations are inscribed below:—

Miss Louisa Anne Ryland	£1000
Abraham and George Dixon Esquires . .	2000
Thomas Lloyd, Esquire	1000
George Frederick Muntz, Esquire . .	1000
William Middlemore, Esquire . .	500
Richard Greaves, Esquire } Edward Greaves Esqre, M.P., and } Jeffery Bevington Lowe, Esqre. }	500
Archibald and Timothy Kenrick, Esqres. .	500
Sampson Samuel Lloyd, and } George Braithwaite Lloyd, Esquires. }	200
Alfred and Duglas Evans, Esquires . .	200
Charles and James Shaw, Esquires . .	100

THOMAS STANDBRIDGE,

Town Clerk.

The building (which has already been fully described in our chapter on the Holte Family), was converted into a museum by the energetic assistance rendered to the Company by Sir Francis E. Scott. Many examples of industrial art, etc., had been collected previous to the acquisition of the hall and park by the Corporation, and many of these were retained. A few years ago the principal contents of the museum of Natural History were removed from the Queen's College, and deposited in Aston Hall. They comprise a large collection of British and Foreign Birds, Mammalia and Reptiles, and are placed in the entrance hall, the 'Yellow Room,' the 'Cleopatra Room,' and 'Lady Holte's Room.' In the splendid department formerly known as the 'Great Drawing Room' (now called the Queen's room), is arranged an interesting collection of Chinese and Japanese productions, originally lent by Ambrose Parsons, and since purchased from that gentleman by the Corporation for permanent exhibition; also the handsome state palanquin and chair of state, presented to Her Majesty by the Major King of Siam. Sir Francis Scott's collection of the Arundel Society's reproductions of works of art, a collection of Specimens from the Great Exhibition of 1851 (comprising models of fruit, articles used in manufactures, etc.), a collection of Geological Specimens, Machinery, Models of Statues, plaster casts, etc., fill the various other rooms,

and are fully described in the excellent Hand-book to the Museum, compiled by the Curator, Mr. Alfred Rodway. During the re-building of the Corporation Art Gallery, the collection of pictures and examples of industrial art has been removed to Aston Hall and is arranged in the Great Gallery and the Glass Pavilion. The latter, which extends along the entire length of the west front of the building was erected subsequent to the purchase of the hall, by the Company.

In 1873, a piece of land fronting Park Road, was purchased by the Corporation, and added to the Park, the total area of which is now 50a 0r 23p.

In 1859, the second set of public baths was erected, in Woodcock Street, near Aston Road, the first stone being laid July 25th.

In October, in the same year, a report was presented to the Council by the Burial Board Committee, respecting the establishment of a Borough Cemetery; and in accordance with the recommendation of the Committee, it was resolved that an estate of one hundred and five acres, at Witton, be purchased for the sum of £16,350, being at the rate of about £150 an acre. The Council further instructed the Finance Committee to obtain a loan of £25,000 for the purchase and laying out of the said land, and for other necessary works in connection therewith. The Cemetery was opened May 27, 1863.

Once more the question of adopting the Free Libraries' Act was brought to the front, in August, 1859. At a meeting of the Council on the 16th of that month, Councillor (now Alderman) E. C. Osborne moved "That this Council doth hereby request the Mayor (Mr. Thomas Lloyd) to convene a public meeting of the Burgesses, to determine whether they will adopt for this Borough an Act passed in the 18th and 19th years of her present Majesty, . . . for the establishment of Free Public Libraries and Museums in Municipal Towns, &c." An amendment was, however, adopted for the appointment of a Committee to consider and report upon the matter.

This report, which was most exhaustive and interesting, was not presented until January, 1860. The Committee reported that since the first attempt to introduce the Act into Birmingham, seven years previously, several large towns had adopted it ; they had, therefore, "the means of estimating its value by their experience, and of thus ascertaining if it is productive of those beneficial results which its friends anticipated." During this period, too, the Act under which Free Libraries were established had been amended. If it had been adopted in 1852, only one halfpenny in the pound could have been taken from the rates towards the cost of maintaining the Libraries, and none of the public money could have been expended in the purchase of books. But in 1855 a new Act was passed, repealing that of 1850, and empowering Town Councils to levy a rate of one penny in the pound, which may be used, not merely for the maintaining of the Library, but also for the purchase of "books, newspapers, maps, specimens of Art and Science," and for all other Library purposes. About twenty towns had adopted the Act, and amongst the number, Manchester and Liverpool. In these, as more nearly resembling our own town, the Committee had made enquiries as to the working of the Act, and reported fully ; it may suffice here, however, to condense from their report the following facts :

Manchester was the first town to adopt the Act of 1850, and, on account of the limited provisions of that enactment, found it necessary to appeal to the inhabitants for voluntary subscriptions, and the sum of £12,823 was raised in this manner, £7,013 was expended in the purchase of a suitable building and site. 18,028 volumes of books were purchased, at a cost of £4,156, and about 3,200 others were presented by various donors ; but of the latter only about 500 were of special value, thus confirming the Birmingham committee in their opinion, "that casual donations is a totally untrustworthy source for the formation of public libraries under any circumstances." The 21,000 volumes acquired at the opening of the library had increased during the seven years to 51,240, including 33,224 Specifications of Patents, bound into 2,306 volumes, presented by her Majesty's Com-

missioners. During the seven years of the existence of the library the total issue of books amounted to 2,000,329.

At Liverpool the results were equally gratifying. The library was established in 1854, and comprised at the time of opening only 4,437 volumes ; which, in five years, had increased to 53,018. The aggregate issues in 1854 were 35,978 ; in 1859 they amounted to 639,043, being an actual circulation of 12,290 volumes per week.

"After the examples given," continues the report, "it is, perhaps, unnecessary to give further illustrations of the working of these institutions. It may, however, be observed, that from every town from which reports have been obtained—Salford, Sheffield, Birkenhead, and Oxford, being among the number — similar encouraging results are recorded ; and in every instance the establishment of a Free Library has been hailed by the inhabitants as an important agent towards the mental and moral improvement of all classes of society."

The result of this report was that, at a meeting of the Burgesses held in the Town Hall, February 21, 1860, presided over by the Mayor (Mr. Thomas Lloyd), the resolution for the adoption of the Act was carried by an overwhelming majority. The Free Libraries' Committee was appointed March 6th, and presented its first report to the Council on the 15th of May, recommending the establishment of a Central Reference Library, Lending Library, Newsroom, and Art Gallery, near the Town Hall, and of three Branch Libraries ; one for the northern district, near St. George's Church ; another near Gosta Green, for the eastern district ; and a third in the vicinity of Bradford Street, for the southern district. These recommendations were approved by the Council, and the Committee was authorised to carry them into effect. Premises for the accommodation of the Northern Branch Library, in Constitution Hill, were obtained from Mr. Cartland, on a lease for twenty-one years, at an annual rent of £45, subject to the Council keeping the premises in proper repair and condition. Meanwhile the Committee was not slothful in carrying out the more important measure authorised by the Council, of erecting suitable premises for the Central Libraries and Art Gallery. On the 4th of September, 1860, a report was presented to the Council on this subject ; the Committee recommended the selection of the piece of vacant ground adjoining the Midland Institute, which the Council of the Institute offered to transfer to the Corporation on condition that the latter should undertake to errect the library buildings thereon, in accordance

On the 21st of February, 1861, the Committee reported the acquisition of the Constitution Hill lease; the purchase of about 6,500 volumes of standard literature from the committee of the

STATUE OF THE LATE PRINCE CONSORT, BY FOLEY.
(Temporarily located in the Corporation Art Gallery).

with the plan of Mr. E. M. Barry (with such internal variations as might be necessary), and that certain leasehold interests, amounting to about £500, together with an annuity of £40, per annum, be paid by the Corporation.

Birmingham New Library, Temple Row West (referred to in earlier chapters), which at this time was about to be amalgamated with the Old Library; and the engagement of Mr. Edward Lings as librarian. With reference to the proposed erection of the Central Buildings on the land adjoining the Institute, they reported that they were in communication with Mr. Barry, the architect, upon the subject, and would shortly be prepared to lay before the Council plans of the intended buildings for approval.

The first Free Library (Constitution Hill Branch) was opened to the public on the 3rd of April, 1861, by Mr. Arthur Ryland, the then Mayor of the Borough. The members of the Council, and the principal inhabitants interested in the cause of education, were hospitably entertained by the Mayor at Dee's Royal Hotel, after which they proceeded to the Library for the purpose of inaugurating it. Addresses were delivered by the Mayor, the Rev. Canon Miller, George Dawson, and others, and the Library was then formally declared open. The arrangements for the issue of books were not, however, completed until the 22nd of April. Crowds of persons presented themselves on that day for borrowers' tickets, and so great was the excitement—we are told in the first annual report of the Committee— that for several weeks applicants had to wait upwards of an hour before their turns arrived to be attended to, as many as two hundred persons applying at one time.

The Committee further reported that they had obtained land for the Southern Branch Library, at the junction of Heath Mill Lane with Deritend, and that efforts were being made to obtain a suitable site for the eastern district, and proposed to erect both these branch Libraries before commencing the central. Notwithstanding several delays, however, in the latter undertaking, it was completed before either of the branches; but of this we shall make fuller record at a later date.

In connection with the park provided by Mr. Adderley (Lord Norton), a free library and a small museum were founded by that gentleman, and opened on the 11th of January, 1864. Being in an out-of-the-way locality, however, they were but little used at first, and it was found desirable after a time to open the library and

newsroom only in the evening, from six to nine o'clock; and the contents of the museum were removed to Aston Hall. The library, which has since been added to by the Free Libraries' Committee, now contains 2,819 volumes.

During the year 1860, that eccentric individual Mr. George Francis Train, applied to the Town Council for permission to lay down a tramway in one of the streets of our town; but, although he obtained the desired sanction no use was made of it, for the tramway was never laid. The public of Birmingham had not as yet any confidence in the scheme; and, it was reserved for the corporation itself to undertake the work of constructing street tramways.

During the year 1860, the Council was occupied with the discussion of a proposed bill for obtaining additional powers for the improvement of the town. On the 5th of December a town's meeting was held to consider its provisions, and amid much noisy interruption a poll was demanded, and fixed for the three following days. The official declaration of the result, which was made on the 17th of the same month, showed a majority of 95, 2,729 votes having been recorded in favour of the bill, and 2,634 against it. The Act was obtained during the following session of Parliament, at a cost of £11,000.

In February, 1862, the Town Council adopted for Birmingham the Adulteration Act, which had just become law through the efforts of our townsman Mr. John Postgate, F.R.C.S., (who has applied himself unremittingly to the task of obtaining the utmost security from adulteration, both of food, drinks, and drugs); and a borough analyst was appointed forthwith, in the person of Mr. Alfred Hill, M.D. We shall refer more particularly to the important part taken by Birmingham in the movement against adulteration in a future chapter.

As an illustration of the value of land in Birmingham in 1864, as well as of the energy and enterprise of the Council in the improvement of the town, we may note here the fact that in the above-named year the sum of £53 10s. per yard was given by the municipal authorities for the land at the corner of Worcester Street, for the improvement of the corner now occupied by "The Quadrant."

We now return once more to the history of the Free Libraries. Owing to the cost which would have been involved in carrying out the plans of Mr. Barry for the Central Libraries, (the lowest tender, after the committee had deducted all unnecessary or nonessential provisions, being £12,250 10s., or, including the Art Gallery, £14,250 10s.), the work was placed in the hands of Mr. William Martin, and the tender of Messrs. Branson and Murray, for the erection of the buildings at a cost of £8,600, was accepted. Owing to a strike in the building trade the work of erection was considerably delayed, but in April, 1865, the buildings were so far advanced that the Committee reported to the Council that it was now desirable to appoint a Chief Librarian, in order that the new officer might enter upon his duties in time for the opening of the Central Lending Library and Newsroom. Thirty-two applications were received from candidates for the new and honourable municipal office, and out of these, three names were submitted to the Council, viz: Mr. George McWhea, Mr. J. D. Mullins, and Mr. Edward Lings, the librarian of the previously-established branch library at Constitution Hill. The Committee recommended Mr. McWhea as the most suitable candidate, but the Council elected Mr. J. D. Mullins (who had for some time previously occupied the post of librarian at the Birmingham Old Library), as Chief Librarian, and, although he has at all times borne the character of an exceedingly strict disciplinarian, he has obtained and maintained the confidence of the Committee and of the Council both as a bibliographical scholar and keeper of the books and manuscripts committed to his care, and as the head of a large and important department of the public service of the town.

The Central Lending Library was appropriately opened on the first day of the British Association meeting in the town, September 6, 1865; a short religious service being celebrated by the Lord Bishop of Worcester, and addresses delivered by the Mayor (Mr. H. Wiggin), Lord Stanley, M.P. (now Earl of Derby), the Rev. Dr. Miller, and Mr. George Dawson, M.A.; and at the conclusion the Library was declared open, free, to the people of Birmingham, for ever. The issue of books commenced on the 19th of the same month, and a large number of borrowers' tickets were speedily issued, the average daily issue of books being 575, and of persons using the Newsroom, 300.

Meanwhile the work of collecting valuable and standard books for the formation of a Reference Library was being steadily proceeded with, and land had been purchased by the Committee, at the corner of Legge Street and Aston Road, near Gosta Green, as a site for the eastern branch library; the plans of Messrs. Bateman and Corser, for the erection of Deritend branch library, at a cost not exceeding £1,000, were approved, and the building commenced. The way was thus prepared for the triple ceremony which took place on the 26th of October, 1866, comprising the opening of the Deritend Branch Library, the laying of the foundation stone of the Gosta Green branch, and the opening of the Central Reference Library. The ceremonies in each case were performed by the Mayor (Edwin Yates, Esq.), and an Inaugural Address on the opening of the Reference Library was delivered by Mr. George Dawson, M.A.,—an address which has ever been considered one of the happiest efforts of "the first of English talkers." Space forbids our quoting more than the closing sentences of this eloquent oration, which, when read in the light of recent events, possess a melancholy interest for us :

"Now, Mr. Mayor, we probably could not part without some little looking forward to the future. For man's part in immortality is so great that he always looks beyond that day when 'the earthly house of this tabernacle shall be dissolved'; beyond the day when these earthen vessels, so gloriously shaped by the Almighty potter, shall have fallen back again into shapeless clay; and he longs, with a pardonable desire, that his name may be remembered, when the place that knew him knows him no more. That glorious weakness I hope we all of us share—that we would fain haunt some place in this world even when the body is gone; that we desire that our names shall be gratefully spoken of when we have long past away to join the glorious dead. If this be your passion, there are few things that I would more willingly share with you than the desire that, in days to come, when some student, in a fine rapture of gratitude, as he sits in this room, may for a moment call to mind the names of the men who, by speech and by labour, by the necessary agitation or the continuous work, took part in founding this Library. There are few places I would rather haunt after my death than this room, and there are few things I would have my children remember more than this, that this man spoke the discourse at the opening of this glorious Library, the first-fruits of a clear understanding that a great town exists to discharge towards the people of that town the duties that a great nation exists to discharge towards the people of that nation—that a town exists here by the grace of God, that a great town is a solemn organism through which should flow, and in which should be shaped, all the highest, loftiest, and truest ends of man's intellectual and moral nature. I wish, then, for you, Mr. Mayor, and for myself, that, in years to come, when we are in some respects forgotton, still now and then, in this room, the curious questions may be asked: Who was Mayor on that famous day? Who said grace before that famous banquet? Who returned thanks for that gracious meal? Who gathered these books together? Who was the first man that held that new office of librarian? I trust his name will be printed whenever the name of this Corporation

appears. What his title is to be I don't know—whether it is to be Town Librarian or Corporation Librarian—but I envy him whatever it may be, and I am glad the Corporation has given itself an officer who represents intellect—that it looks upward deliberately and says, 'we are a Corporation who have undertaken the highest duty that is possible to us; we have made provision for our people—for *all* our people—and we have made a provision of God's greatest and best gifts unto man.'"

On the 1st of August, 1867, the Corporation Art Gallery was opened, in the room provided in the Central Library block, with a small but valuable collection of pictures, some of which had been presented to the town, and others obtained on loan. Among the former may be mentioned *Detected Correspondence*, by Opie; a fine group of *Dead Game*, by Coleman; *An Old Oak, Forest of Arden*, by F. H. Henshaw (presented by the Art Gallery Association); Weigall's portrait of Sir Charles Adderley (Lord Norton), previously referred to; a large picture by Etty, deposited in the Gallery (with several others), by the Birmingham Society of Arts. A number of valuable pictures by J. V. Barber, H. Harris, Samuel Lines, and others, were deposited in the Gallery by the Council of the Birmingham and Midland Institute.

In the spring of 1868 the Reference department was enriched by the presentation of the unique Shakespeare Memorial Library, brought together by the patient and loving labour of Mr. George Dawson and Mr. Sam: Timmins. The Library was founded in commemoration of the Tercentenary of Shakespeare's birth, many of the books being given by Shakespearian scholars and collectors, notably by the two gentlemen above-named, and by Mr. J. O. Halliwell and the late Charles Knight. Other works were purchased by voluntary subscription, and the future growth and completeness of the Library was provided for in like manner by annual subscribers. Donations of valuable books were also received from Mr. J. Payne Collier, F.S.A., Mr. Howard Staunton, Mr. and Mrs Cowden Clarke and other 'good Shakespearians,' as well as by the publishers of editions of the works of Shakespeare and of Shakespeariana.

During the same year the Gosta Green Newsroom and Lending Library were opened, the former on the 1st of February, and the latter in month of June.

In the spring of 1869 the treasures of the Reference Library were rendered more accessible to the public by the issue of an admirably compiled catalogue, which, while affording all the advantages of classification, as well as of a full and complete alphabetical list, had the great merit of brevity and cheapness. The credit of compiling this model catalogue is due to the Chief Librarian and his invaluable assistant Mr. F. T. Barrett, who has since been appointed Chief Librarian of the Mitchell Library, Glasgow, —a post which he is eminently qualified to fill with credit both to himself and to the Library over which he presides. We may here also mention as a circumstance worthy of remark, that there are few public libraries from which so many subordinate officers have been elected to preside over similar establishments in other towns, as those of Birmingham, which have thus proved a valuable training-school for librarians. Mr. F. T. Barrett, of Glasgow, Mr. C. Madeley, of Warrington, Mr. J. H. Wright, of Stockton-on-Tees, Mr. Johnson, of the Medical Institute Library, Birmingham, Mr. A. Cotgreave, of Wednesbury, and Mr. G. Catlin, of Handsworth, are among those whom the present writer (himself a member of the same fraternity, trained at Birmingham) can call to mind as having received their first lessons in library management under Mr. J. D. Mullins.

The annual report of the committee for the year 1868, records several very valuable additions to the Art Gallery. First among these should be mentioned Foley's noble statue of the late Prince Consort, (of which we give an engraving on page 514), which was deposited in the Art Gallery by the Albert Statue Committee until a suitable site should be found out-of-doors for it. The Council of the Midland Institute had handed over to the committee the bust of David Cox, by Peter Hollins, the cost of which was defrayed by public subscription; a bust of Matthew Davenport Hill, Esq., by Hollins, was also placed in the Gallery; and, later in the year, another bust, by Mr. Hollins, of the late Mr. William Scholefield, M.P., presented to the town by the Mayor (T. Avery, Esq.), was handed over to the care of the Art Gallery sub-committee. During the same year three large landscape pictures (views in the Dolomite Mountains) were presented to the Art Gallery by the Artist, Mr. Elijah Walton. The Gallery was further enriched (temporarily) by the loan of a fine collection of armour, jewellery, and other art workmanship, from South Kensington Museum.

The value to art students of the South Kensington loans led the Committee to attempt the formation of a permanent museum of industrial art, and a meeting of gentlemen interested in the movement was held June 14th, 1870; a committee was thereupon appointed to collect funds for this purpose, resulting in the subscription of upwards of £1,100, which was expended in the purchase of examples of Indian workmanship, carving, metal-work, jewellery, and textile fabrics, examples of ancient and modern Venetian glass, purchased from Messrs. Salviati, and of English glass, manufactured by Messrs. Barnes, artisan glass-workers, of Birmingham.

Among the other objects of art which have since been added to the Industrial Art Museum at the Art Gallery may be mentioned the beautiful silver shield, by Messrs. Elkington (known as the " Elkington Challenge Shield "), deposited by the Birmingham Volunteers; the exquisite example of engraved glass, (a vase, by Northwood), presented by Mr. J. B. Stone; a collection of metal-work, purchased out of Mr. Chamberlain's donation of £1,000; a collection of old Roman pottery, glass, and terra-cotta, presented by Signor Castellani and W. Scott, Esq.

The collection contains memorial portraits (chiefly painted by subscription) of Dr. Birt Davies, George Dawson, Peter Hollins, and Alderman Osborne (all painted by W. T. Roden); of Sir Josiah Mason, by H. T. Munns; of David Cox and Arthur Ryland, by Sir J. W. Gordon; of Joseph Goodyear, by Room; of Hugh Hutton, by Blakiston; and of Joseph Sturge and "Poet Freeth," by unknown artists.

The growth of the older department of the Art Gallery—the department of pictorial art—has been to some extent provided for by the establishment of a Public Picture Gallery Fund, for which the town is indebted to the munificence of the late T. Clarkson Osler, Esq., who originated the fund by an anonymous donation of £3,000. Several additions have since been made to the fund, which is invested on behalf of the trustees, and produces about £80 or £90 per annum interest. The latter alone is used for the purposes of the Art Gallery, and two magnificent works of art have already been purchased out of the interest thus accumulated, viz., "A Condottiere," by Sir Frederick Leighton, P.R.A., and "A North-west Gale off the Longships Lighthouse," by John Brett.

In October, 1871, the Free Libraries' Committee applied to the Council for permission to open the Reference Library and the Art Gallery, on Sunday afternoon and evening. The proposal met with great opposition, but was ultimately carried, and the Library and Art Gallery were opened on Sunday for the first time on the 28th of April, 1872.

At the Annual Dinner of "Our Shakespere Club," April 23rd, 1873, an announcement was made of another valuable gift to the Reference Library, viz., a complete collection of the various editions of the works of Cervantes, with all the criticisms and annotations thereon, collected by William Bragge, Esq., F.S.A., by whom they were presented to the Library. A separate Hand

List was compiled by the Chief Librarian, who also compiled and issued (1872-1876) the first three parts of an annotated Catalogue of the Shakespeare Memorial Library (comprising the English Editions of Shakespeare's Works, the English Editions of the Separate Plays and Poems, and the English Shakespeariana), and a useful Hand List of the Birmingham Books in the Reference Library, in 1875.

In 1875 the Committee came into possession of one of an exceedingly rich and valuable collection of books, Manuscripts, Prints, Coins, Seals, etc., relating to the County of Warwick, and of rare early English literature generally; a collection rich in black letter lore, as well as in original editions of the older English Poets, and including, perhaps, the largest number of tracts, etc., relating to the Civil War ever brought together. Space would fail us to tell of the many rarities of this priceless collection,—of the large paper copies of our great county history, and of other topographical works, of the famous Manuscript Cartularies of Knowle and Thelesford, of the treasures of early typography, (among which ought to be mentioned the first Latin edition of the *Navis Stultifera* or "Ship of Fools," and the curious black letter edition of *Reynard the Fox*, both illustrated); of the innumerable collection of Warwickshire pamphlets (including some twenty or more little quartos relating to Robert Dudley, Earl of Leicester); or of the almost unique series of Warwickshire prints, and the altogether unique MS. Collections of William Hamper, Thomas Sharp, of Coventry, and other antiquaries. We have reprinted in our chapter on the Battle of Birmingham the four precious quartos relating to that event, all of which were included in the collection, and the fourth of them, as the present writer believes, and there stated, *only* in that collection, being undoubtedly unique. We have not the heart to go on with the catalogue, for we have to record that nearly all these priceless treasures perished in the lamentable fire of January 1879, of which we

66

have to speak presently. We need only add here, what the reader has already guessed for himself, that this was the far too little known Staunton Collection, formed by the late Mr. Staunton, of Longbridge, Warwick.

The collection was purchased for the Library, at the suggestion of Mr. Sam: Timmins, at a price considerably below its market value, viz: about £2,000, half of which amount was raised by private subscriptions, the remainder being voted out of the funds of the Free Libraries' Committee.

On the 26th of April, 1876, a bust of Sam: Timmins, Esq., J.P., one of the oldest members of the Free Libraries' Committee, was placed in the Reference Library in recognition of his services in the selection of the books, for the library, and as a liberal donor himself to that valuable collection. It met with a melancholy fate, being broken in pieces by the fall of a portion of the roof during the fire in January last.

On the 17th of August, 1876, a Museum of Arms, collected and arranged by the Guardians of the Proof House, was presented by that body to the Corporation to be exhibited free of charge,* and was handed over to the care of the Free Libraries' Committee. It consisted of nearly a thousand specimens of Armour, Crossbows, Guns, Pistols, Swords, etc., many of them being finely ornamented, and the whole illustrating the History of Arms from an early period to the present time. The popularity of this interesting Museum may be gathered from the fact that during the year 1877, upwards of one hundred and eighty thousand persons visited it.

Among the treasures of the Reference Library, at the latest date of which we can speak of it, mention should be made of the rich collection of Books and Pamphlets relating to Birmingham, collected, for the most part, by the assiduous research of the Chief Librarian; a set of the magnificent works on Roman Antiquities by the

Piranesi; a fine copy of the famous *Nuremberg Chronicle*, the best edition, adorned with many hundreds of quaint woodcuts in the earliest style of that art; sets of the Publications of nearly all the learned societies and printing clubs; a file of *Aris's Gazette*, from 1760, or thereabouts, to the present time; the *Description de l'Egypte*, issued by order of the French Government; Lord Kingsborough's *Antiquities of Mexico; L'Antichita di Ercolano;* Walton's celebrated London Polyglot; the series of Photographs of the Antiquities in the British Museum, presented by W. Middlemore, Esq.; many of the most valuable county histories, and other scarce topographical works; a choice selection of works on the fine arts, including the works of Ruskin, Pugin, and others, and engravings from all the principal galleries; the Photographs and Etchings issued by the South Kensington authorities (purchased out of the Industrial Art Museum fund); the Engravings from Ancient Marbles in the British Museum (presented by the Trustee); and many other equally valuable works, in every department of knowledge.

Let the reader add to this catalogue the brief list we have already selected from the Staunton collection, the choice contents of the Shakespeare Memorial Library and the Cervantes Library, and a valuable collection of old books bequeathed to the Library by the late W. Reynolds Lloyd, Esq., and he will form some idea of the richness of that treasure-house of thought and research, and will at the same time be enabled to comprehend, to some extent, the sense of inestimable loss, and the overwhelming grief, which was manifested by every intelligent citizen of Birmingham, when, on the afternoon of Saturday, January 11th, 1879, the mournful intelligence was carried to every quarter of the town, that the Reference Library was in flames! We need not refer particularly to what has so recently transpired and is so generally known; suffice it to say that nearly all that we have enumerated (with the exception, happily, of

---

* It had previously been exhibited, for about two years, in the premises attached to Messrs. Spurrier's Manufactory, in Newhall Street, at a charge of sixpence for admission.

the Gild Book of Knowle, and some few hundred volumes of the Shakespeare and Reference Library books), perished in the flames. The contents of the Art Gallery had fortunately been removed to Aston Hall, (together with the Seals, Coins, and other miscellaneous curiosities of a museum character belonging to the Staunton Collection and the Shakespeare Library), during the alterations which were being made in the Library buildings. It transpired that the origin of the fire was the sudden flickering of a small jet of gas in one of the pipes which a workman was engaged in repairing. The room in which it was situated happened to be strewed with chips and shavings, and one of these became suddenly ignited ; and the flame spread among the shavings so rapidly that it became impossible to arrest it in its destructive career. The statue of the Prince Consort (which had been temporarily placed in the lower reading-room), survived the ravages of the flames and the falling-in of the roof, uninjured, as did also two models by Foley of statues of Burke and Goldsmith. The contents of the lending library were for the most part saved, by the exertions of the assistants and the crowd.

A movement was at once set on foot for restoring the Reference Library, and in addition to many valuable donations of books (including one of a selection of choice and rare volumes from Her Majesty the Queen), upwards of £12,000 has already been subscribed for that purpose.

No report has been issued by the Free Libraries' Committee for the year 1878, owing to the destruction of most of the registers containing statistics ; we can only give the total number of volumes therefore up to the end of 1877, at which date they were as follows :

DEPARTMENTS.	Theology, Moral Philosophy, & Ecclesiastical History.	History, Biography, Voyages, and Travels.	Law, Politics, and Commerce.	Arts, Sciences, and Natural History.	Poetry and Drama.	Magazines and Periodicals.	Prose Fiction.	Miscellaneous Literature.	Juvenile Books.	Embossed Books for the Blind.	Totals.
Reference Library	3,358	10,221	3,884	6,936	†8,199	3,706		8,215			44,519‡
Central Lending Library ...	731	3,431	245	1,856	621	1,910	6,611	1,373	674	91	17,543
Constitution Hill Library...	319	1,872	140	862	160	648	2,033	759	343		7,136
Deritend Library	296	1,684	83	617	292	486	2,511	693	314		6,976
Gosta Green Library	357	1,416	83	707	288	509	2,733	619	382		7,094
Adderley Park Library ...	174	522	53	200	76	238	1,245	259	52		2,819
Totals	5,235	19,146	4,488	11,178	9,636	7,497	15,133	11,918	1,765	91	86,087

† Includes 6,739 Volumes forming the Shakespeare Memorial Library.

‡ This number does not include the Publication of the Patent Office, which make from 2,000 to 4,000 Volumes, according as they are bound.

During the year 1877, no less than 259,144 references were made to books in the Reference Library, on week days, and 21,924 on Sundays—281,068 in all; and the joint issue of volumes during the year in the several lending departments amounted to 398,886; total issue of the various departments in twelve months, 679,954. The Art Gallery and Museum of Arms were visited during the year by 394,645 persons. These figures need no comment. They indicate as adequately as figures can indicate, the immense influence exerted by the Free Libraries and Art Gallery on the intellectual life and progress of the people of Birmingham; and when taken in connection with the eager readiness with which the town

the history of the Free Libraries down to the present time, to the general history of the Corporation.

At a meeting of the Council on the 15th of June, 1869, the Estate and Buildings' Committee reported on the proposed New Municipal

STATUE OF JAMES WATT IN RATCLIFF PLACE.

has set about the work of restoring the invaluable Reference Library, and of repairing the loss it has sustained, they serve to show the high value at which our townsmen estimate these intellectual privileges which they have purchased for themselves, by a voluntarily imposed rate, and have evidently determined to make use of to the utmost of their ability.

We must now return, having traced briefly

Buildings for which a site had been obtained with a frontage to Ann Street, Congreve Street Edmund Street, and a new street or thoroughfare called Eden Place. According to the report of the Committee the cost of these erections would be, as nearly as could be estimated, as follows Corporate Buildings, £37,000; Assize Courts, £76,000; Judges' Lodgings, £12,500; total £125,000. Upon this report being read it was resolved "that the Committee be authorised to advertise for plans for the new corporate buildings, and submit the same to the Council for approval; and that the Estate and Buildings Committee confer with the General Purposes Committee, with the view to ascertain if it is tion, the high and important office of Town Clerk, and, by his uniform courtesy to all who had occasion to consult him, by the able, conscientious, and faithful discharge of his numerous and important duties, and by the loyalty which ever characterised his conduct as

STATUE OF DR. PRIESTLEY, IN CONGREVE STREET.

the intention of Her Majesty's Government to introduce a bill in Parliament founded on the report of the Judicature Committee, and to report the same to the Town Council."

In February, 1869, the town lost an old and esteemed public servant, in the person of Mr. Thomas Standbridge, who died on the 10th of that month, in his 52nd year, having, as expressed in the resolution of the Council on the occasion, "for fifteen years filled with honour and distinc-

the chief officer of this Council, of whose honour and interests he was at all times scrupulously jealous, had gained the esteem and admiration of every member of this Council, and the well-deserved approbation of his fellow-burgesses." A neat and handsome memorial, in the form of an obelisk, has been erected by the Council, in the Episcopalian portion of the Borough Cemetery, at Witton.

On the 9th of March, the place left vacant by

his death was filled up by the appointment of Mr. E. J. Hayes, who still holds the same office.

At a meeting of the Town Council on the 3rd of August, 1869, the following communication from Mr. Josiah Mason, respecting the transfer of the noble Orphanage at Erdington to the care of the Council, was read by the Mayor :—

Norwood House, Erdington,
August 2nd, 1869.

Dear Mr. Mayor,

I herewith send you a printed copy of the foundation deed of the Orphanage and Almshouses which I have lately built here, and endowed with upwards of a thousand acres of freehold land, in the neighbourhood of Birmingham, besides land and buildings in Birmingham itself. This deed of endowment, although made more than twelve months ago, is, as you may be aware, not legally complete until twelve months after its execution. That period having now elapsed, it is proper I should make this communication to you officially, for the following reason :—One of the most serious difficulties I had in settling the endowment scheme was how to provide against the administration of the charity falling under the exclusive control of any religious sect or party, or the funds being diverted from their proper purpose. After much consideration I have concluded that the most effectual means of accomplishing my object was to place my trust under the superintendence of my fellow-townsmen, acting, through their municipal representatives, in such a mode that whilst it should impose the smallest amount of trouble upon the Town Council, should really place in their hands the means of securing the efficient administration of property, which is already considerable, and which, from its nature, must increase with the prosperity of Birmingham. During my own life, or so long as I have health and strength, I trust to be able, with the assistance of the seven gentlemen I have named trustees, to continue the administration of the charity. Immediately after my death, if the Town Council will do me the honour to render the slight assistance I ask in the promotion of my scheme, they will have to elect an equal number of trustees to those I have named, making the number fourteen, viz., seven private and seven official trustees. The seven official trustees may be either members of the Council or not, as the Council for the time being may determine. Whenever any vacancy shall happen in the number of official trustees, nominated by the Council, the Council will fill up such vacancy. Whenever any vacancy happens in the number of private trustees, the whole body of trustees (in which the Town Council will always have the advantage of seven votes to six) will fill up that vacancy. The only restriction I have imposed on the trustees is that they shall be Protestant laymen, resident within ten miles of the Orphanage. In order also that the Town Council may have more frequent opportunities of supervising the finances of the trust than would be afforded by the appointment of trustees (which after the first appointment would be infrequent), I have provided that the accounts of the charity shall be audited by a public accountant once a year, and that a copy of such accounts shall be transmitted to the Town Clerk of the borough. By these means I trust that my charity may always have the advantage of a small executive body elected by, and therefore commanding the respect of, their fellow-townsmen, and preserved from all improper influences, by being placed under the control of the public opinion of the town. It will be a great satisfaction to me to know that the Town Council of the borough of Birmingham will be willing to accept the trust I have reposed in them, and for that purpose I shall be glad if you bring the matter before them in due course.

I am, dear Mr. Mayor,
Yours truly,
JOSIAH MASON.

Henry Holland, Esq.,
Mayor of Birmingham.

On the 14th of July, 1870, the first stone was laid of a new Fish Market Hall, in the Bull Ring, at the corner of Bell Street, by Alderman Phillips.

On the 27th of December, 1871, a public meeting of the inhabitants was held to authorise the Corporation to apply for an Act to lay down tramways in the principal streets ; about twelve routes were included in the bill, which was passed during the following session, but as yet only two lines have been laid. The first from Monmouth Street, along Snow Hill, Constitution Hill, Great Hampton Street and Hockley Hill, to the borough boundary, was opened September 7th, 1873, having cost £12,000 ; it was leased to the Birmingham and District Tramway Company. The same company also hold a lease of the second line (from Monmouth Street to Bristol Road, by way of Colmore Row, Ann Street, Paradise Street, Suffolk Street, the Horse Fair, and Bristol Street.) which was opened on Whit Monday, June 5th, 1876.

On the 14th of June, 1872, H.R.H. Prince Arthur visited Birmingham in order to open the Royal Horticultural Society's Show, at the Lower Grounds, Aston. This was the first royal visit to the town since 1858, and the Town Council received their illustrious visitor with every manifestation of respect. An address was read at the Town Hall, and in the evening the exterior of the Hall was brilliantly illuminated, at the public expense, whereat some few republican ratepayers grumbled at the "waste of public money."

On the 15th of October, 1872, an order in Council was approved by Her Majesty for dividing the borough into sixteen wards. The ward-division was now as follows:

Rotton Park.	Market Hall.
All Saints'.	St. Thomas's.
Ladywood.	St. Martin's.
St. Paul's.	Edgbaston.
St. George's.	Deritend.
St. Stephen's.	Bordesley.
St. Mary's.	Duddeston.
St. Bartholomew's.	Nechells.

If the reader will turn for a moment to the list printed on page 492, he will see at a glance the changes made by this new arrangement. The old Hampton and St. Peter's wards are abolished, and in their places we have three new wards italicised in the first column above. The large wards of Deritend and Bordesley, and Duddeston-cum-Nechells were divided. One alderman and three councillors were apportioned to each ward, thus keeping the total number as before, viz., twelve of the former and forty-eight of the latter.

The plans for the Corporation Buildings were submitted to the Council on the 11th of February, 1873, and, at the recommendation of Mr. Waterhouse (who had been engaged to report on the designs of the various competing architects), those of Mr. Yeoville Thomason were selected as the most suitable. Objections were taken, however, to the elevation (which was of a totally different character from that which was finally adopted), and it was remodelled in accordance with the wishes of the committee. The first stone was laid, June 17th, 1874, by the Mayor, Mr. Joseph Chamberlain, at whose invitation the principal inhabitants met and celebrated the event by a luncheon at the Great Western Hotel. A display of fireworks took place in the evening at Aston Park, also at the charge of Mr. Chamberlain.

The western wing of the buildings (comprising the Council Chamber, ante-rooms, and certain of the offices), was opened without ceremony, on the 7th of November, 1878. The remaining portion of the building (in which are included the grand staircase and reception room), are not yet ready for opening. A full description of the buildings will be given in chapter X.

In April, 1873, a new experiment was made in street paving, by laying the road-way of Moor Street with blocks of wood (rendered hard and impervious to water by hydraulic pressure); and on the 9th of June, 1874, the Council decided to pave New Street, Paradise Street, Dale End, High Street, and Bull Street with the same material. The work was completed in 1875, but a portion of the paving has recently been taken up and re-laid, in order to substitute a concrete foundation for the original one of transverse boards, which was found to be unsuitable.

An interesting presentation in connection with the local jewellery trade took place at the meeting of the Council, June 27, 1873, when a valuable diamond, worth £150,—the first ever cut in Birmingham, was presented to the town, (to be worn with the Mayor's chain,) by Mr. W. Spencer, by whom it was cut, and set in a handsome gold badge, upon which the arms of the borough are emblazoned. This interesting and valuable example of local workmanship is deposited, when not in use, in the Corporation Art Gallery.

On the 1st of September, 1873, the town was enriched by the acquisition of a noble park in the neighbourhood of Moseley, the gift of Miss Ryland, of Barford Hill, Warwick. The munificent donor modestly declined to allow the park to be called after her own name, as the Council by a unanimous resolution wished to do, and it bore simply the name of the old estate out of which it was formed, viz., Cannon Hill Park. At the request of Miss Ryland the park was opened without any public ceremony; a few members of the Council, with the Mayor (A. Biggs, Esq.), came to the park, and simply declared it open for the use of the people. To every visitor on that day was presented, as a memento of the occasion, a card, bearing the following inscription :

Cannon Hill Park, opened 1st September, 1873.— Through the bounty of God, I have great pleasure in giving Cannon Hill Park to the Corporation of Birmingham for the use of the people of the town and neighbourhood. I would express my earnest hope that the park may prove to be a source of healthful recreation to the people of Birmingham, and that they will aid in the protection and preservation of what is now their own property.

LOUISA ANNE RYLAND.

Barford Hill, Warwick.

The park is fifty-seven acres in extent, and is situated in Worcestershire, on the borders of Warwickshire, being divided from the latter county by an arm of the river Rea; the other boundaries of the park are Moseley Road, Pershore Road, and Edgbaston Road, the principal entrance being in the latter. We quote the description given by the curator, Mr. Rodway, in his useful little "Handbook."—

The ground is beautifully undulating, is well wooded, and was laid out with great taste by Mr. J. Gibson, of Battersea, the expense being borne by Miss Ryland. Several acres are devoted to ornamental gardening, including shrubberies, in which are planted many choice and rare evergreens. The natural attractions have been very much enhanced by the formation of large pools, which are surrounded by plantations and pleasant walks. Swans, Canadian geese, ducks, and other water-fowl, are kept on these pools, which are also used for boating, a small charge being made by the lessee of the pools for the use of boats. Near the boat-house are landing stages, at which *alone* persons are allowed to embark or land. The bathing-pool is 216 feet by 100 feet, with a depth varying from 2 feet 6 inches to 5 feet 6 inches. The bottom is concrete, and the water is kept fresh and pure by a small stream passing through it. On one side of the pool a number of dressing sheds are erected for the convenience of bathers.

There is a pleasant retreat at the south-east corner of the Park, called the "Fernery." Here is a small pond, in which grow aquatic plants, and nearly every variety of English Fern may be found on its banks. From this point is gained a delightful view over the adjacent country.

Accommodation is provided for both driving and riding ; an excellent carriage drive, nearly a mile in length, winds

round the Park, and another road, three-quarters of a mile long, is reserved for equestrian exercise only. At the junction of these two roads the Refreshment Pavilion is erected : it is an ornamental structure, chiefly of varnished pine, and measures 45 feet by 25 feet, and is fitted up with a due regard to the comfort and convenience of visitors. It is surrounded by a kind of arcade, under which rustic seats are placed. This pavilion and the Entrance Lodge were erected at the entire cost of Miss Ryland.

We may here briefly notice the satisfactory solution by the Council of what was long known as the Sewage difficulty. Injunctions had been served on the Corporation, against the further pollution of the river Tame, by Sir Charles Adderley and the inhabitants of Gravelly Hill; valuable information had been collected and published by the Sewage Committee, respecting the various modes in operation in other large towns for the treatment and utilisation of sewage; and experiments had been made for years as to the best method of sewage farming. At length, after long and careful consideration, what is known as the Rochdale, or "pan system," was adopted, and the sewage conveyed by boats to the Corporation farms.

At the end of March, 1874, a poll was taken of the ratepayers of the borough, as to whether the Council should have power to increase the borough rates beyond 2s. in the pound, but at the close of the poll, (which lasted three days,) it was found that the proposed increase was defeated by a majority of 2,654.

On the 8th of June, 1875, the Council resolved, after an animated discussion, to abolish the time-honoured Whitsuntide and Michaelmas pleasure fairs, which had long become a nuisance and a serious hindrance to business, blocking up as they did, some of the busiest thoroughfares in the town.

During the parliamentary session of 1875, two important bills were passed, transferring to the care of the Corporation the extensive business and valuable plants of the Gas and Water Companies. The successful piloting of these important measures through the various parliamentary stages is

FORWARD

RICHARD TANGYE.

PHOTOGRAPHED BY WHITLOCK.

BIRMINGHAM: HOUGHTON & CO., SCOTLAND PASSAGE.

due to the energy and practical knowledge of our junior representative, Mr. Joseph Chamberlain, M.P., who was at that time Mayor of Birmingham.

ness at once accepted the invitation, and visited Birmingham, with the Princess of Wales, on the 3rd of November, where he was received with

THE ELKINGTON CHALLENGE SHIELD, IN THE CORPORATION ART GALLERY.
(From a photograph by J. T. Haden.)

In November, 1874, H.R.H. The Prince of Wales paid a visit to the Earl of Aylesford, at Packington, Warwickshire; and was invited by the Mayor (Alderman Chamberlain) to pay a visit to the hardware capital. His Royal High-

the utmost enthusiasm. After receiving the address of the Town Council, at the Town Hall, the Royal Party proceeded to the rooms of the Society of Artists, where luncheon was provided; they afterwards visited the Show

Rooms of Messrs. Elkington, Gillott's Pen Manufactory, and the Mint, and then returned to Packington. The illuminations in the evening were said to have been on the grandest scale ever witnessed in Birmingham.

On the 25th of May, 1875, the Council decided to purchase, for the sum of £5,390, a piece of waste land (eight acres in extent) near the Moseley Road, called Hollier's Charity Land, and to convert the same into a public park. It was at first intended to be called Camp Hill Park, but as this was supposed to bear too close a resemblance, in sound at least, to "Cannon Hill Park," and this might lead to confusion, it was resolved to call it "Highgate Park." The new park was opened June 2, 1876, by the Mayor, Joseph Chamberlain, Esq.; and no one who had aforetime crossed the dismal piece of land, crowded with brick-ends and other unsightly refuse,—the once pleasant greensward worn bare and brown—would have readily identified it with the exquisite little park, with its broad terrace and winding walks, its shrubberies and bright parterres, and its smooth trim lawns, as it appeared after the transformation accomplished under the direction of the Baths and Parks Committee. From the upper portion of the park a better view is obtained of the town than from any other spot in the vicinity. The lower end, near Alcester Street, is paved with asphalte, and serves admirably as a playground for the juvenile population of that neighbourhood.

On the day of the inauguration of Highgate Park another noble gift was announced from Miss Ryland, of about 43 acres of land for a new Park at Small Heath; and four days later, June 6th, the Council decided upon the purchase of yet another park,—the Summerfield estate, situated between the Dudley Road and Icknield Port Road, Winson Green,—for £9,000. This latter, which is about twelve acres in extent, and contains some fine old trees, was opened to the public by the Mayor (Alderman Baker) on the 29th of July in the same year.

The Small Heath Park, which was opened April 5th, 1879, was laid out at considerable expense (£4,000 of which was generously contributed by Miss Ryland), from plans prepared by the Borough Surveyor. A carriage drive was formed, and an ornamental structure erected in the centre of the park, as a Refreshment House, and from the elevated ground upon which this building stands, a good view of the whole park, and of the ornamental lake, may be obtained. The principal entrance is in Coventry Road, but for the convenience of visitors arriving by railway at Small Heath Station, another entrance has been made in Wordsworth Road.

We may here close the list of our Public Parks and recreation grounds by recording the opening, on the 1st of December, 1877, of the Recreation Grounds presented to the town by W. Middlemore, Esq., comprising about four acres of land situated in Burbury Street, Lozells. During the present year (1879) the Gas Committee have temporarily thrown open to the public, as a recreation ground, a piece of land at Nechells.

The breathing places of Birmingham may, with advantage to the reader, be here tabulated as follows :—

	SIZE.			OPENED.
	A.	R.	P.	
Adderley Park ...	10	0	22	... 1856.
Calthorpe Park ...	31	1	13	... 1857.
Aston Park ...	50	0	23	... 1858.
Cannon Hill Park ...	57	1	9	... 1873.
Highgate Park ...	8	0	28	... 1876.
Summerfield Park ...	12	0	20	... 1876.
Burbury Street Recreation Ground	4	1	3	... 1877.
Small Heath Park ...	41	3	34	... 1879.

In all, therefore, the people of Birmingham now possess nearly 220 acres of parks and playgrounds, and by the Birmingham Closed Burial Grounds Act of 1878 they will shortly acquire several other pleasantly laid-out open spaces within the town itself; so that it will, hereafter, compare favourably with almost any in the provinces in this particular. The attention paid, too, by the Corporation to the beautifying of all our open spaces by planting trees and shrubs, will, in course of time, make bright and cheerful those places which were, in many instances, little better than waste howling wildernesses,—deserts of brick and mortar.

On the 6th of June, 1876, the Council appointed a new Chief of Police, in the place of Superintendent Glossop, who had been superannuated, at £400 a year, in the April of the same year. The candidate selected for the office was Major Bond, under whose *regime* the tone and condition of the force has been considerably improved.

Under the Artisans' Dwellings Act of 1875, a scheme was approved by the Council, November 9th, 1875, for the clearing of a large area of insanitary dwellings, lying between Bull Street, Dale End, and Steelhouse Lane, and the construction of a new and important thoroughfare from New Street, opposite Stephenson Place to the junction of Bagot Street with the Aston Road, and also for constructing two lesser thoroughfares, leading out of the new street into High Street and Dale End.

A Government enquiry was held respecting the proposed scheme, in 1876, and the Act obtained for carrying out its proposals. Nearly all the properties have now been purchased, and a small portion of the area lying between New Street and Bull Street has been cleared, and the commencement of the new street formed, upon which buildings are now being erected. The clearing of this vast area of insanitary buildings, (most of which have been standing upwards of a century,) may be regarded as one of the most gigantic undertakings in the annals of the Corporation; and the project (like the purchase of the valuable properties of the Gas and Water Companies) is mainly due to the enterprise of our junior member, Mr. Chamberlain, although much praise is due to the hard-working Chairman of the Improvement Committee, Councillor White. Much remains yet to be done, but the manner in which the work has been commenced gives every assurance that, in a few years to come, such a transformation will be effected in this locality as will render it one of the most important and flourishing districts in the town.

And with this brief notice of an undertaking, which, to describe fully, would occupy far more space than we have at our disposal, we bring to a conclusion our sketch of the history of the Corporation.

CHAPTER II.

POLITICAL HISTORY, 1841-1879.

The Anti-Corn-Law Agitation—General Election, 1841—The Chartists and the Anti-Corn-Law Association—The Complete Suffrage Association—The Anti-Corn-Law League—John Bright's First Speech in Birmingham—Death of Mr. Joshua Scholefield—Defeat of the Liberals—Repeal of the Corn Laws—Free Trade—General Election, 1848—The Birmingham Political Council—The Catholic Question—General Election, 1852—The War with Russia—General Election, 1857—Death of Mr. G. F. Muntz, M.P.—Return of John Bright—The Reform Agitation—The Birmingham Reform Association—Defeat of the Government—General Election, 1859—A New Reform Bill—Withdrawal of the Bill by the Government—The Radical Reform League—General Election, 1865—Mr. Gladstone's Reform Bill Defeated—Great Reform Demonstration at Brookfields—Mr. Disraeli's Bill—Second Meeting at Brookfields—The Reform Bill Carried—Death of Mr. W. Scholefield, M.P.—Return of Mr. George Dixon—Formation of the Liberal Association—The Irish Church Suspension Bill—General Election, 1868—Return of the Three Liberal Candidates—Disestablishment of the Irish Church—Formation of the National Education League—Passing of the Elementary Education Act—Election of the first School Board for Birmingham—The Religious Difficulty in the Board Schools—Resignation of Mr. George Dixon, M.P.—Return of Mr. Joseph Chamberlain—General Election, 1874—Opposition to the Foreign Policy of the Government—Present State of Parties in Birmingham.

OUR next task in the history of our own times, from the year 1841 to the present day, is to record briefly those political events which have to a certain extent, a lasting interest, as apart from the merely ephemeral movements which have exerted no abiding influence either upon the constitution or in the political life of the town.

The agitation for the Repeal of the Corn Laws during 1841, brought about a Parliamentary crisis; the vote of want of confidence in Her Majesty's Ministers, moved by Sir Robert Peel, on the 24th of May, was carried by a majority of one in a House of 623 members, and on the 23rd of June Parliament was dissolved. Mr. Joshua Scholefield and Mr. G. F. Muntz, issued addresses in advance of the expected dissolution, seeking re-election, (the latter after only a year and a half of service, having been elected for the first time in January, 1840); and the Conservatives were not far behind their opponents in bringing out candidates for the anticipated elections, in the persons of Mr. Richard Spooner and Mr. W. C.

Alston. The nomination was fixed for June 30th, and, in addition to the four gentlemen named, Mr. G. White, the Chartist, was also nominated. Although the show of hands was manifestly in favour of the Liberals, a poll was demanded for Mr. Spooner, and was taken with the following

NEW LINE OF STREET, COLMORE ROW AND ANN STREET.

result : for Mr. Muntz, 2,175 ; for Mr. Scholefield, 1,963 ; and for Mr. Spooner, 1,825.

Meanwhile the Birmingham Branch of the Anti-Corn-Law Association had taken up in earnest the work of spreading information on the subject of Free Trade, by means of pamphlets, leaflets, weekly meetings, sermons, and other methods. A medal was struck by Mr. Joseph Davis, of Newhall Hill, bearing appropriate devices, and the two mottoes : " *Undo the heavy burdens, deal thy bread to the hungry* "—and on the reverse, " *Free Trade with all the World.*"

A meeting of delegates was held January 26, 1842, at the Waterloo Rooms, Mr. W. Scholefield, presiding, at which reports were read respecting the state of trade in the vicinity; the workmen in the fancy steel toy trade reported that the rate of wages had been reduced one-half, and that where, in one manufactory, in 1815, 120 persons had been employed, there were at that time only forty. In the plating trade the number of *employés* had been reduced by one third, and the remainder were working only for stock, and were not fully employed; the wages in that trade had also been reduced 35 to 40 per cent. Similar reports were presented from the Brassfoundry trade, from lamp-makers, gun-makers, silver workers, tin-plate workers, jewellers, and others; while the pawnbrokers reported " that they would not be able much longer to lend money on pledges, the business had increased so rapidly, and so few pledges were being redeemed." Another feature in the commercial depression was exhibited in the statement of the number of void houses in Birmingham, which, by the last census, (1841) were reported to number 4,000, although the population was increasing at the rate of $12\frac{1}{2}$ per cent., or more than 4,000 a year. In the principal streets alone there were void houses representing an annual rental of little less than £4,200, and an annual levy of about £360. A deputation was appointed to wait on the Government, and a petition to the House of Commons was approved; and in the evening a public meeting was held in the Town Hall, addressed by Mr. Curtis, of Ohio, U.S., and Mr. Cobden.

The facts thus brought before the public, as to the misery and want inflicted by the Corn Laws, impelled the worthy pastor of Carr's Lane, the Rev. J. A. James, to address his congregation on the subject of the iniquitous restrictions. Had the question been one of commercial reform, or of general politics merely, he would not, he said, have brought it before them; but, as a minister of a religion which was pre-eminently one of mercy, he felt impelled to come forward.

He concluded by reading a petition, praying for the total repeal of the Corn Laws, as impolitic, unjust, and unscriptural. This petition was presented to the House of Commons by Mr. Joshua Scholefield on the 14th of February, signed by upwards of 50,000 of the inhabitants of Birmingham; and on the following Friday, February 18th, an enthusiastic town's meeting, on the same subject, was held in the Town Hall, at which the Chartists (who had hitherto proved rather doubtful allies) gave their hearty support to the Anti-Corn Law Association.

The year 1842 was also marked by the attempt to establish on a firm foundation the Complete Suffrage Association, of which Mr. Joseph Sturge was one of the leaders. It was, in effect, a system of Chartism divested of its ugly element of " physical force." The conflict with the old Chartist body, however, rendered all the efforts of this association unavailing. A conference was held in the town during the month of April, at which delegates from forty-four towns were present, and on the 9th of that month a meeting of the Association was held in the Town Hall, to receive a report of the proceedings of the Conference. Another meeting was held on the same evening in Duddeston Row (their head-quarters at that time) by the old Chartists. Riots were occurring in various parts of the country during the two months which followed, and were repressed with no gentle hand by the Government; and it was not long before the Birmingham adherents of the Charter were up in revolt, issuing placards, and otherwise inciting the people to acts of violence. On the 22nd of August a meeting was announced to be held in Duddeston Row, the placard calling upon the Men of Birmingham to " WORK NO MORE until Liberty be established," and was otherwise couched in language which seemed likely to incite the proposed meeting to riot. Some little disturbance did actually occur, but by the prompt interference of the police it was immediately quelled; and the convener of the meeting—the well-known George White—was arrested and committed to the sessions on a charge of issuing the seditious and inflammatory placards.

In consequence of the Royal Proclamation against illegal meetings, the Town Hall Committee declined to grant the use of that building for a proposed Conference of the Complete Suffrage Association; a special meeting of that association was therefore held instead, on September 12th. On the 14th of November another meeting was held, to elect delegates to the conference, which was to be held during the following month. It seemed to resolve itself into a struggle between the Chartists and the members of the association; the former mustered strongly, and were determined to oppose the appointment of Mr. Sturge as chairman, proposing instead that a Mr. Fellows, a working man, should preside. Mr. Sturge was then nominated, and the meeting declared in his favour, by a large majority. Once more the Town Hall was refused for the Conference, and it was held in the room formerly occupied by the Mechanics' Institute, in Newhall Street. The sitting of the Conference commenced December 27, and at its opening there were nearly 300 delegates present; but again the conflict between the two parties divided the meeting, one party declaring in favour of the word "Bill" being used in a certain resolution, and the other of the word "Charter," and so, after much wordy warfare over one unlucky word, the Conference dissolved without accomplishing any useful purpose.

Less than a month afterwards, a political assembly of a more useful and successful character was held in the Town Hall, On the 22nd of January, 1843, a "Great Anti-Corn-Law Tea Party" took place, at which upwards of 1,700 persons were present. After tea, the meeting was addressed by the leading Liberals of Birmingham and Manchester, including, among the latter, John Bright, who delivered his first speech in Birmingham on this occasion in denunciation of the "oppressive impost." At the

close of the meeting nearly £200 was subscribed towards the funds of the Anti-Corn-Law League.

On the 22nd of May, in the same year, a similar tea party was held in the Town Hall, in the interests of the Complete Suffrage Union, and in honour of the twenty-six members of the Birmingham Town Council, who, on the 3rd of March, had voted for the motion of Mr. Alderman Weston, to petition Parliament for Complete Suffrage, Vote by Ballot, Equal Electoral Districts, Abolition of Property Qualifications, and Annual Parliaments—the five points of the Charter in fact—which had been carried by a majority of one.

Another great Anti-Corn-Law meeting was held in the Town Hall, February 5th, 1844, at which Mr. Cobden, Colonel Thompson, and Mr. Moore were present as a deputation from the League. Some little disturbance was created by George White, who made an attempt to speak in favour of the Charter, but subsequently left the hall, and the members of the deputation then addressed the meeting. The sum of £850 was afterwards subscribed towards the funds of the League.

During this year, the town had to mourn the loss of its oldest representative, the colleague of Mr. Attwood in the first Reformed Parliament, —Mr. Joshua Scholefield—who died in London, on the 4th of July, in the 70th year of his age. Of the three candidates who were proposed for the vacant seat,—Mr. William Scholefield, nominated by the "Liberal Electors," Mr. Joseph Sturge, by the "Radical Electors," and Mr. Richard Spooner, by the Conservatives, the last named gentleman was elected, and had the honour of being the only Conservative who has ever sat in Parliament for Birmingham. The voting was as follows: for Mr. Spooner, 2,095; Mr. Scholefield, 1,735; and Mr. Sturge, 346. If the latter, therefore, had followed the admirable example of George Edmonds, (who, as our readers will remember, honourably refused to be the means of dividing the Liberal party at the first

Birmingham election,) the roll of our Parliamentary representatives would have presented an unbroken series of Liberal victories, from the time of our enfranchisement to the present day.

During the session of 1846 the Bill for the Repeal of the Corn Laws was being discussed in the House of Commons, and the utmost efforts of the League were exerted to enlist the sympathy of the nation in its fovour. Pamphlets and fly-leaves, containing facts, arguments, rhymes, catechisms and conversations were done up in neat packets, bearing an appropriate pictorial design, and circulated gratis in all parts of the country. On the 25th of June, the Bill was read a third time in the House of Lords, and passed without a division ; and the rejoicing in Birmingham on the success of the movement was both hearty and general. A public meeting was held July 8th, at which the following resolution was passed :—

That this meeting regards with feelings of the highest satisfaction the Repeal of the Corn Laws and the Customs Tariff, and considers that the gratitude of the country is due to Sir Robert Peel for his noble and successful exertions in support of their Repeal and Reform.

An address, " containing the expression of much gratitude " was also adopted and signed by nearly 8,000 persons, and was presented to Sir Robert Peel in London, July 27th.

In view of the General Election, which was fixed to take place in July 1847, the Liberals of Birmingham began early in June of that year to work for the return of two members of their own party, and thus to wipe out the disgrace of their defeat at the previous election, whereby a victory had been obtained by the Conservative candidate. It was unanimously resolved that Mr. William Scholefield should be invited to become a candidate, and a deputation was appointed to wait upon Mr. Muntz to ascertain whether he would unite with Mr. Scholefield in canvassing the electors.

Mr. Muntz, however, declined the proposal, and refused to " coalesce with anybody," or to make any personal canvass, " never having done so, and believing that such a practice is equally

degrading both to the constituency and the candidates." In his address to the electors he quoted and applied to himself Goldsmith's well-known lines—

" Unpractised he to fawn or seek for power,
By doctrines fashioned to the varying hour."

Mr. R. Spooner offered himself again for re-election in the Conservative interest, and on the same side Mr. Sergeant Allen sought the suffrages of the electors, issuing an address wherein an attempt was made to blend Liberal with Conservative principles—a combination which has of late years been styled Liberal-Conservatism. The polling took place on the 30th of July, and resulted in the regaining of the second seat for the Liberal party, by whom every subsequent Parliamentary election has since been won, Mr. Spooner being the only Conservative member who has ever sat for Birmingham. The numbers were as follows :—for Mr. Muntz, 2,830 ; Mr. Scholefield, 2,829 ; Mr. Spooner, 2,302 ; and Mr. Allen, 89, the last-named gentleman having retired from the contest at an early hour on the polling day.

During the political excitement which followed upon the French Revolution in 1848, and in order to counteract the violence of the Chartists, a new Liberal society was established for the peaceable agitation of various reforms, under the title of the Birmingham Political Council, the preliminary meeting of which was held on the 31st of March in that year, Mr. J. Baldwin being elected chairman, and Mr. G. Mantle secretary. Following on the lines of the old Political Union, its motto was " Peace ! Justice ! Prosperity ! "

In the following April a declaration in favour of obtaining by all peaceful and constitutional means, Household Suffrage, Vote by Ballot, Triennial Parliaments, and electoral Districts, was signed by 9,000 persons, and on the 1st of May another political society was established, under the name of the Reform League, of which Mr. G. F. Muntz, M.P. was elected president, with Messrs. W. Scholefield, M.P., George Dawson,

Thomas Weston and R. K. Douglas as Vice-presidents. A large Executive Committee was also appointed, and W. E. Timmins was elected Secretary.

An impetus was given to the Reform agitation during this month by the passing of the Jewish Disabilities Bill in the House of Commons by a majority of 61 votes, and its subsequent rejection by the Lords by 163 against 128 votes. Notice was given by Mr. Joseph Hume in the House of Commons that on the 20th of June he should move the following resolution :—

That this House, as at present constituted, does not fairly represent the population, the property, or the industry of the country, whence has arisen great and increasing discontent in the minds of a large portion of the people ; and it is therefore expedient, with the view to amend the National Representation, that the elective franchise shall be so extended as to include householders ; that votes shall be taken by ballot ; that the duration of Parliament shall not exceed three years ; and that the apportionment of members to population shall be made more equal.

As might be expected Mr. Hume's resolution was accepted in Birmingham with the utmost satisfaction. A petition in support of the motion was adopted by a large and enthusiastic meeting of the Reform League, in the Town Hall, on the 31st of May ; a meeting of the Political Council was held in the Town Hall, June 7th, in favour of Universal Suffrage and in support of Mr. Hume's motion ; and a somewhat noisy and violent out-door gathering of the Chartists was held in Loveday Street, near the People's Hall, on Sunday June 11th. The attendance of a large body of police at the Staniforth Street station, and of two companies of infantry from Weedon, who were stationed near the railway, prevented any serious breach of the peace, however ; and their services were, happily, not in requisition.

Mr. Hume's motion was not brought forward until the 6th of July, when it was rejected by a majority of 267, only 84 votes being recorded in its favour.

The efforts of Louis Kossuth in the Hungarian struggle for liberty, in 1849, awakened the sympathy of the people of Birmingham, in common with that of the nation in general, and one of the first meetings for the expression of that sympathy was held in the Odd Fellows' Hall in this town, on the 23rd of May in that year ; when the following resolutions were adopted unanimously :—

That by us, Englishmen and Freemen, no struggle for the defence or attainment of national liberty, can be looked upon with indifference ; and all efforts to secure it should have the advantage of an expression of sympathy from the people of this Country.

That the present struggle in Hungary is eminently an effort which demands the sympathy and support of English Freemen, as it at once seeks the preservation of long-enjoyed liberties and the confirmation of newly-acquired freedom ; thus uniting our sympathies as true Conservatives and friends of progress.

That this Meeting pledges itself to aid the Hungarian cause by every available means open to individual effort, and consistent with our duties as citzens of a neutral state.

Another meeting was held on the 23rd of June, for the same purpose, and to petition Parliament on the same subject ; and a third, a Town's Meeting, was held at the Corn Exchange, on the 13th of August, when the following resolutions were passed :—

That as Englishmen, as lovers of all freedom, civil and religious, as true Conservatives, and as friends of progress, this meeting feel it a sacred duty to express their earnest, entire, and unreserved approbation of the Hungarian struggle for Independence, and their humble and hearty admiration of Hungarian heroism.

That we look with deep and unmitigated abhorrence upon the savage and horrible manner in which Austria carries on the war ; and as friends of the rights of nations and the freedom of the world, emphatically protest against the unrighteous intervention of Russia.

That a petition be presented to the Queen, praying the Government to give an emphatic expression to these universal feelings of the people, by immediately recognising the de facto Government of Hungary ; and that the Mayor be requested to sign the same on behalf of the meeting, and to secure its presentation.

After a season of political repose, party feeling of a religio-political character was roused, in the town and throughout the country, in 1850, by the creation of Dr. Wiseman Cardinal Archbishop of Westminster, and the establishment of a Roman Catholic Hierarchy in England. A Town's Meeting was held in Birmingham on the 11th of December, which has been described as one of the most extraordinary gatherings ever assembled in our Town Hall.

"The building," says Dr. Langford, "was literally crammed; it being estimated that not deafening; and the number of witticisms uttered by many of the auditors was not the least remarkable occurrence of this most remarkable meeting.

"Mr. James Taylor proposed the following address:—

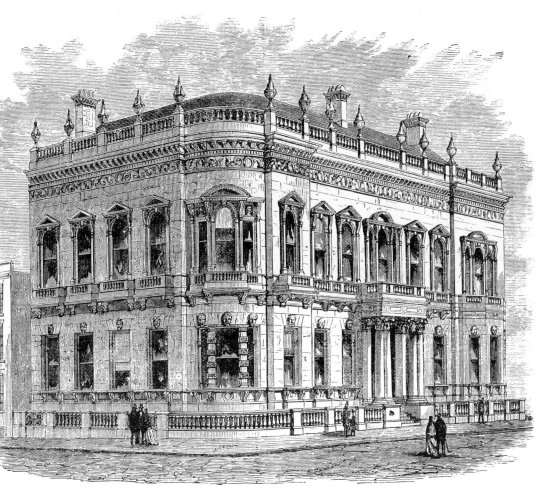

THE UNION CLUB HOUSE, COLMORE ROW.

fewer than 10,000 persons were present. The platform presented an unusually lively appearance. On the right of the Mayor were arranged the requisitionists, and on the left the leaders of the opposition. The cheers and counter-cheers, the groans and hisses which greeted those best known, as they appeared on the platform, were

"TO THE QUEEN'S MOST EXCELLENT MAJESTY.
    "*May it please Your Majesty.*

"We, Your Majesty's faithful subjects, Inhabitants of the Borough of Birmingham, beg permission to assure Your Majesty of our dutiful and loyal attachment to your throne and person; we have learned with feelings of indignation of the Bull recently promulgated by the Pope of Rome, in which he arrogantly assumes the power to parcel out this, Your Majesty's Kingdom of England, into several dioceses, under the government of a Roman Catholic Archbishop and Roman Catholic Bishops, with territorial jurisdiction ; and we humbly submit an opinion that the Roman Pontiff has been greatly influenced in his policy towards this Country by the information which must have reached him concerning the existence in the Church of England of a certain number of the clergy, whose teaching and practice approximate to those of the Church of Rome.

" We regard the proceedings of the Pope as an insult to Your Majesty, as a violation of the constitution under which we live, and as an audacious attack upon our civil and religious liberties. We protest against the recognition of the authority in this nation of any foreign potentate, as subversive of order, good government, and freedom ; and we earnestly pray Your Majesty to take immediate steps to vindicate the prerogatives of the Crown, and to maintain the liberties of Your Majesty's subjects.

" This address was seconded by J. B. Melson, M.D., and supported by the Rev. J. A. James, R. Spooner, M.P., and the Rev. R. Vaughan.

" Mr. Joseph Sturge proposed the following amendment :—

" To the Queen's Most Excellent Majesty, The humble address of the Inhabitants of Birmingham, in Town's Meeting assembled.

" *May it please Your Majesty*,

" We, Your Majesty's loyal subjects of the Borough of Birmingham, in Town's Meeting assembled, for the purpose of expressing our sense of the recent appointment of a Roman Catholic Hierarchy in this Country, beg respectfully to represent to Your Majesty, that in our opinion such appointment does not require any legislative interference.

" We dutifully, yet earnestly, deprecate all restrictions upon the free enjoyment by every religious body within Your Majesty's dominions, of its spiritual order and discipline.

" We therefore entreat Your Majesty to sanction such measures as may be proposed for securing the maintenance and extension of civil and religious liberty.

" The amendment was seconded by George Edmonds and supported by George Dawson, the Rev. Brewin Grant, and Mr. Stokes, a Roman Catholic. It was, of course, put first to the meeting. I quote the scene from the graphic report of a contemporary chronicler :—

" The Chairman then proceeded to read the original address, and the amended one submitted by Mr. Sturge, during which the meeting preserved the strictest silence until the conclusion of each address, when there was a burst of cheering from the supporters of each.

" A profound stillness then fell upon the vast multitude that filled the hall, so that a pin could be almost heard to drop, while 10,000 men contentedly held their breaths in a state of most intense excitement, as the Chairman advanced to the front of the gallery to put the question.

" The amendment was first put, and a forest of hands and a sea of moving hats and handkerchiefs was instantly displayed, while the pent-up excitement of the mass gave way in a tremendous burst of cheering.

" The question was then put in the negative, or against the amendment, and an apparently equal numerical display of hands, and an equally enthusiastic manifestation of feeling, followed. When silence was restored, the Chairman, after a pause said, I find it so exceedingly difficult to decide, that I wish to try it again. (Great laughter and cheering.)

" The question for and against the amendment was again put, with nearly the same results, and the same vociferous applause. The Chairman, after silence had been obtained, said, I feel extreme difficulty in deciding this question, particularly as there are scattered in different parts of the hall groups of persons on both sides. I feel, as I say, extreme difficulty in deciding this question, BUT MY OPINION IS THAT THE AMENDMENT IS NOT CARRIED. A tremendous shout of applause, followed by waving of hats and handkerchiefs, burst from the supporters of the original address, their excitement being of the most rapturous and enthusiastic kind, no doubt stimulated by the expectation that they had obtained a triumph. At length silence having been with some difficulty restored—the Chairman, advancing to the front said, I will now put the original address. Those who are in favour of the original address will hold up both hands. In a moment thousands of hands were held up, and cheers and other demonstrations of excited congratulation followed. When the prolonged cheering had somewhat subsided—the Chairman said, those who are against the original address will hold up both their hands. A still larger number of hands were then held up, followed by the same noisy demonstrations. The Chairman then advanced to the front of the orchestra, amidst the most intense excitement, and said, I feel the same difficulty that I did before in coming to a decision, but it is my opinion, and I DECIDE THAT THE ORIGINAL ADDRESS IS LOST. A tremendous burst of cheering, which seemed to shake the building, followed this announcement, while the utmost consternation and disappointment exhibited itself amongst the requisitionists. The uproarious thunders of applause were prolonged again and again amongst the supporters of the amendment.

" The Mayor, on the motion of Mr. Sturge, then left the chair, amidst cries of " a most unfair decision," from some of the requisitionists, who were taunted by Mr. Edmonds with gross insult to the Mayor, and as being very inconsistent sticklers for law and authority. Mr. James Taylor, shaking his head at the Mayor, said (as we understood him), " You have disgraced yourself." Mr. Edmonds then suggested that Mr. Spooner should take the chair, while a vote of thanks was given to the

Mayor ; but this Mr. Spooner positively decline1 to do, amid confusion, during which the Mayor left the Hall. Ultimately, however, Mr. Weston was moved into the chair, and on the motion of Mr. Edmonds, seconded by Mr. Sturge, the vote of thanks was put to the meeting and carried *mem. con.*, the requisitionists declining to take any part in the vote.

"Three cheers were then given for the Mayor, three for liberty, and three for the Queen ; and the proceedings of this, one of the most numerous and important meetings ever held in Birmingham, terminated by the supporters of the amendment singing " God save the Queen," which was received with silence, and in some instances by hissing from the right-hand side of the hall and platform. The proceedings occupied about six hours ; and although the meeting was occasionally in such an excited state that many of the speakers could not be heard beyond a short distance from the platform, yet the assembled multitude were remarkably good humoured, and separated very quietly."

The excitement continued during the first few weeks of the new year, and among other local contributions to the controversy lectures were delivered by the Rev. Dr. Miller, Dr. Dixon, (Wesleyan minister), and Mr. George Dawson, M.A. Ultimately the question was set at rest by the passing of the Ecclesiastical Titles Bill, a mere *brutum fulmen* which never accomplished, and perhaps was never intended to accomplish, its avowed purpose, and was most wisely altered in 1871.

The question of Parliamentary Reform was again brought to the front in 1852 ; a public meeting was held in the Town Hall, January 16, addressed by George Edmonds, George Dawson, the Rev. Brewin Grant, Sir Joshua Walmsley, M.P., and G. Thompson, M.P. ; and in February a new Reform Bill was introduced into the House of Commons by Lord John Russell, for extending the franchise in the counties to occupiers of premises rated at £20, and in cities and boroughs to householders rated at £5. Another meeting was held on the 24th of that month to support the Bill, but the intention was frustrated by an amendment, which was carried, declaring that "any measure of Reform that does not include the shortening of the duration of Parliament, the abolition of the property qualification of Members of Parliament, universal suffrage, and

a fair distribution of members corresponding with the population of each district, will not give satisfaction to the people of this country."

As most of our readers know, the Reform Bill of 1852 did not become law, and the cause of Parliamentary Reform was shelved for a time. For several years afterwards the country was too busily engaged with the affairs of Eastern Europe to pay much attention to other political questions affecting the interests of the people of Great Britain.

On the 21st of February, 1852, Lord John Russell resigned, and the Earl of Derby formed a Ministry, in which Mr. Disraeli was for the first time Chancellor of the Exchequer, that being, moreover, his first office in any administration. On the 1st of July, in the same year, Parliament was dissolved ; the nomination for Birmingham took place on the 10th, when the old representatives, Messrs. Muntz and Scholefield, were returned unopposed.

Another attempt was made by Lord John Russell, in 1854, to carry his Reform Bill (which provided for the enfranchisement of £10 householders in the counties, and £6 householders in boroughs) ; but the country was too much engrossed by the Crimean War to take much notice of it. A meeting was, of course, held in Birmingham, in support of it (March 15th), but the Bill was withdrawn in April, and once more shelved.

The " annual attempt to disfranchise the freeholders and other legally qualified voters " for North Warwickshire, by the numerous objections raised as to their eligibility to vote, stimulated the Liberals of Birmingham, in 1856, to form a Liberal Registration Society. Mr. W. Scholefield, M.P., and Messrs. James Taylor, jun., H. Allbutt, W. Harris, H. Smith, J. S. Wright, and Councillors Sadler and Jackson were the leaders in this useful movement; at the first meeting, held October 1st, nearly £100 was subscribed towards the objects of the society.

In March, 1857, Parliament was dissolved,

and once more the two representatives " walked over," being re-elected without opposition. But in the case of the senior member, Mr. G. F. Muntz, the parliamentary honours thus renewed were enjoyed only for a few short months; for on the 30th of July, in the same year, he died, at the age of 62, having represented the borough in Parliament for seventeen years.

It happened at that time, that a member of the former Parliament, who had already become famous both as an orator and a sound politician, was without a seat, having been ungraciously rejected by his former constituency, Manchester, on account of his views on the Crimean War, and his consistent advocacy of a peace policy, and to this gentleman,—" the foremost man in the House of Commons," Mr. John Bright—" the Liberals of Birmingham almost instinctively turned,"* in order to fill up the blank caused by his temporary absence from the national legislature,—a place which no other living statesman could have filled.

Another Liberal candidate came forward, Mr. Baron Dickenson Webster, of Penn's Mills—but at the public meeting for the selection of candidates, held August 4th, it was obvious that he would meet with the support of only a small minority of the Liberal electors, and before the day of nomination Mr. Webster wisely withdrew from the contest, so that, on August 10th, Mr. Bright was elected without opposition. " The peculiarity of this election," says Dr. Langford, " was, that Mr. Bright was not in Birmingham at the time, and had issued his address only two days before the nomination. It was the spontaneous tribute of a great constituency to a great man—which could overlook even great differences of opinion on some subjects for the sake of securing a representative of the highest eloquence, the most unswerving consistency, the most sterling honesty, and of

the broadest Liberal views."*   The Mayor (Mr. John Ratcliff), immediately telegraphed the result to Mr. Bright, and received the following reply :

Rochdale, August 10th, 1857.
Dear Mr. Mayor.
I have to thank you, and I do most sincerely, for your kindness in sending me the telegraphic message, which informs me that I am one of the Parliamentary Representatives of the great community over which you have the honour to preside. I hope I may have the power hereafter to show that I am not wholly unworthy of the confidence your townsmen have placed in me.
Believe me, with great respect,
Yours faithfully,
JOHN BRIGHT.

To the electors who had thus returned him, unsolicited, to his old accustomed place in the House of Commons, he issued the following address :

Rochdale, August 10th, 1857.
Gentlemen,
Your respected Chief Magistrate has informed me by telegraph, that he has this day declared me to be duly elected one of your Representatives in Parliament, and I have learned from other sources that such was the feeling manifested in my favour that no other Candidate was presented to you at the hustings, and that therefore my election has been without contest or opposition from any quarter.
When I addressed you two days ago, I had no expectation of a result so speedy and so tranquil of the then impending struggle ; I accept it as a conclusive proof of the bias of your political views, and of a confidence in me which I shall strive to maintain undiminished.
It is a matter of real regret to me that I have not been able to be with you during the past week, and at the hustings this day ; I shall hope, however, that on some not distant occasion I may be permitted to meet you in your noble Town Hall, and to become more intimately acquainted with a constituency from whom I have received an honour as signal as it was unexpected, and towards whom I can never entertain other feelings than those of respect and gratitude.
With heartfelt thanks for your kindness, which I trust I may have the health and opportunity in some measure to repay,
I subscribe myself,
Very faithfully yours,
JOHN BRIGHT.

In October of this year the first Congress of the Social Science Association was held in

* Dr. Langford : Modern Birmingham, ii., 9.

* Modern Birmingham, ii., 10.

Birmingham, and among other distinguished visitors who were present on that occasion was the author of the second Reform Bill, Lord John

My Lord,—We, members of the political party that delight in the name of Liberal, rejoice in the presence of your lordship in our town, and cannot suffer you to depart without expressing to you our constant and

ILLUMINATION OF ST. PHILIP'S CHURCH,
On the occasion of the Marriage of the Prince of Wales, March 10th, 1863.

Russell. Advantage was taken by the Liberals of his presence in Birmingham to present the following address :

grateful remembrance of the distinguished services you have rendered to the cause of Political Reform, and Civil and Religious Liberty. We need not recount these services. They are written in our Country's history.

We also desire to express our hope that your lordship may long live to write your name on many another page of our national history ; certain, that however we may differ from you in details, all your future, like your past life, will be devoted to the furtherance of the political enfranchisement of your countrymen, and to the removal of the last remnant of religious intolerance and sectarian exclusion.

This is not the time to press upon your lordship our views on particular measures. We desire simply to express to you our gratitude for your past services, our admiration of your character, and our earnest hope that your lordship may be spared to consummate those political and religious reforms with which your name will be ever associated.

At the commencement of the year 1858 a Reformers' Union was formed in Birmingham (chiefly through the exertions of some of the old Reformers), its bases being : 1st, a much wider extension of the suffrage ;—2nd, a re-distribution of electoral districts ;—3rd, the ballot;—4th, abolition of property qualification ;—and 5th, shortening the duration of Parliament." The first great meeting of the new Union was held in the Town Hall, February 2nd, being called by the Mayor, in response to a requisition signed by upwards of 4,000 inhabitants. An important and lengthy letter from Mr. Bright (who was unable to attend) was read, in which he reviewed the several bases of the Union :

I beseech you, he said, to watch well what is proposed, [in Parliament,] and what is done. Be the measure great or small, let it be *honest* in every part. Include as many as you can in the right of the franchise. Insist upon such a redistribution of seats as shall give the House of Commons fairly to the industy, the property, the intelligence, and the population of the country. Demand the ballot as the undeniable right of every man who is called to the poll ; and take special care that the old constitutional rule and principle by which *majorities* alone shall decide in Parliamentary elections shall not be violated.

I give my hearty support, as I have heretofore done, to the propositions contained in your circular. I lament that I cannot join in your meeting to-morrow, for I esteem it a great honour to be permitted to act with the inhabitants of Birmingham on that question, which, a quarter of a century ago, they did so much to advance, and on which their potent voice is once more to be heard.

On the 27th of October, 1858, after three years of enforced absence from public life, during which

he had been reduced by ill-health "to a condition of weakness exceeding the weakness of a little child," Mr. Bright met his constituents for the first time since his election. It need scarcely be said that he met with such a reception as Birmingham men well know how to give to those whom they delight to honour,—a reception which, in its ardent demonstrations of enthusiasm, fell but little short of that which, three months before, had been accorded to their beloved sovereign herself. We have not the space to describe the speech itself, which dealt with the still vexed question of Reform, but there is one paragraph which should not be omitted from this record, referring as it does, to the distinction which Birmingham conferred upon itself by the spontaneous election of Mr. Bright as their representative :—

I shall not attempt, he said, by the employment of any elaborate phrases, to express to you what I felt at the time when you conferred upon me the signal honour of returning me as one of your representatives to the House of Commons. I am not sufficiently master of the English language to discover words which shall express what I then felt, and what I feel now towards you, for what you did then, and for the reception which you have given me to-night. I never imagined for a moment that you were prepared to endorse all my opinions, or to sanction every political act with which I have been connected ; but I accepted your resolution in choosing me as meaning this, that you had watched my political career ; that you believed it had been an honest one ; that you were satis-fied I had not swerved knowingly to the right hand or to the left ; that the attractions of power had not changed my course from any view of courting a fleeting popularity; and, further, that you are of this opinion—an opinion which I religiously hold—that the man whose political career is on a line with his conscientious convictions, can never be unfaithful to his constituents or to his country.

The sight of the vast surging mass which filled the great hall to its utmost capacity, " com-posed," as he afterwards remarked, " to a great extent of our countrymen who have no political power, who are at work from the dawn of day to the evening, and who have, therefore, limited means of informing themselves on great ques-tions," doubtless moved the great orator to renewed efforts in obtaining for the great mass of his constituents their political rights ; and early in the session of 1859 he introduced in the House of Commons a new Reform Bill, based upon the principles of the Reform Association, which had been formed in Birmingham in November, 1858—viz., a large extension of the suffrage, vote by ballot, and a more equal apportionment of Members to population. A town's meeting was held in the Town Hall, February 1st, for the purpose of considering the proposed measure, and resolutions were adopted by an overwhelming majority in its support, and expressing entire faith in the integrity of its promoter, pledging themselves " to give him their most hearty support in his endeavours to promote such a scheme of Parliamentary Reform as shall be satisfactory to the great body of the people."

A rival Bill was introduced, however, during the same session by the Earl of Derby, which included several " fancy franchises " — as Mr. Bright happily termed them—giving a vote to persons having £10 per annum in the Public Funds, Bank Stock, or India stock, or £60 in a Savings Bank, to recipients of pensions in the Public Services amounting to £20 a year, to dwellers in a portion of a house whose aggregate rent was £20 a year, to graduates of the Universities, ministers of religion, members of the legal and medical professions, and to certain schoolmasters. The only praiseworthy feature in the Government Bill was the proposed assimilation of the county franchise to that of the boroughs, thus reducing it to £10.

A great town's meeting was held in Birmingham, to consider the Government measure, on the 9th of March, at which both representatives of the borough were present, and strongly condemned the bill. A resolution to the same purpose was adopted by the meeting, as was also a petition, which received upwards of forty thousand signatures in two days.

The obnoxious bill was defeated on the second reading, April 1st, by a majority of 39 (291 *for* and 330 *against*), and on the 19th of the same

month Parliament was prorogued, preparatory to a dissolution, which followed immediately afterwards.

Messrs. Scholefield and Bright offered themselves for re-election, the latter issuing an important address on the question at issue. The Conservatives found a candidate in the person of Dr. G. Bodington, of Sutton Coldfield, who, in his address, however, stated that he would not engage in the contest unless Birmingham bade him do so ; and as no response was given by the electors, he wisely declined to court what seemed certain defeat. Later on, the Conservatives brought forward another candidate, Mr. Thomas Dyke Ackland ; but, notwithstanding the support which he received from a number of timid Liberals who feared " the extreme and dangerous principles of Mr. Bright," he was defeated by a large majority, the numbers being—for Mr. Bright, 4,425 ; Mr. Scholefield, 4,282 ; and Mr. Ackland, 1,544.

The new Ministry under Lord Palmerston introduced, early in the session of 1860, another Reform Bill, providing for a considerable extension of the franchise, which was received with great satisfaction by the people of Birmingham, to whom it was proposed to give a third representative. The bill was passed through the Commons successfully by the beginning of June, and a few days later, to the surprise and grief of all true Liberals, Lord John Russell announced that the Government intended to withdraw it. And so from this time the question of reform was shelved until the "rest and be thankful" policy came to its end with the death of the Premier in 1865.

During the session of 1860 the cause of Free Trade was advanced by the financial policy of Mr. Gladstone, and more especially by the negociation of the French Treaty. But one of the most important fiscal reforms introduced by this great statesman was the abolition of the paper duty, one of the heaviest and most oppressive " taxes on knowledge." This reform, as our readers are doubtless aware, was strongly opposed by the House of Lords, who, contrary to all modern precedent, at first rejected this portion of the Budget, and thereby called forth much discussion as to the right of the Upper House to deal with money bills. A Committee of the House of Commons was appointed to inquire as to the precedents for the course adopted by the Lords, and their report was drawn up by Mr. Bright.

While the cause of Reform slumbered peacefully within the Legislature, it was not permitted to do so in Birmingham, " the home of Reform," as its citizens loved to call it. The Radical Reform League held meetings from time to time, and were not slow to record their dissatisfaction at the apathy displayed by the Government in regard to this question. At a meeting held on the 4th of March, 1861, the following resolution was adopted :—

That the deliberate and dishonourable abandonment of Reform by her Majesty's Government having again thrown the question before the country, it is the duty of Reformers and all classes promptly and earnestly to combine to force upon the attention of the House of Commons the national desire for a thorough reform. This League, therefore, calls upon the attention of the people in every town in the kingdom to petition Parliament during the present Session, praying for an immediate consideration of the subject, and for the adoption of a measure which shall satisfy the just requirements of the people, by including manhood suffrage, vote by ballot, and equal electoral districts.

Again, at the annual meeting to receive the addresses of their representatives, held January 26th, 1864, the town declared that :—

The present House of Commons having been elected on the question of reform, and the majority of its members having pledged themselves to promote an extension of the franchise, this meeting records its opinion that the Parliament has failed in its duty in not having passed a measure which would have admitted a large number of the unenfranchised to a real share in the government of the nation. This meeting believes the present period to be favourable to the passing of such a measure, the necessity for which has on various occasions been enforced by her Majesty's Ministers, and by the leaders of both political parties.

On the 17th of February, 1865, a new Asso-

ciation was founded, which was destined to become one of the most powerful organizations for the advancement of the cause of Liberalism ever established—exceeding in its influence and results even the famous Political Union of Thomas Attwood. A meeting was held on that day in the Committee Room of the Town Hall of all the leading members of the Liberal party in Birmingham, and the result of their deliberations was the formation of the *Liberal Association*.

The following were the officers and committee for the first year :—President, Mr. P. H. Muntz ; treasurer, Mr. John Jaffray ; hon. secretary, Mr. George Dixon ; committee, Messrs. Councillor J. Baldwin, G. Baker, George Dawson, R. Fletcher, Alderman W. Holliday, W. Harris, B. Harris, Councillor H. Holland, G. J. Johnson, J. T. Keep, Alderman T. Lloyd, Alderman H. Manton, J. S. Manton, W. Middlemore, C. E. Mathews, Alderman T. Phillips, J. Pickering, Alderman C. Sturge, J. Taylor, jun., Alderman A. Ryland, and J. S. Wright. *

In July, 1865, another general election took place. The two members for Birmingham were elected without opposition ; but in North Warwickshire one of the seats was contested by Mr. G. F. Muntz, at the instance of the newly-organised Liberal Association. He was unsuccessful, however, in wresting the seat from either of the Conservative members, who were supported by a safe majority. The numbers were as follows :—For Mr. Newdegate, 3,159 ; Mr. Davenport Bromley, 2,873 ; Mr. Muntz, 2,408. The Conservative victory was celebrated in Birmingham by a banquet at the Exchange Assembly Rooms, on August 7th, at which Mr. (afterwards Sir Charles) Adderley (now Lord Norton) presided.

The proposed Reform Bill about to be introduced by the Russell administration in the session of 1866 formed the principal political topic of the previous autumn. A meeting of

---

* Langford : Modern Birmingham, p. 345.

69   EXTERIOR OF ST. MARTIN'S CHURCH, AS RE-BUILT IN 1875.

the local branch of the National Reform League was held in the Town Hall, November 23, Mr. J. A. Partridge in the chair. Mr. Edmond Beales and Mr. Mason Jones attended, and the following resolutions were passed :—

That this meeting adopts as a principle the right of manhood suffrage ; as a protection the ballot ; and as a policy the duty of accepting such instalments as may be attainable.

That having regard to the time-honoured name of Russell, and the great services and high reputation of Mr. Gladstone, this meeting expresses its confident hope that a large instalment of political rights will now be conceded to the working manhood of this country, and that the principle of manhood suffrage will be recognised as the basis of our representation.

Another meeting was held in the same building on the 13th of December, at which Mr. Bright delivered one of his great Reform speeches. On the 25th of the same month was published the return of householders, prepared by the Government in anticipation of their Reform Bill. The number of houses in the parish of Birmingham, with their respective rentals (so far as affected by the proposed measure), were as follows :—

Under £4 rentals	974
£4 and under £5 ,, ...	2,114
£5 ,, ,, £6 ,, ...	5,943
£6 ,, ,, £7 ,, ...	8,478
£7 ,, ,, £8 ,, ...	5,150
£8 ,, ,, £9 ,, ...	4,801
£9 ,, ,, £10 ,, ...	565
£10 and upwards	13,204
	41,229

The new Bill was introduced in the House of Commons by Mr. Gladstone, on the 12th of March, 1866 ; and the local agitation on its behalf commenced forthwith. A town's meeting was held in the Town Hall, March 26th, at which letters were read from the borough members, and a petition was adopted which received the signatures of 44,236 persons, and was presented to the House of Commons. On the 18th of June the Government were defeated by a majority of 11, and, after an adjournment of a week, resigned office. A new administration by Lord Derby on the 9th of July, and the business of the Session

was brought to a close as speedily as possible, leaving the question of Reform unsettled.

During this time several great open-air meetings were held in Birmingham ; one at the back of the Town Hall on July 4th, at which from 6,000 to 10,000 persons were estimated to have been present ; another, on the 9th, at Gosta Green, and a third, at the same place, on the 25th.

"The failure of the franchise bill of the late administration," says Mr. Molesworth,* "made it abundantly evident to those who regarded themselves as unjustly excluded from the franchise that their claims would never be conceded by the legislature unless, as in 1832, they took the matter into their own hands, and showed in an unmistakeable manner, both to friends and foes, that they were thoroughly in earnest, and that whatever Conservative reaction there might be among the enfranchised classes it did not extend to those who were denied a share in the election of representatives to the House of Commons." For this purpose the Reform League was established, partly through the instrumentality of Mr. Edmond Beales, "a highly respectable barrister, who had been appointed to be its president.'† Open air meetings were held from time to time during the spring and summer of 1866, and on the 23rd of July in the same year a monster demonstration was appointed to be held in Hyde Park. Owing, however, to the Home Secretary, and Sir Richard Mayne, the head of the London police, the reformers were refused admission into the park, and, by the direction of Mr. Beales, the procession was led back to Trafalgar Square, where, after the passing of the usual resolutions in favour of reform, the vast throng dispersed peaceably to their homes. Unfortunately, however, the usual contingent of idle and ruffianly hangers-on remained behind, scenting with unerring instinct a disturbance,

* History of England from the year 1830—1874. By William Nassau Molesworth. *Vol. III., people's edition, p. 289.*
† Ib.

and a riot ensued, wherein the park palings on either side of the Marble Arch were torn down and considerable damage done, the cause of reform being greatly discredited thereby.

A similar demonstration was organised in Birmingham, and was held at Brookfields, near Icknield Street East, on the 27th of August, 1866. Many of the factories and workshops in the town were closed and large numbers of people poured into the town from the neighbouring districts. A monster procession was formed to the place of meeting, and thither flocked thousands upon thousands of earnest men, until it is estimated that more than 200,000 persons were present at the vast assembly. A number of stands were erected on the ground, and addresses delivered from each of them, the following resolution being put simultaneously to the entire meeting : " That the present House of Commons has, by its rejection of the very moderate measure of Parliamentary Reform proposed by the late Government, proved itself utterly unworthy of our confidence and support, and that it in no sense represents the wishes of the Commons of Great Britain. We, therefore, hereby pledge ourselves to demand, agitate for, and use all lawful means to obtain registered, residential manhood suffrage, as the only just basis of representation, and the ballot to protect us from undue influence and intimidation in elections." The borough members were present at this gathering, but Mr. Bright found himself unequal to the task of addressing a great crowd in the open air ; so he and his colleague reserved their speeches until the evening meeting, which was held in the Town Hall. The building was densely crowded, and, after addresses warmly recognising the services of Messrs. Bright and Scholefield in the cause of reform had been read and presented, speeches were delivered by the two members and by Mr. Edmond Beales, who told his hearers, amid cries of " shame," that what he had done in the cause of reform (in connection with the Hyde Park meetings) had

entailed upon him the loss of his post as Revising Barrister for Middlesex.

In February, 1867, Mr. Disraeli introduced the Government proposals for Reform in a series of thirteen resolutions ; and on the day following the Committee of the Birmingham Liberal Association, considering that the said resolutions were " formed with the intention of delaying the settlement of the question of Reform and of opposing the just demands of the people," instructed the officers of the Association "to confer with the members for the borough as to the action which ought to be taken by the Liberal party in the present condition of affairs. Several public meetings were held by the Liberal party during the few weeks which followed ; and on the 22nd of April (Easter Monday) another great Reform Demonstration was held at Brookfields, at which from 200,000 to 250,000 persons were present. Addresses were delivered simultaneously from eight platforms in various parts of the immense area, and the resolutions, which were signalled by the blowing of a trumpet, were put at once throughout the entire assembly, and by nearly two hundred and fifty thousand voices the cry went forth for a satisfactory measure of reform.

We need not refer particularly here to the events which followed during the session of 1867. After numerous alterations and revisions, the Conservative Ministry carried a Reform Bill, which, as all our readers know, extended the suffrage to every householder, and gave to the large constituencies (including Birmingham) an additional representative, a provision hampered, however, by the " minoity clause," by which electors in those constituencies can vote only for two members, thus providing, as was supposed, for the return of a representative of the weaker party in each case.

On the 9th of July, 1867, our respected senior member, Mr. W. Scholefield, died, in his 58th year. Two candidates were nominated for the vacant seat : Mr. George Dixon (who was at that time Mayor) being supported by the Liberal party, and Mr. Sampson Lloyd. The nomination took place in the Town Hall on July 22nd, and the polling on the following day, Mr. Dixon being elected by a majority of 1,605. The numbers were—for Mr. Dixon, 5,819 ; for Mr. Lloyd, 1,605.

During this year a new political society, called the "Constitutional Association," was formed, and Mr. Sebastian Evans was elected honorary secretary. A Working Men's Liberal-Conservative Association also came into existence, and several lectures were delivered under the auspices of the two societies during the following winter. Lectures were also delivered by leading Liberals, at the instance of the Reform League. The Working Men's Liberal-Conservative Association held their annual meeting on the 9th of December, at which a report was read showing that the society numbered 2,000 members.

The year 1868 was spent chiefly in preparing for the election contest, which it was felt must come during the ensuing autumn. The defeat of the Government on Mr. Gladstone's Irish Church resolutions led to a dissolution ; and now the canvass commenced in earnest "for decidedly the most remarkable general election that has taken place since that which followed the passing of the Reform Act of 1832.* In Birmingham five candidates entered the field— three in the Liberal interests, Messrs. Bright and Dixon, the former members, and Mr. P. H. Muntz, one of the first members of the Town Council ; and two Conservatives, viz., Messrs. Sampson S. Lloyd and Sebastian Evans, LL.D. Meetings were held almost nightly in all parts of the town ; comic journals were issued weekly by both parties—"Toby" being the Liberal "organ" and "The Third Member" the Conservative—and each lampooned the opposition candidates in ill-drawn and wretchedly executed cartoons ; and the machinery of the several

political associations was put in motion to compass the ends of each party. The Liberals, determined to win the three seats in spite of the "minority clause," made elaborate arrangements for equalising the voting in each ward ; in one the Liberal electors were instructed to vote for Bright and Dixon, in another for Dixon and Muntz, and in a third for Bright and Muntz, and so on throughout the borough. It was a marvellous example of discipline that these regulations were successfully carried out ; the temptation to disobey orders in wards instructed not to vote for Mr. Bright was exceedingly strong ; and added to this came the taunts of the Conservatives, who dubbed the obedient electors the "Vote-as-you-are-told party"—but the Liberals remained loyal to their Association. The nomination, contrary to the usual custom, was fixed to take place in the open air, at the back of the Town Hall, on the 16th of November. Upwards of 20,000 persons were present, and the show of hands was largely in favour of the three Liberal candidates, but a poll was demanded for Messrs. Lloyd and Evans. This took place on the following day, and so well was the work of distributing the votes between the three Liberal candidates carried out, that the clause which was expected to have ensured the return of a Conservative "third member" proved wholly ineffectual. The result was as follows :—

					Votes.
For Mr. Dixon .	.	.	.	.	15,098
,, Mr. Muntz .	.	.	.	.	14,614
,, Mr. Bright .	.	.	.	.	14,601
,, Mr. Lloyd .	.	.	.	.	8,700
,, Dr. Evans .	.	.	.	.	7,061

The overwhelming majority of Liberal members returned to the new Parliament led Mr. Disraeli to place his resignation in the hands of Her Majesty, and Mr. Gladstone was sent for to form a Cabinet. Mr. Bright, for the first time in his parliamentary career, was invited to take office in the new Government, and consented to become President of the Board of Trade. It need scarcely be said that in his second appeal to his constituents

* Molesworth : History of England, iii. 349.

he was not opposed, and the re-election took place with the utmost quietness on the 21st of December.

The first session of the new Parliament saw the disestablishment of the Irish Church; and

During the following session (1870), the Elementary Education Act was passed, and was speedily adopted in Birmingham, the election of the first School Board for the town taking place

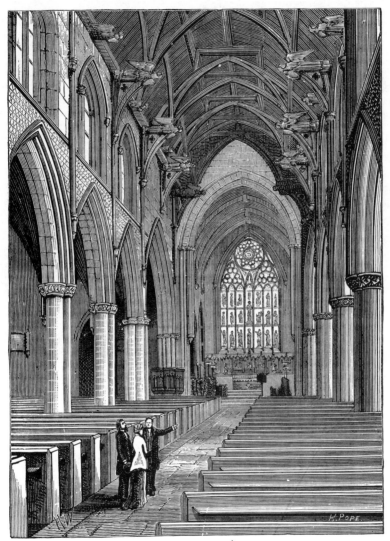

INTERIOR OF ST. MARTIN'S CHURCH.

during the progress of the Bill through the two Houses, the Liberals of Birmingham accorded their hearty support to the Government, by public meetings held in the Town Hall and elsewhere at each stage of the proceedings.

in November of that year. The Liberal party unwisely attempted to carry fifteen candidates, the total number required to form the new Board, but miscalculated the relative strength of parties as affected by the cumulative system of voting, by which an elector might, if he chose, give the whole of his fifteen votes for one candidate. The Conservatives, on the other hand, attempted only to secure a narrow majority, nominated only eight candidates, the whole of whom were elected. The Roman Catholics also secured the return of one member, thus leaving the Liberal party with only six successful candidates. At the first meeting of the Board, Mr. W. L. Sargent was elected Chairman, Mr. Sampson S. Lloyd, Vice-Chairman, Mr. G. B. Davis, Clerk, and Messrs. Martin and Chamberlain, Architects to the Board. For the first three years (the term of office) the Church of England party on the Board ruled, and a system of religious teaching embracing sectarian principles was adopted. But at the expiration of their term of office, in November, 1873, the Liberals, profiting by their former experience, restricted themselves to eight candidates, and ejected them by an overwhelming majority, and the position of parties was, therefore, exactly reversed, the second Board consisting of eight Liberal or "secular" members, six Churchmen, and one Roman Catholic. The policy of the Board was immediately afterwards reversed, and all distinctively religious teaching (including even Bible-reading) discontinued ; but an unsectarian Religious Education Society was formed for the purpose of supplying the deficiency by voluntary agency out of the ordinary school-hours, to such scholars as cared to attend.

In 1876 the election was uncontested and the Board now consists of the following members : Mr. G. Dixon, J.P., Chairman, Mr. T. Beston, Rev. R. B. Burgess, M.A., Rev. H. W. Crosskey, Mr. R. W. Dale, M A., Mr. W. J. Davis, Mr. W. H. Greening, Miss C. M. Kenrick, Mr. J. Jones, Mr. J. A. Langford, LL.D., Rev. Canon Longman, Rev. E. F. M. MacCarthy, M.A., Rev. H. C. Milward, M.A., Rev. W. H. Poulton, M.A., and J. S Wright, J.P., Vice-Chairman.

In November of this year (1879) the Board will have been in existence for nine years, and during that period have built aud opened 24 schools all of them architecturally considered, ornaments to the town. The following is a list of these schools with the date of opening, and the number of scholars for whom accommodation is provided, including boys, girls, and infants :—

Name of School.	Date of Opening.	No. Accommodated.
1. Farm Street.	July, 1873.	1055.
2. Bloomsbury.	March, 1873.	1059.
3. Jenkins Street.	May, 1873.	1136.
4. Steward Street.	July, 1873.	1055.
5. Garrison Lane.	July, 1873.	967.
6. Elkington Street.	May, 1874.	983.
7. Lower Windsor St.	November, 1874.	1055.
8. Allcock Street.	April, 1875.	1052.
9. Rea Street South.	July, 1875.	1070.
10. Osler Street.	November, 1875.	1025.
11. Dartmouth Street.	May, Oct., 1876.	1053.
12. Smith Street.	June, 1876.	972.
13. Bristol Street.	October, 1876.	1023.
14. Nelson Street.	November, 1876.	971.
15. Norton Street.	November, 1876.	994.
16. Moseley Road.	January, 1877.	1017.
17. Fox Street.	January, 1877.	1017.
18. Brookfields.	November, 1877.	1018.
19. Summer Lane.	September, 1877.	1352.
20. Oozells Street.	January, 1878.	807.
21. Dudley Road.	June, 1878.	1220.
22. Little Green Lane	August, 1878.	1347.
23. Hutton Street.	January, 1879.	1095.
24. Montgomery Street	July, 1879.	1000.*

The total amount expended in the erection of school-buildings and purchase of sites, is £349,575 19s. 1d., and the total cost of school maintenance for eight years has been £94,928, of which £52,574 has been provided by the School Rate.

The following information as to Prizes and Scholarships is given in Dr. Langford's interesting and valuable Handbook :

Mr. J. Chamberlain resigned his connection with the Board in 1876, and gave the sum of £500 to be invested for the purpose of founding scholarships, and Mr. J. S.

---

* Langford, Birmingham: *A Handbook for Residents and Visitors* (just issued), pp. 60-61.

Wright gave a donation of £20 a year, to be continued for three years, for the same purpose. These scholarships are open to boys and girls in all the schools under the control of the Board. There is a trust endowment of £250 5s. 9d. belonging to the Birmingham and Edgbaston Day School for Girls which has been transferred to the Board, and Messrs. Cassell, Petter and Galpin have presented 20 copies of their "National Educator" in six volumes to be given as prizes. Prizes are also given for regular attendance, and through the indefatigable exertions of Miss Julia Goddard, prizes are also given for pupils who pass the best examination on kindness to animals. In 1878, 536 books were thus awarded ; and a silver medal, given by Mrs. J. H. Chamberlain, as the "Dawson Memorial Prize," for the best paper by a pupil teacher ; special prizes by Mr. Flower and the Mayor, Mr. Alderman Jesse Collings.

In 1873, after a long period of rest, necessitated by the utmost physical prostration, Mr. Bright returned to public life, and again accepted office in the Cabinet, as Chanellor of the Duchy of of Lancaster. The election to this office (without opposition), took place on October 18th, 1873.

In January, 1874, Parliament was dissolved, and at the same time Mr. Gladstone tendered his resignation of office. The legislation of the two previous sessions had partaken, to a great extent of a sanitary and social character, and interfered with many existing "interests," the representatives of which felt themselves aggrieved and "harassed ;" and adding to this the fact that certain members of the Government had become exceedingly unpopular, from various causes, it is not to be wondered at that a reaction had set in against the Government as a whole. But the Liberal party were scarcely prepared for the wholesale rejection of their candidates which took place throughout the country, and surprised even the Conservatives themselves by the overwhelming majority returned in favour of a change of administration. While this was the case, Birmingham was even yet regarded as unassailable, and an attempt was made to divide the Liberal party and thus afford an opportunity to carry a Conser-

vative candidate, it failed, and no contest took place ; the three members were therefore returned without opposition. The election took place on the 30th of January, 1874.

In June, 1876, Mr. George Dixon, on account of domestic affliction, accepted the Stewardship of the Chiltern Hundreds—in other words resigned his seat—and on the 27th of the same month Mr. Joseph Chamberlain was elected, without opposition, to fill the vacant seat.

Since that date the " spirited foreign policy " of the Conservative government has occupied the attention of the country, almost to the exclusion of home legislation. Political subjects have been fully discussed, however, in Birmingham, at the annual meeting of the constituency to hear adddresses from the borough members. Against the war policy of the Government, Birmingham has protested, from time to time, in large and enthusiastic meetings. On the 31st of May, 1877, the Right Hon. W. E. Gladstone visited Birmingham to promote the federation of the Liberal Associations, and after meeting with a splendid reception as he passed through the streets, addressed a densely packed meeting in Bingley Hall, at which it was estimated there were, at least 20,000 persons present.

The influence of Birmingham, as will be seen from the foregoing outline of our political history, has at all times during the present century, been exercised chiefly on behalf of the cause of Liberalism ; and we doubt not that when once more the attention of the country is turned towards domestic politics, the broad and earnest Liberalism of Birmingham will again exercise a potent influence for good on the destinies of the nation in general; and we hope to see, in the not very distant future, many great reforms, in the accomplishment of which Birmingham may play an important and honourable part.

CHAPTER III.

PUBLIC LIFE AND EVENTS, 1841-1879.

The Church Rate Question—The People's Hall—Death of Mr. G. Hollins—Murder in Heneage Street—Death of Mr. W. Hollins, Architect—Visit of H.R.H. the Prince Consort—The Licensed Asylum—Death of Miss Hutton—New Street Central Railway Station—The County Court—Riot at Snow Hill—The Corn Exchange—South Stafford Railway—Death of James Watt, of Aston—The Odd Fellows' Hall—Exhibition at Bingley House—Visit of Prince Albert—The First Cattle and Poultry Show—Erection of Bingley Hall—Death of the Rev. Rann Kennedy—The Stour Valley Railway—The "Baroness Von Beck" Case—Visit of Kossuth—Banquet to Charles Dickens—Aston Hall Fêtes—Death of T. C. Salt—Death of Joseph Sturge—Statue of Thomas Attwood—Death of David Cox—The Volunteer Movement—Hospital Sunday—The Sturge Statue—The Marriage of the Prince of Wales: Rejoicings in Birmingham—The Birmingham Lifeboat—Monetary Panic in 1865—Elihu Burritt—Working Men's Exhibition, 1865—Curzon Hall Opened—The First Dog Show—Monetary Panic in 1866—The Murphy Riots—Albert Statue—Death of George Edmonds—Watt Statue—Last Visits of Charles Dickens to Birmingham—Sir Rowland Hill Statue—The Priestley Statue—Great Western Arcade—Recent Events.

WE have now to record briefly the general history of the period under notice, classifying the various occurrences of each year, so as to form, to some extent, a connected narrative, rather than a mere disjointed list of events chronologically arranged.

The principal event of interest in the first year of this period, was the attempt made by the Rector of St. Martin's to levy a church-rate. The first notice of this intention was issued about the end of August, as follows:

In obedience to a mandate of the Archdeacon of Coventry to the churchwardens of Birmingham, a vestry meeting of the inhabitants of Birmingham who are entitled to be present and vote in vestry will be holden at the Town Hall, on Friday, the 10th of September next, at eleven o'clock in the forenoon, for the purpose of making a church-rate to defray the charges incident to the churches and chapels of Birmingham.

On the 31st of the same month a crowded meeting was held at the Public Office, Mr. C. Sturge in the chair. Speeches were delivered by Messrs. Edmonds and Pare, and a resolution was passed unanimously appointing the whole of the gentlemen present to form a committee to watch over and protect the interests of the inhabitants at the proposed vestry meeting.

The meeting was held on the 10th of September as announced, in the Town Hall; after a scene of indescribable confusion," arising out of the election of a chairman, in the absence of the Rector from ill-health, and as soon as the voting

for the chairman was completed (whereby **Mr.** Thomas Weston was elected by 2,162 votes, as against 97 recorded for Mr. T. Gutteridge), the meeting was dissolved, as no proposition was offered by any ratepayer present.

The polling for the rate took place on the 21st of October, when it was found that only 728 votes were recorded in its favour, while there were 7,281 against it.

During the year 1841 the People's Hall was erected in Loveday Street, at a cost of £2,400. It afterwards became a gun manufactory.

On the 16th of December in this year, Mr. George Hollins (the organist of the Town Hall and of St. Paul's Church) died, in the 23rd year of his age; upon which the *Gazette* observed:

The loss of such an individual as Mr. George Hollins, is no ordinary bereavement. To his aged father, to a large circle of immediate relatives, to a young and amiable wife, to three infant children, who are unconscious of what has befallen them, the privation is one of the most severe character. The more direct object of these remarks is to express what is known to be the feeling of public sympathy on this painful occasion—and upon this subject it is scarcely possible to say too much. Every lover of music, and every mind that is capable of appreciating real genius, will feel a deep interest in this premature calamity.

Mr. Hollins's place as organist of the Town Hall organ was filled by the appointment, on the 17th of February in the following year, of Mr. James Stimpson, of Carlisle Cathedral.

FORWARD

J. H. CHAMBERLAIN, ESQ.

PHOTOGRAPHED BY WHITLOCK.

BIRMINGHAM: HOUGHTON & CO., SCOTLAND PASSAGE

Another attempt was made in 1842 to levy a Church Rate on the inhabitants, but once more it was defeated by an overwhelming majority ; there

the parish of St. Martin's Lane, have *resolved* to tax JOHN BOUCHER and NATHAN KIMBERLEY, Church-wardens of the aforesaid Parish, to the amount of 15s. 3d. for tobacco, snuff and cigars, *which they have never had,*

THE GREAT WESTERN ARCADE.

being against the rate 3,889 voters, while in its favour no more than the odd 89 could be polled. Dr. Langford prints the following advertisement as an illustration of the public feeling on the subject :—

10, Digbeth, and 60, Snow Hill, Birmingham, March 17th, 1842.

KNOW ALL MEN by these presents, that we, the under-signed, being "A VERY SMALL MINORITY," residing in

to enable us to pay their unjust demand of 15s. 3d. for Church Rates, towards the repairs of the Church, *which we never attend.*

BRADLEY AND HOLLINGSWORTH,
Shopwardens.

Among the events of this year mention may briefly be made here of a tragic affair which occurred on the 7th of January, 1842 ; a woman named

Stapenhill being shot by her husband, in Heneage Street.

In January 1843, Birmingham mourned the loss of a worthy townsman, in the person of Mr. William Hollins, who died on the 12th of that month, in his 80th year. As we have pointed out, in our notices of the several buildings, Mr. Hollins was the architect of the Public Office, the Birmingham Old Library, the General Dispensary, and other local edifices. " The later years of his life were devoted to introducing a more correct taste into mural monuments, upon which he spared no cost in collecting information from Italy, France and this country. His numerous productions in this department are impressed with a purity of taste, and propriety of character, rarely to be met with in a metropolitan studio."* His son, Peter Hollins, Esq., sculptor, is still living, and has contributed to the adornment of the town by several statues and busts, which are noticed elsewhere in this volume.

On the 29th of November in this year, the town was honoured by a visit from His Royal Highness the Prince Consort, who was at that time the guest of Sir Robert Peel, at Drayton Manor. The royal party were met at the Midland Railway Station, Lawley Street, by the Mayor, the members of the Town Council, and several of the nobility of the neighbourhood, and an address was read and responded to by His Royal Highness. The party afterwards visited the principal manufactories; also the Town Hall, the Grammar School, and the Proof House. Addresses were presented by other representative bodies, including the Rural Dean and the Clergy, the Governors of the Free Grammar School, the Council of the Queen's College, and various local Committees.

On the 23rd of September, 1844, the Philosophical Institution lost its esteemed curator, Dr. William Ick, who died at the early age of 44. The following notice of this worthy disciple

* Obituary notice, quoted by Dr Langford, *Modern Birmingham*, i., 32.

of science has been kindly written for us by Mr. Joseph Hill :

No history of our town would be complete without alluding to the scientific researches of the energetic Curator of the Birmingham Philosophical Institution, Dr. Wm. Ick, F.G.S. At no other period could his laborious researches have been of such value. The railway and canal excavations prior to 1840, and the cuttings through the red sandstone above Bell's Barn, were a constant strain upon his enthusiasm ; and, pencil and book in hand, he was ever on a tour of discovery, and every section laid open was a field for a series of remarkable pourtrayals in colour of their minute characteristics, whilst his pen has described the various formations with great clearness and power. The valley of the Rea is dilated on in various papers, notably in one printed in the *Midland Counties Herald*, June 7, 1842. The whole of the valley he brought under careful examination. The various beds of vegetable-peat, gravel, drift coal, quartzose, crystaline boulders, chalk, flints, &c., and results of igneous disturbances are descriptively pourtrayed. Near Nechells he discovers antlers of the stag *cervus elephas* and horns of an ox. At Edwards' Wire Mills the tibia of an ox, and near the river bed bones of stags, hares, &c., fresh water shells, beetles, shrubs, willow and hazel nuts in abundance ; and in the four feet clay large trunks and branches of willows and old oaks, with several feet of overlying beds. His researches extend past Lawley Street to Digbeth, and onward to Vaughton's Hole and Speedwell Mill. The excavations at the General Cemetery and various parts of Edgbaston and the Lozells, are also brought under careful investigation. Dr. Ick died in 1844, a comparatively young man, not too young, however, to have left a name as a philosopher and scholar, as a successful botanical, geological, and scientific lecturer.

At the anniversary dinner of the Licensed Victuallers' Society, 1845, presided over by the Mayor, (the late Alderman Phillips,) it was resolved, at the instance of that gentleman, that an asylum should be founded in connection with the society, for decayed members of the trade and their widows. Mr. Phillips began the subscription with £50, (which he subsequently increased to £100,) and about £600 were subscribed at the dinner towards this laudable object. The fee simple of a suitable piece of land in the Bristol Road was secured at a cost of £1,118 3s., and the first stone was laid by Mr. Phillips, on the 30th of August, 1848. The building was erected from the designs of Mr. D. R. Hill, and was opened for the reception of the first inmates in 1849. The sum of seven shillings a week is allowed to a widow or widower in the asylum, and ten shillings a week to a man and his wife; medical attendance and all other requisites are provided in case of sickness. The claims for admission having, of late years, greatly exceeded the accommodation, and instead of enlarging the premises, the system of out-door pensions was extended, whereby a weekly allowance is made, and the recipients reside chiefly with their relatives. Every member of the trade in the borough contributes six shillings a year towards this excellent institution, and is, therefore, entitled to its provisions, in case of need.

Among the visitors to our town in 1845 we had a "chiel" from the Land 'o Cakes, "takin' notes," which he afterwards "prentit" in his *First Impressions of England and its People*, our critical visitor being none other than the famous geologist and journalist, Hugh Miller. He entered the town from the western end, and was disappointed with the "long low suburb," and its "particulary tame-looking houses," and was beginning to lower his expectations "to the level of a flat, mediocre, three-mile city of brick," when, he says, "the coach drove up through New Street, and I caught a glimpse of the Town Hall, a noble building of Anglesea marble, of which Athens in its best days might not have been ashamed." The whole street he considered "a fine one," and admired specially "a stately new edifice—the Free Grammar School of King Edward the Sixth;" and, descrying "through the darkening twilight a Roman looking building that rises over the market-place," he infers that "the humble brick of Birmingham . . . represents merely the business necessities of the place; and that, when on any occasion its taste comes to be displayed, it proves to be a not worse taste than that shown by its neighbours."

He observes that "almost all the leading towns of England manifest some one leading taste or other," and that of Birmingham he naturally enough conceives to be a taste for music.

"In no other town in the world," he says, "are the mechanical arts more noisy: hammer rings incessantly on anvil; there is an unending clang of metal, an unceasing clank of engines; flame rustles, water hisses, steam roars, and from time to time, hoarse and hollow over all, rises the thunder of the proofing house. The people live in an atmosphere continually vibrating with clamour; and it would seem as if their amusements had caught the general tone, and become noisy like their avocations. The man who for years has slept soundly night after night in the neighbourhood of a foundry, awakens disturbed if by some accident the hammering ceases: the imprisoned linnet or thrush is excited to emulation by even the screeching of a knife-grinder's wheel, or the din of a coppersmith's shop, and pours out its soul in music. It seems not very improbable that the two principles on which these phenomena hinge—principles as diverse as the phenomena themselves—may have been influential in inducing the peculiar characteristic of Birmingham; that the noises of the place, grown a part of customary existence to its people—inwrought, as it were, into the very staple of their lives—exert over them some such unmarked influence as that exerted on the sleeper by the foundry; and that, when they relax from their labours, they seek to fill up the void by modulated noises, first caught up, like the song of the bird beside the cutler's wheel, or coppersmith's shop, in unconscious rivalry of the clang of their hammers and engines. Be the truth of the theory what it may, there can be little doubt regarding the fact on which it hinges. No town of its size in the empire spends more time and money in concerts and musical festivals than Birmingham; no small proportion of its people are amateur performers; almost all are musical critics; and the organ in its great hall, the property of the town,* is, with scarce the exception of York, the largest in the empire, and the finest, it is said, without any exception."†

On the 31st of March, 1846, Catherine Hutton died, at the advanced age of 90. She was, as many of our readers are doubtless aware, the only daughter of William Hutton, and was born on the 11th of February, 1756. We have already made frequent reference to her letters in the course of this history, and it is to her graphic narrative of the riots that we are indebted for several of the incidents of that local reign of terror. Her life was perhaps one of the busiest ever spent in our midst, owing, chiefly, as she herself said, to

* The organ is not the property of the town, (although placed in the Town Hall,) but of the General Hospital, having been purchased for the Triennial Musical Festivals.—R. K. D.

† HUGH MILLER: *First Impressions of England and its People,* pp. 208—9.

her admirable rule of life, never to be "one moment unemployed when it was possible to be doing something." Besides writing three novels, "Oakwood Hall," "The Miser Married," and "The Welsh Mountaineer," and editing her father's "Life," she contributed sixty papers and short stories to various periodicals; she collected upwards of 2,000 autographs (adding to many of them notes and anecdotes of the writers); and

on the coast, and five inland." Truly a remarkable life!

Towards the close of this decade a large area in the older part of the town (comprising Peck Lane, King Street, Little Colmore Street, and the Froggary) was cleared away for the erection of a great central railway station. With the destruction of this mass of worn-out and tumble-down buildings many interesting fragments of

THE LATE GEORGE DAWSON, M.A.

(From a Photograph by Thrupp).

was also a collector of prints of costumes from eleven years of age almost up to the time of her death, and arranged them chronologically in eight large folio volumes,—indexing and annotating them with the same care which she displayed in the collection of autographs. Besides all this, she read extensively, "geography, history, poetry, plays, and novels," and made "patchwork beyond calculation, from eleven years old to eighty-five,"—had "ridden in every sort of vehicle except a wagon, a cart, and an omnibus," and had "been in thirty-nine of the counties of England and Wales, twenty-six times at London, twenty-one at watering places

old Birmingham were also removed; among these we may make mention of the site (in the Froggary) of the first synagogue, in Birmingham, wherein the remnant of the House of Israel were permitted to worship, unmolested, after their ancient form, "hallowed by the holiest traditions, through countless ages;"* and near it, in King Street, the neat Gothic church which had been newly erected for the members of Lady Hunting-don's Connexion, together with the old meeting-house of the same society, which had been originally the first local theatre of importance,—

* W. Bates: *Pictorial Guide*, p. 74.

the predecessor of the Theatre Royal. The old Minerva Tavern, better known as "Joe Lyndon's," the resort of the "Anti-Jacobin" or Conservative party, in Peck Lane, and the school, on the site of the old prison, at the corner of Peck Lane and Pinfold Street, were also among the landmarks of the past which were swept away to make way for the new station.

This important addition to our public buildings was opened June 1st, 1854, and is thus described in Dr. Langford's interesting *Handbook :*

"The most remarkable feature of the station is the roof, the work of Messrs. Fox, Henderson, and Co., and was constructed under the direction of Mr. Phillips. This splendid piece of engineering skill rests on 45 Doric pillars, which spring on the one side, from the station wall, and on the other side is supported on iron columns of the same order. The roof is a perfect span, having no intermediate supports. The spring of the roof begins at 30 feet above the platform, and consists of 36 principals or arches of iron, each weighing about 25 tons ; these are firmly framed together, and the principals are placed at intervals of 24 feet apart, and each is composed of five pieces riveted together. The pillars are each 5 tons 12 cwt. in weight. The roof is composed of glass and corrugated iron ; there are more than 120,000 feet of glass, weighing upwards of 115 tons, and nearly 100,000 feet of iron sheeting : the total weight of iron used in the construction of the great work is over 1,400 tons, and the ribs of iron by which the roof is supported are 25 tons each ; but so admirably proportioned is the work, and so skilful the arrangement of the various parts, that the whole has a light and elegant appearance. The work is creditable alike to the designer and contractor, and we fear that but few of the many thousands who are yearly under this wonderful roof pause for even a few moments to notice and admire the skill and taste which have been employed in its construction."

The *New Small Debts Act*, which took effect throughout England and Wales on the 15th of March, 1847, effected an important reform in the recovery of small debts, and during that year a County Court was established in Birmingham, at the Waterloo Rooms, Waterloo Street. A site has been selected for a new Court House, in the new street about to be constructed in carrying out the Birmingham Improvement Scheme.

We need only mention, in passing, a somewhat serious disturbance which occurred at Snow Hill Flour Mills—the scene of several similar disturbances in past times,—on the 29th of June, 1847, in consequence of the seizure of false weights.

It will hardly be believed by strangers that until the 1847, all the business of the grain trade of Birmingham was transacted in the public streets, in all weathers, to the great inconvenience of the farmers and others interested in the trade. Through the exertions of Mr Lucy and some other gentlemen, however, the much needed shelter was provided, by the erection of a neat and useful structure at the back of High Street, "suitable for all the purposes either of a convenient market or an assembly room." The Corn Exchange Hall is built in the Italian Doric style, and including the vestibules, is 172 feet long, and from 30 to 40 wide ; it is a remarkably light and elegant building, and has entrances from High Street and Carr's Lane. It was built from designs by Mr. Hemming, and was opened on the 28th of October, 1847. Seven years afterwards it was enlarged, in consequence of the greatly increased trade of the district. The corn market is held on Tuesday and Thursday, and a Grocers' Exchange is held in the same building every Wednesday.

On the 1st of November in the same year, 1847, the South Stafford Railway was opened, communicating with Walsall and Lichfield.

On the 2nd of June, 1847, James Watt, the last surviving son of the inventive partner in the great Soho firm, died at Aston Hall, in his 80th year. "Inheriting a large share of the powerful intellect of his distinguished father, to the extension of whose fame he had for the last thirty years shown the most zealous and truly filial devotion, he united to great sagacity and a masculine understanding the varied acquirements and literary taste of a well cultivated mind. His name will long be remembered in association with that of the late M. Boulton, as they were for nearly half a century successfully engaged in carrying out those inventions and improvements by which the genius of his father was immortalised." *

The British Association paid a second visit to Birmingham during the September of 1849, and to add to the attractions of the place an Exhibition of the Manufactures of Birmingham and the Midland Counties was prepared on a more extensive scale than anything which had previously been attempted. The site selected for the Exhibition was the quaint old red brick house in Broad Street, to which we have several times referred in our narrative—the residence of the Lloyd family—known as "Bingley House." In the spacious grounds attached to this residence a large timber building was erected, and a temporary corridor was constructed connecting it with the house itself, so that the entire block might be used for the purposes of the Exhibition, which was opened on Monday, September 3rd, and proved an extraordinary success. Exhibits in artistic metal work were contributed by Messrs. Messenger and Sons, Winfields, Hardmans, Salt and Lloyd, and other leading firms ; choice specimens of glass work from Osler's stood side by side with the beautiful stained glass of Messrs. Hardman and Messrs. Chance, the medals of Allen and Moore and others, and the porcelain of Wedgwoods, Mintons, and Copelands ; and from the looms of Manchester, of Spitalfields and of Kidderminster, came the best examples of English textile fabrics, in carpets, silks, and cotton goods, from the manufactory of Messrs. Elkington came choice reproductions of the artistic work of bygone days in gold and silver, together with the most beautiful examples of modern design, telling of the great change which had already come over the spirit of "Brummagem workmanship." Jewellery, steel 'toys,' and trinkets of all sorts, together with the other distinctive products of Birmingham, were also exhibited in great profusion, and helped to increase the brilliancy and interest of the first great Exhibition ever held ; which was

destined to pave the way for the world's show of two years later.

Notices of the various objects exhibited appeared from week to week in the *Illustrated London News,* and in the monthly parts of the old *Art Union,* the predecessor of the present *Art Journal.* The Prince Consort made a special journey from London in order to visit the Exhibition, and made a careful and minute examination of the various exhibits, and took copious notes, doubtless with a view to the elaboration of the modest attempt, thus successfully carried out, which eventually led to the great Exhibition of 1851.

On the 2nd of December in this year the Odd Fellows' Hall was opened, in Temple Street.

In 1849 the first great Cattle and Poultry Show in the Midland Counties was held in Birmingham, in a temporary building erected in Lower Essex Street. It was opened on the 11th of December, and there were upwards of 800 entries of Cattle and a proportionately large number of exhibits in the Poultry department of the show. Upwards of 25,000 persons visited the exhibition, and the receipts amounted to nearly £900. A new building was erected during 1850 on the site of Bingley House, the old residence of the Lloyd family, for the accommodation of the annual Cattle Show. This structure, which covers upwards of an acre and a quarter of land, and is consequently one of the largest halls in the kingdom, was finished in time for the second annual show in December, 1850, and was called after the house which it had displaced, Bingley Hall. It has been in recent times the scene of great political meetings, addressed by Mr. Gladstone and the members for the borough. The Cattle Show is still held every year, about the first week in December ; on the last occasion (1878) the hall was illuminated by the electric light, and upwards of 65,000 persons visited the show, the amount received being £2,010 1s. 0d.

On the 2nd of January, 1851, the Rev. Rann

---

* Obituary Notice, quoted by Dr. Langford.

Kennedy, M.A., died, in his 79th year. He had been for many years Incumbent of St. Paul's Chapel. "He was," says a contemporary, "for upwards of half a century, one of the most useful and eloquent members of this community, and singularly guileless, benevolent, and upright in private life. His religious teaching was always entirely free from bigotry or intolerance, and it caused him to be loved and honoured by good men of all persuasions, through the whole of his long and exemplary career. He was a man of great and varied powers of mind, an elegant poet, and an accomplished classical scholar. It may be truly said of him, as of Playfair, that, independent of his high attainments, he was one of the most amiable and estimable of men, upon whose perfect honour and generosity his friends might rely with the most implicit confidence, and on whom it was equally impossible that, under any circumstances, he should ever perform a mean or questionable action, as that his body should cease to gravitate or his soul cease to live."

On the 19th of August, in the same year, the Stour Valley Railway was opened, communicating with the mining district of South Staffordshire, with stations at Spon Lane, Oldbury, Dudley, Tipton, Wolverhampton and other places in the "Black Country."

During this month, an incident occurred which "led to the display of a great deal of unmerited censure, and to an outburst of general, but misplaced indignation *" A lady, known as "the Baroness Von Beck," came to Birmingham, and passed herself off as a Hungarian exile, who had rendered good service to the cause of independence. She had previously published a volume of "Personal Adventures during the Recent War of Independence in Hungary;" and was at that time preparing another work, "The Story of her own Life," and, accompanied by her secretary, Constant Derra, visited the principal towns in England, to obtain subscribers for the new book. Many of the Liberal leaders in

* Langford.

Birmingham assisted her, and as she fell ill during her stay in the town, she was invited by Mr. H. W. Tyndall, to stay at his house, where she was treated with great kindness and consideration. Subsequently it transpired, by accident, that the *soi-disant* "Baroness" was an impostor, and was suspected, moreover, of being a spy, in the pay of the Austrian Government. She was identified by M. Hajnik, Ex-chief Commissary of Police in Hungary, as a woman of indifferent reputation, whose real name was Wilhelmina Racidula, and was arrested and conveyed to the Moor Street prison. On the 30th of August the case came before the magistrates, but while the "Baroness" was being led from her cell to the dock, she died in the ante-room of the Court. The excitement was, of course, intense, but the case against M. Derra was proceeded with, notwithstanding, on a charge of obtaining money under false pretences, but he was dismissed.

The Mayor said "the bench showed by their decision that they were not satisfied that the prisoner had been guilty of conspiring with the woman. He thought they had been not only justified in arresting the woman under such circumstances, but in taking the prisoner also. He begged, on his part, to express his thanks to those humane gentlemen who had taken part in affording shelter to persons whom they considered destitute strangers. He regretted, for the cause of Hungary, that such deception had been practiced. Had the two parties been before the Bench in place of the one, the decision might have been different."

In July 1852, M. Derra brought an action against Messrs. George Dawson, H. W. Tyndall, Arthur Ryland and Richard Peyton, for false imprisonment, estimating the damages at £5,000, but was non-suited. A new trial was applied for and granted, and the case was heard at Warwick Assizes, August 2, 1853, before Mr. Justice Maule, when a verdict was returned for the plaintiff, damages £800. Mr. Dawson's portion of the costs and damages was raised by subscription, by the members of his congregation.

The illustrious exile with whom the unfortunate woman had claimed friendship, Louis Kossuth, visited Birmingham on the 10th of November 1851. "The whole town," says Dr. Langford, "kept holiday; nearly all the manufactories were closed, and a procession of from 60,000 to 70,000 men was formed to meet Kossuth at Small Heath and escort him into the town. Since the day that the Political Union met Thomas Attwood at the same place, Birmingham had not witnessed such a magnificent display of generous enthusiasm. Flags, banners, and trade symbols were carried in profusion; six bands of music were placed in different parts of the procession, and almost every person wore the Hungarian tri-colour. The streets were lined with people, every window on the line of route were lined with gazers,—men, women, and children,—all displaying the popular colour. Platforms were erected in every convenient place, and were crowded with spectators. As the carriage containing Kossuth passed along the streets he was greeted with the loudest demonstrations of welcome and the heartiest enthusiasm—surpassing in this respect any public event ever witnessed in Birmingham, not excepting those in connection with the Political Union."

A few days after the illustrious patriot left Birmingham, the sum of £750 was forwarded to him, to be applied as he might think fit, in the cause of his country.

In the autumn of 1852, a committee of working men met at the Trees Inn, Hockley, and inaugurated a shilling subscription to present a testimonial to the delightful author who was at that time charming the reading public with his charming fictions, which he sent forth from year to year within their ever welcome green leaves of their welcome instalments, to testify to the genial creator of *Pickwick*, the high esteem in which he was held by the working men of Birmingham.

The presentation, which consisted of a copy of the "Iliad" salver of Messrs. Elkington, and a diamond ring was made on the 6th of January, 1853, at the old rooms of the Society of Artists, in Temple Row. In the evening a banquet was given at the Royal Hotel, at which Mr. Dickens delivered one of his happiest speeches, which, if space permitted, we should be happy to transfer to these pages entire; one passage, however, we may quote, as showing the interest he felt, even at that time, in the, as yet, only projected Midland Institute :—

He was rejoiced to find that there was on foot a new Literary and Scientific Institution, which would be worthy of this place, even if there were nothing else of the kind in it. It was to be an Institution where the words "exclusion" and "exclusivism" should be quite unknown; where all classes and creeds might assemble in common faith, trust, and confidence. It was designed to graft on it a great gallery of painting and sculpture, and a museum of models, where industry might exhibit the various processes of manufacturing machinery, and thereby come to new results. Nay, the very mines under the earth and sea would not be forgotten, but would be presented in little to the enquiring eye. It would be an Institution by which the obstacles which now stood in the way of the poor inventor would be smoothed away, and if he had anything in him he should find encouragement and help. He observed, with unusual interest and gratification, that a large body of gentlemen had agreed for a time to lay aside their individual opinions, and at an early day to meet to advance this great object, and he would particularly call upon the company, in drinking this toast, to drink success to their endeavours, and to make a pledge to promote the welfare of the Institution.

In 1855 the town paid a well-deserved tribute to the memory of Sir Robert Peel, by the erection of a bronze statue, designed by Mr. Peter Hollins and cast by Messrs. Elkington and Mason, being "the first colossal work of the kind ever produced in one piece in Birmingham."* Upwards of three tons of metal were used in the casting of this work, which is eight feet and a half in height. It stands on a fine pedestal of polished granite, resting on a sub-plinth of grey stone; and was originally surrounded by a handsome railing, the bars of which represented large clusters of wheat-ears, to commemorate the repeal of the Corn

* Dr. Langford : *Guide*, p. 187.

Laws. These, however, have lately been removed and the position of the statue slightly altered, so as to harmonise with the Priestley statue in the and Paradise Street, and was unveiled on the 27th of August, 1855, being presented to the Corporation, on behalf of the Committee, by the

THE CHURCH OF THE MESSIAH (UNITARIAN), BROAD STREET.

same locality, to which reference will be made at the date of its erection. The Peel statue was erected at the junction of New Street, Ann Street, Hon. and Rev. Grantham Yorke (now Dean of Worcester), Chairman. The cost of the statue was 2,000 guineas.

71

In the spring of 1856, the question of purchasing Aston Hall being prominently before the public, Mr. John Walsh Walsh conceived the happy idea of organising a grand fête at Aston Hall on behalf of the Queen's Hospital, the finances of which were at that time, at a very low ebb. Permission being granted for holding the proposed fête, preparations were made on a large scale, and it was fixed to be held on the 28th of July. When the day arrived, it soon became evident that such a fête was about to be held as had not been heard of before even in Birmingham, the home of monster gatherings of various kinds. Upwards of fifty thousand persons, from Birmingham, from the Black Country, and from the surrounding rural districts, poured into the usually quiet little village of Aston, which was gaily decorated for the occasion; and from the belfry of the fine old village church chimed forth such a joyous welcome as had not been heard since the unfortunate Stuart king had visited the mansion of Sir Thomas Holte, while it was yet in all its pristine grandeur.

Through the noble avenue of the park thronged the delighted thousands, and in and out of the quaint old corridors and noble state apartments of the Hall; old English games, and innocent fun and pleasure of every description, occupied the afternoon, and in the evening the avenue was illuminated with thousands of variegated lamps; and the fête was brought to a close with a grand display of fireworks, chief among which was a device which bore the legend "Save Aston Hall!" and which doubtless first led the working men of Birmingham to resolve upon carrying out the glowing injunction. The receipts amounted to £2,222 12s. 5d., of which £1,500 (profit) was handed over to the Queen's Hospital. Mr. Walsh was elected a life governor of the Hospital, and in commemoration of the splendid services thus rendered to that institution, a marble tablet recording the event was erected in the vestibule of the building.

There had been some jealousy on the part of certain persons, that the proceeds of the fête had not been divided with the General Hospital, and in consequence, Mr. Walsh and his friends organised a second fête on behalf of that institution, which was, if possible, a greater success than the first. It took place on the 15th of September in the same year, and Birmingham again poured its tens of thousands into the noble park so soon to become their own "for ever." A contemporary report says, "from the corner of Dale End to the park, the road was one continued procession of cabs, carts, and omnibuses, four abreast," and the total number of visitors was estimated at little less than 90,000. A cheque "on account" was handed over to the governors of the hospital, for the sum of £1,700, and at the next committee meeting it was resolved that the aggregate amount received from the two fêtes should be ascertained, and the entire profits equally divided between the two hospitals.

In the spring of 1859, Birmingham had to mourn the loss of two worthy citizens, Thomas Clutton Salt, an old reformer of '32, and the noble hearted philanthropist, Joseph Sturge.

Mr. Salt died on the 27th of April, at the ripe age of sixty-nine years, having been born on the 26th of April, 1790.

Joseph Sturge died suddenly, on the 14th of May, at the age of sixty-five. His labours on behalf of the oppressed slaves of the West Indies and the United States, and in the interests of Peace, are too well-known to need re-counting here; we may, however, appropriately quote the words of Mr. Bright:

"To me, his life, so far as I was acquainted with it, was a great lesson. I knew him most intimately in the last years of his life, when there was about him a ripeness of goodness which is rarely seen among men. In looking back to him,—in recalling that which was striking in his conversation, his temper, his habits of thought, and his actions, I often say to myself,—'What a glorious man he was! what courage and what meekness! what benevolence in action, and what charity in thought! what a charming unselfishness, and what a following of that highest example afforded to us in the New Testament history.'"

Our third statue was erected during the year 1859, viz., that of Thomas Attwood, "the Father of Political Unions." It was the work of the late Mr. John Thomas, of London, and cost about £800. The figure is cut from a block of Sicilian marble, and is nearly nine feet in height; it represents Mr. Attwood in the attitude of addressing one of the great gatherings of the people recorded in an earlier chapter of our narrative. The left hand holds a roll, bearing the word "Reform," resting on a Roman fasces (typifying unity, and obedience to the Law); and on the bands thereof are the words "Liberty, Unity, Prosperity." The statue is placed on a bold pedestal of grey granite, which rests on a broad rustic base of freestone. It was unveiled June 7th, 1859. An engraving of this statue was given on page 351 of this work.

This was a year of losses for us; death was very busy with the famous men of Birmingham, and in less than a month after the death of Joseph Sturge, the glorious landscape painter, David Cox, fell beneath the scythe of the mighty reaper. He was a native of Birmingham, and is said by his recent biographer, Mr. Solly, to have been born in Heath Mill Lane, but an old resident informs us that Cox's father (a blacksmith) lived at the house now occupied by Mr. Corbett as a Temperance Hotel, at the corner of Hill Street, opposite the Town Hall, and that this house was pointed out to him in his early days, by his father, as the birthplace of David Cox. However this may have been, he was intended to have been brought up to his father's business, but it proved unsuitable, not only to his tastes, but, what was of far more importance at the time, to his strength also, as he was a rather weakly lad; and his attention was directed to drawing. He began by painting miniatures for lockets and for the tops of snuff-boxes; and afterwards became a scene-painter at the Theatre Royal, then under the management of Macready, with whom he afterwards travelled to Leicester, and at length found his way to London. His

parents disapproved of his connection with the Theatres, and he turned his attention to the production of little sketches for the print-seller. He became acquainted with Varley, and was permitted to visit him and watch him at his work, and thus he became familiar with that artist's style and method of work. He afterwards went to Hereford as a drawing-master, and settled there for a time; but returned by-and-by to London, and obtained the appointment of drawing-master at one of the military colleges. But the love of nature had taken too strong a hold upon him, and before long he was again free, and pursued his art at his leisure. His frequent visits to Bettwys-y-Coed rendered that quaint, old-fashioned little Welsh village famous throughout England, and helped to make it a general rendezvous for tourists in North Wales. About the year 1840 he returned to his native home and took up his residence at Harborne, where he died, on the 7th of June, 1859, and was buried in the churchyard of that beautiful suburb.

One of his greatest admirers and friends was the late Mr. Gillott, whose collection of pictures included many of the finest of Cox's works; and at the sale of the collection, in 1873, they realised £25,324.

The Rev. John Angell James also died during this year; but the notice of his life belongs more particularly to the religious history of this period.

During this year a successful attempt was made to organize a Volunteer Rifle Corps for Birmingham. The project had been attempted in 1852, but was not attended with success; in 1859, however, after some correspondence and "beating up," a company was formed, and the first general muster was held in Bingley Hall, on the 12th of October, there being "as many as 116 members assembled on the occasion." This was not considered satisfactory, in a great centre like Birmingham, and in the following December a vigorous effort was made to increase the number with the result that, by the end of February, 1860, the number of men enrolled was nearly

WYCLIFFE CHAPEL (BAPTIST), BRISTOL STREET.

1,000 ; and on the 28th of the same month the first " march out " of the newly-formed corps, and its first public drill took place at Calthorpe Park.

The year 1859 is also memorable in our annals as having seen the inauguration of the "Hospital Sunday" movement; whereby on one Sunday in every year, a collection is made at all the places of worship in the town. This movement was originated chiefly through the exertions of the Rev. Dr. Miller, and the first year's collection which was made on the 13th of November, brought to the funds of the General Hospital the noble sum of £5,200 8s. 10d. Of its subsequent results we shall give a tabulated statement in the history of our charitable institutions during this period.

On the 14th of December, 1861, the nation was plunged into grief on account of the death of the Prince Consort, at the comparatively early age of forty-two. The day of the funeral (December 23rd) was observed in Birmingham with every token of the sincerest grief on every hand.

"From an early hour in the morning the deep-toned bells of the various churches in the town tolled forth a melancholy 'minuting,' and kept reviving ever freshly in the mind the depressing recollection of the great deprivation which the Queen and the country have sustained. The aspect of the town as the forenoon advanced was singular in the feeling of sadness and gloom which it excited. Almost without exception in the centre of the town, and Edgbaston, Hockley, Aston, and other suburbs, the blinds were drawn down in the windows of the residents, and scarcely a shop was open after the hour of eleven. A Union Jack floated, at half-mast high, here and there, at the summit of buildings in the town, and mourning garments were generally worn. So universal were these emblems of sorrow, that even the poorest clad women wore some humble expressive 'bit of black.' There was a stillness in the crowded thoroughfares, which seemed to whisper of death; and people spoke to each other with 'bated breath,' so irresistible was the influence of the sad event.

As had been previously arranged, and as was the rule throughout the district . . . . and doubtless everywhere throughout the length and breadth of the land, special church and chapel services were held in the morning, afternoon, and evening, and they were attended by densely crowded congregations. The interiors of the sacred edifices were draped with black, and heart-felt emotion was visible in every countenance." *

A funeral éloge was delivered by Mr. George Dawson, at the public service held on the same day, in the Town Hall, and almost every public body in the town, from the Town Council downwards, adopted and forwarded addresses of condolence to the widowed Queen.

About three weeks afterwards a public meeting was held, at which it was resolved to erect a statue to the memory of the late Prince, and in a short space of time upwards of £2,000 were subscribed for that purpose. The sculptor selected was the late Mr. Foley, and the work was completed by the end of 1867; owing, however, to the difficulty in selecting a suitable site,—it having been the intention of the committee that the statue should be placed under a Gothic canopy —it was located temporally in the Corporation Art Gallery, and was unveiled by the Mayor (Alderman Avery,) April 27th, 1868. The statue is of Carrara marble, and is rather over life size; "the Prince is clothed in the robes of the Order of the Bath, and the heavy cloak falling over and backwards from the shoulders, forms a background to the figure, and by the quietness and order of its folds, gives repose and majesty to the composition. . . The attitude of the figure is exceedingly graceful, natural, and dignified. One leg is a little advanced, and the weight of the body is principally supported by the other. The right arm hangs down, the fingers of the hand just grasping the hem of the heavy robe. The head is well set upon the shoulders, and the face is full of very

* *Birmingham Journal*, Dec. 28, 1861.

noble expression." *. An engraving of the statue appears on page 514.

It was removed in 1878 into the News Room of the Central Free Library, during the erection of the new temporary Art Gallery; and remained in the building through the whole of the conflagration in January last, being only slightly discoloured by the flames. It was subsequently removed, with the plaster models of Foley's statues of Burke and Goldsmith (which did not escape with so little injury as their marble companion), into the lobby of the Council House.

Another addition was made to the "marble men" of our town in 1862 by the erection, at a cost of £1,000, of a marble statue to the memory of Joseph Sturge, an engraving of which appears on page 479 of this volume. It was the work of Mr. John Thomas (the sculptor of the Attwood statue), and is supported on either hand by life-size groups in Portland stone, representing "Charity" and "Peace." From the front and back of the pedestal project bold tazza-shaped basins, out of which, originally, pretty jets of water arose, as shewn in our engraving of the statue; but of late the basins have been filled during the summer with bright bedding plants. The statue was unveiled on the 4th of June, 1862, by Wm. Middlemore, Esq., in the presence of about 12,000 spectators,

The 10th of March, 1863, was a day to be remembered in the annals of modern pageantry, as the occasion of perhaps the most brilliant festivities ever celebrated in the United Kingdom. On that day the loyal subjects of Queen Victoria everywhere celebrated the marriage of the Heir Apparent with the

"Sea-Kings' daughter from over the sea,"

the Princess Alexandra, of Denmark. In Birmingham the streets were hung with flags, banners, which floated gaily in the "merry March air." The Town Council and other public bodies

dined together; the Volunteers had a grand field day at Calthorpe Park; special services were held at St. Martin's Church and at Carr's Lane Chapel; a special fête was held at Aston Park; the poor were feasted, the bells rang out at intervals from steeple and spire, and, as if to show that even the clerk of the weather was determined to contribute to the general rejoicings, the weather was brilliant, the town being, according to a contemporary chronicle, "flooded with the mellow light of a bright spring day."

But beyond all else in the day's festivities will be remembered the unusually brilliant display of illuminations, which, in some respects certainly, have never been equalled in the midland counties. All the public buildings, and most of the houses in the principal streets, displayed more or less elegant devices in gas and coloured lamps; but the palm for brilliancy and effectiveness was undoubtedly borne away by the illuminations with which the whole of the west end of St. Philip's Church (including the tower and dome) were covered, as shown in our engraving on page 539. This *chef-d'œuvre* of illumination is thus described by a contemporary chronicler:—

The arcade of the church, the tower, dome, and cupola were lighted up upon all their architectural lines, and the whole was surmounted by an immense cross of jets, enclosed in ruby-coloured glass. Independent of the erection of the scaffolding, which occupied forty men three days, the preparation of the tubing and the fixing of it was a gigantic achievement in gas fitting. Over 3,000 feet of tubing, varying in diameter from three-quarters of an inch to three inches, were used, and to join it no less than 2,000 "fittings"—joints, sockets, &c. —were required. When lighted up, the illumination displayed 10,000 distinct jets of gas, each issuing from a large batswing burner. And then, in order that there might be no lack of pressure in the supply of gas, the pipes were parcelled out into six divisions, entirely unconnected with each other, and each of these divisions were supplied with gas through an independent service pipe attached, not to the ordinary street mains, but to a six-inch and three-inch main, which drew their supply from a ten-inch main laid down to supply the gasometer in Gas Street, and used for no other purpose. Something like 70,000 feet of gas per hour was consumed, and the effect, as may be well imagined, was brilliant in the extreme. Every architectural outline in the quaint building glowed with a brilliant beadwork of lights, which now sunk with the passing wind to the prettiest of little blue jets, that looked like glow-worms in a hedge-row, and again blazed out with a full proud brilliancy that, while throwing a strange glare on the upturned faces of the multitude below, lighted up the houses all around, and flung grotesque lights and shadows through the trees upon the monuments and graves beneath them in the churchyard. And, as if the illumination of the tower was not sufficient, coloured fires were burnt at intervals, and long rows of variegated lamps were hung in festoons along the railings running through the churchyard, whilst others nestled in the wreaths of evergreens that spanned the gateways.

A most appropriate wedding gift was manufactured by Messrs. Elkington, at the expense of the town, in the form of a silver *répoussé* table, of which an engraving is given in Messrs. Day and Sons' noble volume recording the national celebrations on this occasion. This splendid specimen of Birmingham workmanship was presented to the Princess of Wales at Marlborough House, on the 30th of April; the deputation consisted of the Mayor (Mr. C. Sturge), the Rev. Charles Evans. Messrs. Jaffray, F. Elkington, G. F. Muntz, W. C. Aitken, C. Ratcliff, H. Wiggin, R. Peyton, S. Thornton, T. Kenrick, and Alderman Hodgson.

We have already made reference, in the third portion of our history of travelling, to the inventions of Dr. William Church; this gentleman, who is described as one of the first mechanical geniuses of his age, died at Vermont, in the United States, on October 7th, 1863, aged 85 years. A biographical notice of this local worthy appeared in the *Birmingham Journal* of April 23rd, 1864, and is reprinted by Dr. Langford in his *Modern Birmingham*, vol. 2, p. 253.

On the 21st of November, in the same year, died two worthy disciples of art, the one an artist and the other a collector, whose memory ought to be treasured by every lover of the art they adorned. The first was our townsman Samuel Lines, the well-known artist, who died at his house n Temple Row West, in the 86th year of his age. He was born at Allesley, near Coventry, in 1778, and at the age of nine years, owing to

the death of his mother, he was placed under the care of an uncle, a farmer, and was compelled to take an active share in agricultural work. From an early age he manifested his love for Art, and, proving unsuitable to the work of a farmer, he was apprenticed, in 1794, to a Mr. Keeling, a clock dial enameller and decorator, in Birmingham. He was afterwards employed by Mr. Clay, in making designs for the adornment of his *papier mâché* goods. He also made designs for Wyon, Holliday, and other die engravers, and for the ornamentation of the blades of swords of honour, presented to officers who had distinguished themselves in military and naval engagements. By this work he was brought into contact with Mr. Gunby, at that time the principal local sword-maker, who was in private life an amateur artist and a collector of pictures. Through his assistance and patronage, Samuel Lines took the first step in what was destined to be the occupation and the delight of his future life—the teaching of drawing. He opened his school in Newhall Street, in 1807, occupying two rooms in a house exactly opposite Bread Street. This step was attended with great prosperity, so that, in a short time, he was enabled to build a house for himself, in Temple Row West, where, for fifty years, "until within a very few weeks of his death, he continued his teaching, with honour to himself and profit to the many hundreds of persons who were from time to time enrolled among his pupils." We have elsewhere referred to the part he took in the organization of the first art exhibitions in Birmingham : we need only mention here that a portrait, with one or two examples of his work, have been deposited in the Art Gallery Collection, by the Council of the Midland Institute.

By the death of Sir Francis Edward Scott, of Great Barr Hall—the second to whom we referred as having died on the 21st of November in this year—the Midland Institute was deprived of a friend and patron, who had rendered to that institution invaluable services, " sparing neither his purse nor more active labour, to advance its prosperity and usefulness.* When the Aston Hall Museum was established, he generously fitted up one of the rooms at his own expense, with the casts and prints issued by the Arundel Society, (of the council of which society he was a member,) and at his death he bequeathed to the Midland Institute a fine collection of the Limoges Enamels, which are now deposited in the Corporation Art Gallery. Unfortunately for the town which owes so much to his efforts, his health broke down at the early age of thirty-nine, and he died at St. Leonard's-on-Sea, November 21st, 1863. The brief eulogium contained in the obituary notice in the *Daily Post* may well be quoted here :

True, upright, and honourable, no word of his required anyone to certify it ; no deed of his could reflect shame upon the doer. Open-hearted and liberal, ready to help, quick to praise, a warm friend, a noble adversary, Sir Francis Scott has left to his young children the glorious inheritance of a good and an unsullied name.

During this year an experiment was made to provide for the material wants of the artisan class, by the establishment of a Public Dining Hall, in Slaney Street. Subsequently a second was opened in Cambridge Street, but it soon became evident that a great mistake had been made in selecting as the sites of those institutions such unattractive thoroughfares, and in 1866 the Birmingham Dining Halls Company was wound up.

On the 21st of January, 1863, the foundation stone was laid (by Mr. H. Van Wart), of an Exchange for Birmingham. The building was completed by the end of the following year, and was opened January 2nd, 1865, by the Mayor (H. Wiggin, Esq.) The principal elevation is in Stephenson Place, and its appearance from that side is exceedingly picturesque ; it had originally a narrow frontage to New Street, but this has been recently extended by the enlargement of the building in 1877-8. The ground floor of each front is arranged for retail shops, and behind these is

* Langford

the Exchage Room and the Chamber of Commerce. Above these is a large and convenient Assembly Room, which is chiefly used for musical and other entertainments of a popular character. The remaining space on the upper floors, is devoted to the refreshments, coffee, and smoking rooms, and to private offices of convenient sizes and suites. The entrance to the Exchange Room is in the centre of the principal frontage, under a tower which is carried up to a height of 100 feet or thereabouts. The Assembly Room entrance is in New Street, between the older portion of the building and the recent addition. The cost of erecting the building (exclusive of the enlargement, amounted to £19,300 ; the architect was Mr. Edward Holmes, and Messrs. Branson and Murray were the builders.

On the 5th of April, 1864, the Town Council of Birmingham resolved to invite General Garibaldi to visit the town, he having arrived in London two days previously. On the 8th of that month a laconic message was received by the Mayor, conveying the invitation that "Garibaldi accepts the invitation." A reception committee was formed, to co-operate with the General Purposes Committee of the Council, and a subscription was raised for the purposes of the reception ; but unfortunately the promised visit was never paid owing to the unexpected return of the Italian patriot to Caprera, on the 22nd of the same month ; and the subscriptions were handed over to the fund for the assistance of his efforts on behalf of Italy.

The 23rd of April, 1864, marked the tercentenary of the birth of England's great dramatist, and at Stratford-on-Avon preparations were made for a great festival in his honour, in which many of the leading men of Birmingham took part. Representations were given of Shakespeare's finest dramas, by the most eminent living exponents of the histrionic art ; sermons were preached, (one entitled " Genius the gift of God, by the Rev. R. W. Dale, M.A., the pastor of Carr's Lane); concerts were given, and every form of artistic enjoyment helped to pass the pleasant days by the side of the " soft flowing Avon."

In Birmingham, however, a more enduring form of commemorating the three-hundredth natal day of the great dramatist was resolved upon, in the formation of the Shakespeare Memorial Library, which we have already noticed in a former chapter. A soiree was held in connection with " Our Shakespeare Club," at the Royal Hotel; at which the first of that long

the presence of a large concourse of spectators. The Mayor (Mr. H. Wiggin) presented the boat to Captain Robinson, who represented the National Lifeboat Institution, and it was stationed at Sutton, on the Lincolnshire coast.

A second lifeboat was purchased during the year 1865, and named the *James Pearce* (after the originator of the movement). It was stationed at Caistor, on the Norfolk coast, and was launched at Yarmouth on the 25th of October in that year. Its crew were enabled to render active service on its very first trip, namely, from Yarmouth to

QUEEN'S COLLEGE, PARADISE STREET.

series of annual speeches on Shakespeare, was delivered by the late Mr. George Dawson, M.A., upon whom, as president of the club, devolved the honour of proposing the principal toast every year, until his death, in 1876. A selection from these speeches has recently been published by Mr. C. C. Cattell.

On the 31st of December, 1863, the preliminary meeting was held in connection with a praiseworthy movement for the purchase of a lifeboat by the working men of Birmingham. The movement was so far successful that in the following November, 1864, " The Birmingham Lifeboat, No. 1" was launched on Soho Pool, in

Caistor, by rescuing a vessel off the Crosby Sands; and both the Birmingham boats have since " seen service." It would be an act of injustice not to mention the names of Dr. Langford, Mr. Fulford, and Mr. R. Foreshew in connection with this humane undertaking. The first-named gentleman, in the absence of the Mayor, presented the *James Pearce*, on behalf of the subscribers, to the Royal Institution at Yarmouth.

Our notices of the Birmingham Banks will come in a future chapter, but we must not omit, in this chronicle of passing events, some reference to the commercial panic in 1865, consequent on the suspension of payment by the old-established bank of Attwood, Spooner, Marshall, and Co., on the 10th of March, an event which, says Dr. Langford, astonished "almost all people, not only in the town, but in the country at large." The liabilities amounted to about one million pounds, £700,000 in deposit accounts, and £300,000 customers' balances; and the statement of accounts showed a deficiency of about £340,000. The business of the bank was subsequently taken over by the Joint-Stock Banking Company, on payment by them of a dividend of 11s. 3d. in the pound for the assets and property.

Just one week after the old-established bank in New Street had closed its doors—on the 17th of the same month—the Penny Bank, in which were deposited the hard-earned savings of most of the more provident among the working classes, suspended payment, its accounts showing a deficiency of nearly eight thousand pounds, out of between nine and ten thousand pounds liabilities. A meeting was called by the Mayor (Mr. H. Wiggin), in the Committee Room of the Town Hall, on the 28th of April, to consider a proposal for the relief of depositors of sums under £3, but this was negatived by a proposal appointing a committee to investigate the affairs of the bank. The committee subsequently reported that the realisation of the assets had produced about £2,000, or a dividend of five shillings in the pound. A subscription list was opened for the payment of the depositors in full, but succeeded only in enabling the committee to pay a dividend of 11s. 3d. in the pound. One of the contributors to the fund was the late Mr. William Scholefield, M.P., who had been in its more prosperous days president of the bank. On hearing of the efforts of the committee to pay the depositors in full, he generously forwarded a cheque for £100 on behalf of the movement.

During this year the late Mr. Elihu Burritt, "the learned blacksmith," was appointed Consul in Birmingham for the United States. In the fulfilment of his consular duties he was required to furnish, with his reports of the trade of the

district with the United States, some notices of the industrial character and natural resources of the district, and to this circumstance we owe his pleasant and interesting volume, entitled *Walks in the Black Country and its Green Borderland,** about one-third of which is devoted to a description of Birmingham.

The British Association paid its third visit to Birmingham during this year, and, as on the two previous occasions, an exhibition of the local industrial productions was organised, wherein the members of the association might note the improvement which had taken place in the manufactures of the town since their visit in 1849. The Working Men's Industrial Exhibition was first projected at a meeting held on the 11th of October, 1864, and after great preparations, the exhibition was opened in Bingley Hall, August 28th, 1865. The Rev. Dr. Miller (President) offered up prayer, after which the Prize Ode, written by Mr. Coombe Davis, and set to music by Mr. T. Anderton, Mus. Bac., was performed, and the inaugural address was delivered by the late Lord Lyttelton.

"The well-known hall in which the exhibition is held," says the *Illustrated London News,* "is admirably suited for the purpose; but, large as is its area, it fell short of the space required by the number of persons who were anxious to exhibit. As it is, the catalogue sets forth that there are 753 exhibitors, and the room required is 4,900ft. wall or hanging space, 3,820ft. floor space, and 2,830ft. table face. . . . . The hall itself has been appropriately and elegantly decorated, an abundance of flowers having been used. There are festoons in great variety, bannerets ornamented in gold and silver, busts and vases, statuary, etc. This method of decoration has been employed with such good effect that the appearance of the hall was all that could be desired for such an exhibition. The articles displayed are of a very miscellaneous character. The staples of the local industry of course figure prominently; in stamping, there are one or two wonderful specimens; of mechanism there is a great variety; of iron manufactures, furniture, saddlery, brass-foundry, jewellery, papier-mâché wares, carving and gilding, there is a good display. There are numerous models in which much of skill and clever workmanship is displayed; one of these represents a church which is said to be composed of more than 4,000 separate pieces of wood. The contributions from feminine fingers are numerous and varied; and

*Published by Sampson Low, 1868.

although of less worth, but not, perhaps, the least curious feature of the exhibition, is a quantity of "original poetry," sent in to compete for the prize ode, to be set to music and performed at this inauguration ; "a play," and some compositions in music. This exhibition is in every respect most creditable, and, like all others of its kind, contains much that is instructive as well as useful."

The Prizes were distributed by Lord Leigh at a tea meeting, which was held in the Town Hall, December 19th, presided over by the Rev. Dr. Miller. Thirteen silver and seventy-two bronze medals were awarded ; also 118 certificates of merit. Of the surplus profits (after distributing 200 guineas amongst 17 members of the Committee, 50 guineas to Mr. Kerkhoff, one of the honorary superintendents, and silver medals to 29 others), the sum of £300 was voted to the Hospitals, leaving £700 to be disposed of afterwards, which was done in the following year, at a meeting of the Committee, held on the 14th of May. The balance was then distributed as follows:—"General Hospital, £50 ; Queen's Hospital, £200, as a mark of the high regard of the Committee for Dr. Lloyd, for the services rendered there by him ; Children's Hospital, £75, as a mark of esteem for the services rendered by the Rev. Dr. Miller to the Committee ; Lying-in-Hospital, £25 ; Blind Asylum, £50 ; Orthopædic Institution, £50 ; Penny Bank Relief Fund, as mark of esteem for Mr. Thomas Lloyd, £100 ; the Sanatorium, £50."*

On the 1st of August, 1865, the foundation stone of Curzon Hall was laid by Viscount Curzon, M.P., and the building was sufficiently advanced by December following to allow of the sixth annual Dog Show being held therein. "Although," says Elihu Burritt, "a circus occasionally performs within its walls, it is really devoted to the greatest provincial parliament of dogs in great Britain. Hundreds of every lineage, use, name, size, stripe, and language, are here assembled about Christmas time, and discuss questions of canine and social economy with a gravity and earnestness which few human conventions frequently imitate. Great lion-faced St.

Bernarders and little Scotch terriers, with their spiteful eyes peering through moppy meshes of hair, take part in these animated debates. It is one of the most interesting re-unions in the animal world that an amateur of it can witness."*

The hall is 103 feet long and 91 wide, and is provided with a large stage, specially suitable for panoramas, and is used for that purpose during every winter season by Messrs. Hamilton ; it is also occasionally used as above stated, for circus performances.

On the 14th of July, 1866, another commercial panic was felt throughout the district in consequence of the stoppage of the Birmingham Banking Company, "owing," as the advertisement stated, " to gross past mismanagement recently discovered." The statement prepared by the official liquidator showed assets to the amount of two millions, and liabilities, £1,800,000. A new joint-stock banking company was subsequently formed, and the bank opened under the title of The Birmingham Banking Company, Limited.

On the 16th and 17th of July, 1867, occurred the last of that long series of riots which have rendered the town of Birmingham somewhat infamous in that respect. It originated in the weakness of the chief magistrate of the town in refusing to grant the use of the Town Hall for the purpose of a series of anti-papal lectures by the late Mr. William Murphy, and thus tacitly giving the rough element in the town to understand that Mr. Murphy was not to be protected from any attacks which might be made upon him by such of the said roughs as might feel themselves aggrieved by the—certainly intemperate—language of the lecturer. But whatever might be the character of Mr. Murphy's lectures, he should undoubtedly have received the same protection as would be accorded—and rightly accorded—to the political orator, however intemperate his language might be ; and it is to be regretted that a stronger and a wiser course was not pursued,—the use of the hall granted, and

---

*Dr. Langford, *Modern Birmingham*, ii, 285.

*Walks in the Black Country, p. 91.

the utmost endeavours made to preserve order. Refused the use of the Town Hall, the partisans

delivered on Sunday, June 16th, when it was found extremely difficult to preserve the peace in

SIR JOSIAH MASON'S SCIENCE COLLEGE, EDMUND STREET.

of Mr. Murphy erected a large wooden structure in Carr's Lane, and the first lectures were

the neighbourhood of the lecture hall. On Monday afternoon, the 17th, a number of the lowest roughs, delighted at the opportunity of a "row," and probably not caring two straws for either cause, took possession of Park Street, stripped many of the houses of their contents, tore off the tiles from the roofs of most of the buildings in the street, and there ensued such a scene of destruction as had not been equalled since the Chartist riots of 1839. The services of the military and police were speedily brought into requisition, and by nightfall the riot was quelled and peace restored. The lecturer continued his harangues for some days after the disturbance, but no further breach of the peace ensued. He was subsequently attacked, however, while lecturing in Whitehaven, and died in Birmingham from the injuries thus received, March 12, 1872.

On the 1st of July 1868, the veteran reformer, Mr. George Edmonds died at Northampton, in the 80th year of his age, having been born in Birmingham in 1788. The principal incidents in his public life have already been told, in the several chapters of our political history. In 1838, as we have previously stated, he was appointed Clerk of the Peace immediately upon the establishment of Quarter Sessions, and from that time he took but a small part in political movements. His last public appearance was at the great Reform meeting in the Town Hall, which followed the Brookfields Demonstration of the same afternoon, August 28th, 1866, and on that occasion, "after recalling some of the political events of the past with earnest and pathetic fervour, he took his leave of them 'for ever.'" *

In 1868, Birmingham did honour to the memory of James Watt, and at the same time made a noble addition to the art treasures of our town, by the erection of a beautiful statue, by the late Alexander Munro, to the memory of the great inventor. The statue was unveiled on the 2nd of October, 1868, during the Social Science Congress, which was held in Birmingham in that

* Langford.

year. The *Daily Post*, in describing this beautiful work, said: "It would be difficult to conceive an attitude more thoroughly expressive of a work accomplished. The significant grasp of the fact by the left hand, and the almost dreamy way in which the other hand holds the compasses with their points upturned, tell the whole story of the man's life even to the careless spectator; for, useless as the compasses are now, and, though still held, no longer active, the man rests secure in the knowledge of the greatness of his great invention. Of vulgar triumph there is none expressed about the mouth, or in the eyes, nor in the richly-furrowed forehead, broad and high; but there is an almost tender sadness. The statue is a poem—a great and noble work, which makes us glad when we think that we have such artists among us and of us; for the whole life is there, the innate genius, the long struggle, the many failures, the perfect victory, and the triumph, one, indeed, unsoiled by any ignoble thought, and into which entered no taint of earthly selfishness. The sculptor has seen the whole of Watt's life clearly, and he has made it plain to us also."

In 1868, a statue was subscribed for by the inhabitants, to the memory of the originator of the penny postage, Sir Rowland Hill, K.C.B. It was temporarily located, when completed, in the Exchange Room, until the erection of the new Post Office, and in 1873 it was removed to its present position in the Public Room of the last named building. Sir Rowland Hill is represented as holding a roll of penny postage stamps, and on the dwarf pedestal on which the statue rests is an alto-relievo depicting the homely scene familiar to all, of the postman's daily work. We can only express regret that this memorial is not placed in a more conspicuous position out of doors, where it might be seen by the masses, and especially by casual visitors, who probably never enter the Post Office.

During the Session of 1869-70, the Birmingham and Midland Institute had for its president Charles Dickens, who had ever taken the deepest interest in the welfare of the Institute. He delivered the inaugural address in the Town Hall, on the 27th of September, an address which is full of valuable advice, and was the longest effort in public speaking which the great novelist ever attempted. It was delivered without note of any kind (except in reading a quotation from Sydney Smith), and without a single pause.

At the close of the address, in replying to certain remarks of Mr. George Dixon, (who proposed the vote of thanks to the president), Mr. Dickens summed up his own political creed in the words : " My faith in the people governing is, on the whole, infinitesimal ; my faith in the people governed is, on the whole, illimitable." This statement called forth considerable discussion in the public prints, as to its exact meaning, some alleging that it had reference to the Liberal Government of that day, and others that it implied a disbelief in the capability of the people to govern themselves. But in the following January (1870), when the illustrious president again visited the Institute for the purpose of distributing the prizes and certificates, he explained the use of the phrase as follows :—

" When I was here last autumn I made, in reference to some remarks of your respected member, Mr. Dixon, a short confession of my political faith—or perhaps I should better say, want of faith. It imported that I have very little confidence in the people who govern us—please to observe ' people ' there will be with a small ' p,'—but that I have great confidence in the People whom they govern —please to observe, ' People ' there with a large ' P.' "

This was Charles Dickens's last appearance in Birmingham. In the following June, we in Birmingham, in common with English-speaking people throughout the whole world, mourned the loss of the genial humorist whose death had " eclipsed the gaiety of nations, and impoverished the public stock of harmless pleasure."

The testimonial presented to Mr. Dickens by his Birmingham friends in 1853 was never forgotten by him, and when he sat to Mr. W. P. Frith for his portrait, he made the Birmingham illuminated address form a portion of the picture, whereupon a local artist, Mr. Walker, who " could

scarcely believe that the great novelist had troubled himself to remember the address . . . wrote to know the truth of the matter, when Mr. Dicken's immediately replied :—' I have great pleasure in assuring you that the framed address in Mr. Frith's portrait is the address presented to me by my Birmingham friends, and to which you refer. It has stood at my elbow, in that one place, ever since I received it, and, please God, it will remain at my side as long as I live and work.'" *

In 1874, an act of tardy justice was performed by the erection of a statue to the memory of Dr. Priestley, on the occasion of the centenary of his great discovery of oxygen. The statue was unveiled and presented to the Mayor and Corporation, on behalf of the subscribers, by Professor Huxley, who afterwards delivered an address on the life and work of Dr. Priestley, in the Town Hall, on the 1st of August, 1874. The statue, which is in white marble, was the work of Mr. Alex. W. Williamson, and represents Dr. Priestley at the moment of his experiment which led to the discovery of oxygen ; he is holding a lens in his right hand, directing the rays into a small vessel supposed to contain mercury, which rests on a simple yet beautiful rustic pedestal formed of three unhewn stones, around which a creeping plant has entwined itself. There is no attempt to alter or tone down the costume of the period, by the introduction of a cloak or other more graceful robe, yet the appearance of the work is full of simple grace and dignity, well worthy of the man whose outward appearance it so faithfully preserves for the benefit of future generations of Birmingham men and women. This noble statue is an instalment of that reparation which the town owes to the memory of one of her worthiest, yet most ill-used, citizens.

In November, 1875, an attempt was made by the Town Council to adorn some of the public

---

* Charles Dickens : The Story of his Life, [by " Theodore Taylor, i.e., John Camden Hotten,] page 258.

thoroughfares, by planting trees therein. The first of these were planted in Stephenson Place, November 25th; others were planted in Broad Street, from the Church of the Messiah to the Five Ways, in Bristol Street, Camp Hill, and other thoroughfares. Nechells Park Road was also planted with trees during the autumn of the same year, at the expense of Mr. A. Winkler Wills. Other attempts at beautifying the streets were made, with perhaps greater success, by the Town Council, by laying out small gardens and shrubberies in the principal open spaces, as in little Hampton Street, Lower Lawley Street, Summer Hill Terrace, Nechells Place, and elsewhere, and by planting flowers, in boxes, around some of the public statues.

In 1876 the Royal Agricultural Society's Annual Show was held at Aston Park, from the 19th to the 24th of July, and was visited by 163,463 persons, a number which had been exceeded on one occasion only, viz., at the Manchester Show of 1869, when (partly owing to the presence of H.R.H. the Prince of Wales at the Show), 200,000 persons visited it. Including about £500 paid for season tickets, the receipts amounted to nearly £13,000 at the Birmingham Show, which was, therefore, one of the most successful in the annals of the Society. Among the visitors to the Show was the late Prince Imperial.

During the same year an important addition was made to the "lions" of Birmingham by the erection of the Great Western Arcade, over the tunnel of the Great Western Railway, from Monmouth Street to Temple Row. A company was formed in July 1875 to erect the Arcade, from plans and designs by Mr. W. H. Ward, and the contract for the erection of the building was taken by Mr. Henry Lovett, of Wolverhampton. The Arcade was lighted up, for the first time, on the 19th of September, 1876, in the presence of the Mayor, (Alderman Baker), and other gentlemen. There are forty-two shops on the ground-floor and a like number on the balcony, the latter being used chiefly as offices, and nearly every artistic trade is represented therein. The shop fronts are in ebony and gold, as are also the railings of the balcony, and other fittings, and the roof is of etched glass, with a dome in the centre of the building, 75 feet in height from the floor; the wood-work of the roof as well as of the interior of the dome is richly decorated. The Arcade is 400 feet long, and commodiously wide, and is 40 feet in height, to the centre of the arched roof.

The galleries are illuminated by forty-four four-light candelabra, and the lower part of the building is lighted by the same number of three-light pendants, while from the centre of the dome is suspended a colossal chandelier, 14-ft. high and 8-ft. in diameter, comprising two tiers of lights,— eighteen in the upper, and twenty-four in the lower tier. The Arcade is thus lighted by 350 lamps, each of which is enclosed within opal globes, shedding a mellow light on the building, and when the whole of these lights are lit the effect is magnificent. The cost of the entire building amounted to nearly £70,000.

On the 30th of November, 1876, Birmingham mourned the loss of one of her noblest sons, who was cut down suddenly and mysteriously in the prime of life, after only a few hours' illness,— the able and eloquent preacher and lecturer, and the public spirited citizen, George Dawson. The record of his work in our midst belongs to other sections of our narrative, but we may properly record in this place the fact that, immediately after his death, a memorial was resolved upon by his fellow townsmen, and a statue was subscribed for, which has been entrusted to Mr. Woolner. It is now finished and "has been pronounced by competent judges to be a most successful work,"* and we can only echo the hope expressed by Dr. Langford, "that there will be no unnecessary delay in completing the work, and that the present generation will have the pleasure of seeing the unveiling of the

---

* LANGFORD : *Handbook*, p. 192.

statue of the man they so highly esteemed and so deeply loved."*

We have yet another memorial to record. During the year 1877, it was suggested that a statue or other suitable monument should be erected to commemorate the invaluable services rendered to the town by Mr. Joseph Chamberlain, M.P., in the negociations for the purchase of the great properties of the Gas and Waterworks Companies, and in originating the Improvement Scheme elsewhere referred to. After some delay a memorial fountain, bearing a medallion portrait of Mr. Chamberlain, was decided upon, and is now in course of erection on the open space at the back of the Town Hall, and will shortly be completed.

On the evening of August 26th, 1878, a fire broke out on the premises of Mr. William Dennison, a confectioner in Digbeth, whereby four persons lost their lives. The alarm of fire was given immediately after the inmates had retired to rest. Some time elapsed before the fire-escape arrived on the spot, and when it did arrive it was

---

* LANGFORD: *Handbook*, p. 192.

found too short to be of much service. Mr. Dennison himself escaped, however, by its assistance, and an attempt was made to rescue an infant three months old, but it fell to the ground in the confusion, and shared the fate of the young wife, who was only nineteen years of age, her sister, and a servant girl.

The alleged mismanagement of the Fire Brigade and the police came in for a large share of blame in reference to this melancholy occurrence, and attempts were made to obtain political capital out of the shortcomings of this department of the Corporation work ; but the ratepayers were not induced, on account of a single mistake, to lose confidence in the men who had done so much for the improvement of the town, and had elevated the tone and character of its local government.

The principal events in the public life of Birmingham during the last thirty-eight years have now been briefly recorded ; and we have only to record, in the few remaining chapters, the work done, and the progress made in special departments, by the religious, literary and scientific, musical, and philanthropic institutions of the town.

CHAPTER IV.

THE CHURCHES AND SECTS OF BIRMINGHAM; 1841—1879.

Restoration of St. Martin's—St. Philip's—The proposed "Ten new Churches"—Miss Ryland's Donation—The Excommunication Case at St. Alban's—Later Church Work in Birmingham—The Unitarians—The New Meeting—The Baptists—George Dawson Charles Vince—Arthur Mursell—Independents—John Angell James—R. W. Dale M.A.—R. A. Vaughan—Spring Hill College—Methodists—Roman Catholics—Swedenborgians—Catholic Apostolic Church—George Dawson and the Church of the Saviour—The Society of Friends—Other Denominations.

WE have now to record the later history of the religious societies of the town ; to notice the growth and extension of the various denominations, to describe the numerous churches erected during the past forty years, or thereabouts, and to mark the changes which have taken place in some of the older churches whose previous history has already been written.

First, then, as to the Mother Church, St. Martin's. At the date at which the old church passed out

of our narrative, matters had reached the worst, as regards the appearance of the building. "It is a long lane," says Mr. Bunce, "that has no ending, and so, when all had been done that could be to disfigure the poor Church, affairs mended, and a necessary restoration was effected, to bring back, as nearly as might be, the features of the original edifice. This restoration was projected in 1849, in consequence of rumours that the spire was unsafe, an impression which sub-

A. R. VARDY, M.A.

PHOTOGRAPHED BY WHITLOCK.

BIRMINGHAM: HOUGHTON & CO., LIMITED, SCOTLAND PASSAGE.

ASTON LOWER GROUNDS.

Interior of the Winter Garden. Exterior of the Great Hall and Aquarium. View in the Grounds.
Interior of the Aquarium. Interior of the Theatre.

sequent examination verified. A subscription was consequently begun for the general restoration of the church, from the design of Mr. Philip Hardwick, at the estimated cost of £12,000. About £5,000 were collected, but, through lack of public interest, the project fell through. In 1853, however, it became necessary to restore the tower and spire, by re-casing the former and re-building the latter. The top stone of the old spire was removed July 28th, 1853, and the top stone of the new spire was put on November 22nd, 1855, on the occasion of Prince Albert's visit to Birmingham, to lay the foundation stone of the Midland Institute." *

During the progress of the work, two arched recesses were discovered, at the bottom of the tower, each about seven feet in width, with subsidiary arched traceries of a very beautiful character. The architect conjectured that these were the resting-places of the original founders, and on carefully examining the spot, the workmen having removed a thick crust of lime which covered the tombs, found three skeletons in one recess, and a fourth in the other, in good state of preservation. They were again deposited in their stone coffins and re-interred; and the recesses were appropriately restored in accordance with the period of their date, viz., about the thirteenth century.

The contrast between the restored tower and spire and the ugly building in its encasement of brick, forced itself home, in time, upon the minds of the parishioners, and in 1870, they determined upon rebuilding the fabric. The last sermon was preached in the old church on the 7th of October, 1872, by the former rector, the Rev. Dr. Miller, and in a short time nothing was left standing except the already restored tower and spire. The new building was completed in 1875, and was consecrated July 20th, the total cost, including the reredos, being about £32,000. It was re-built from the designs of Mr. J. A. Chatwin, in the Gothic style of the early decorated period. The

* History of old St. Martin's.

tower opens to the north aisle by lofty arches, remains of the old edifice; the nave is lighted by a well-proportioned clerestory, from which springs a beautiful open timbered roof, a copy to a certain extent of that of Westminster Hall. At the entrance to the chancel is a lofty and well-proportioned arch, rising almost to the full height of the building, 60 feet. The large east window was the gift of Messrs. Hardman and Mr. Riddell, and is an admirable example of the artistic work of the former; in the centre is a representation of the Crucifixion, and above and below are depicted the principal circumstances in the Parables of the Prodigal Son, the Good Samaritan, etc. Below the window is a beautiful marble reredos, containing in the centre compartment, a representation of the Holy Supper, and on either side, statues of the Evangelists. The south transept contains a very fine memorial window, (presented by Mr. T. Ryland in memory of his wife), designed by Mr. William Morris, the poet, containing representations of the typical forerunners of Christ; and exactly opposite, in the north transept, is another in memory of the late Mr. John Gough, churchwarden, representing the Prophets, with Our Lord in the centre as the great theme of prophetic utterances. The great west window is also filled with stained glass, the subject illustrated being the Last Judgment, as described in St. Matthew, xxv., 31. The old east window, by Messrs. Chance, executed in 1851, is now placed in the organ vestry overlooking the old altar-tombs of the Bermingham family. The length of the church from east to west (interior) measures 155 feet; the width (at, and including the transepts) 104 feet, but elsewhere, (including the north and south aisles) 67 feet.

As much of the original building as could be preserved is included in the restored Church; the choir stalls are made from the old timbers, portions of the old stonework are let into the walls, and, as a matter of course, all the old monuments, mural tablets, etc., have been replaced in the new building. We can only add our feeble tribute of

praise to the architect, who has caused the beautiful structure described in our first chapter to live
anew in all its noble grandeur, and has produced
a Church "which we may show with pride to
strangers, and with all the greater pride because
from first to last—designs, buildings, fittings, and
enrichments, it is a Birmingham work."

In 1864 the work of restoring St. Philip's
Church was commenced by the re-building of the
south-west portion, at the charge of Mr. Peter
Hollins, as a memorial of his father. The contrast between the newly-built portion and the
remainder of the church, (which, on account of
the soft, friable nature of the stone originally
used, presented a very dilapidated appearance),
led the members and friends to proceed with the
work of the restoration, and in 1869 the last
portion of the body of the church was finished,
by the restoration of the west front. The tower
however still remains in its original condition,
and suggests to the casual visitor the curious
problem as to how a structure so much older in
appearance found its way to the top of a comparatively new-looking church.

In the pleasant open churchyard are several
monuments worthy of a passing notice. Upon a
tombstone near the south-west corner of the
church, to the memory of one James Barker,
who died January 22, 1781, are the following
curious lines :—

" O cruel Death how cou'd you be so unkind :
  As to take him before, and leave me behind ?
  You should have taken both of us if either :
  Which wou'd have been more pleasing to the survivor"

Near to the footpath behind the east end of the
church is a stone to the memory of Sarah Basker-
ville, the wife of the famous printer ; at the
entrance to the churchyard from Cherry Street is
the base of one of the pillars intended originally for
the Town Hall, which had been wrought by one of
the two men who were killed during the building
of the hall and interred near the spot thus ap-
priately marked ; and at the entrance opposite
Temple Street is a handsome granite obelisk to
the memory of the Birmingham men who fell in
the Crimean War. At the corner of the churchyard, adjoining the rectory, is the quaint little
building erected in 1792 for the accommodation
of the Theological Library, bequeathed by the
first rector (the Rev. William Higgs), for the use
of the clergy of the neighbourhood.

We referred in our last chapter of the Church
History of Birmingham to the Church Building
Society, and the proposed erection of ten new
churches, of which St. Matthew's was the first.

The second of these was St. Mark's, which is
situated in King Edward's Road, Summer Hill,
and was erected from the designs of the late Sir
G. Gilbert Scott, A.R.A., in the early English
style. It cost £3,100, and was consecrated July
29th, 1841.

The third of the churches built by the same
organisation was St. Luke's, in the Bristol Road.
It is in the Norman style of architecture, and was
designed by the late Harvey Egginton, of Worcester. There is a fine stained window by Messrs.
C. and F. Pemberton. The cost of the building
amounted to £3,700, and it was consecrated on
the 28th of September, 1842.

The fourth of this series was St. Stephen's, in
Newtown Row, a plain structure in the " geome-
tric Gothic " style, designed by the late R. C.
Carpenter, and erected at a cost of £3,000. It
was consecrated July 23rd, 1844.

The fifth and last of the series (for it was found
impracticable to complete the ten churches as proposed), was St. Andrew's, which was erected on
the waste land at Bordesley, near the Coventry
Road. The foundation stone was laid July 23rd,
1844, and the church was consecrated on the
30th of September, 1846. There is a beautiful
three-light window at the east end of the aisle,
presented by the architect, Mr. R. C. Carpenter.
The church consists of a nave and chancel, north
aisle, and tower, and follows the style of Gothic
architecture known as the " decorated."

The next district in which new church accommodation was provided was in the heart of the
town, in one of the humblest districts, known as

the Inkleys. A new church was erected, in 1851, in Tonk Street, and is in truth a church in which "to the poor the Gospel is preached." It is a plain brick building, in the early English style, designed by Mr. Orford, and consists of nave, aisle, and chancel. It was consecrated on the 26th of July, 1851, and cost about £6,000.

Ladywood was the next locality in which provision was made by the Church of England for the spiritual wants of the people, by the erection of a handsome church, dedicated to St. John; the first stone was laid September 28th, 1852, and it was consecrated on the 15th of March, 1854. It was erected from designs by Mr. Teulon, of London, and is a good example of the decorated geometrical style, consisting of chancel, nave, aisles, and tower.

On the 30th of May, 1855, a new church was commenced in the growing district north of St. George's, at the corner of Farm Street and Wheeler Street. It was erected from the designs of Mr. Pedley, in the early "middle-pointed" Gothic style, rectangular in plan, consisting of nave, chancel, aisles, north and south chapels, and sacristy, and was consecrated on the 4th of June, 1856, being dedicated to St. Matthias.

On the 30th of August, 1859, the little church of St. Clement, at Nechells, was consecrated. It is cruciform in plan, and consists of nave, aisles, transepts, and chancel, and has a small bell-turret at the south-east angle of the nave. It was built from the designs of Mr. J. A. Chatwin, at a cost of about £3,500.

Owing to the munificence of Miss Ryland, the erection of a new church for the district of Ladywood was commenced in 1857, the foundation-stone being laid by that lady on the 1st of August. Miss Ryland gave the land and a large sum of money towards the cost of the building, which amounted, in all, to about £3,000. The church, which is dedicated to St. Barnabas, is situated in Ryland Street North, and was designed by Mr. Bourne, of Dudley. In plan it is a parallelogram, without aisles, having a large

open timber roof spanning the entire width, and there are galleries on three sides. The tower is at the north-west angle of the building, and is surmounted by an octagonal crocketted turret. It was consecrated on October 24th, 1860.

The erection of new churches within the borough boundaries appears to have ceased from this date, until 1865, when a neat little structure was erected in Broad Street, called Immanuel Church, from designs by Mr. E. Holmes, in the decorated Gothic style. The cost of erection was about £4,400.

In the following year a new church was erected in the densely-populated district south of St. Martin's, in Bissell Street. The land for this church (St. David's) was presented by Mr. John Nicholls, and the building, which is "a handsome Gothic edifice, very broad and vigorous in treatment,"* was designed by Mr. Martin (Martin and Chamberlain), at a cost of £5,000. The spire is visible from a great distance.

In 1867 Miss Ryland contributed £10,000 for building additional churches in Birmingham, and the first church erected out of this fund was St. Lawrence's, in Dartmouth Street,—a Norman Gothic building of brick, with stone facings, consisting of chancel, nave, aisles, and tower. It was consecrated June 25th, 1868.

During the same year, a new church was erected in Great Colmore Street, dedicated to St. Asaph, and was consecrated on the 8th of December, 1868. It consists of nave, chancel, and aisles, and has three stained windows. The cost of erection was about £6,500.

In the same year a new church, dedicated to St. Nicholas, was erected on land given by the Messrs. Elkington, in Lower Tower Street; the cost of building being provided jointly by the trustees of the Ryland fund, and the representatives of Mr. H. Elkington. The east end of the church has since been enriched with carving and with a handsome reredos, at the expense of Mr. F. Elkington. At the western end of the church

*The Stranger's Guide through Birmingham (Cornish), p. 44.

is a fine stained window representing the Twelve Apostles.

On the 5th of January, 1869, St. Gabriel's, a small church in Pickford Street, was consecrated, and in the same year a neat Gothic church was erected in Cato Street, Duddeston, dedicated to St. Anne. It is built of brick, and consists of nave, chancel, and aisles, with galleries supported on iron pillars. It was consecrated on the 22nd of October, 1869.

In 1871 the new church of St. Alban the Martyr was completed, after some years of effort on the part of the curate-in-charge of the previous "temporary church," which had become somewhat notorious on account of the extreme ritualism practised therein; and, in consequence, assistance had been refused by the Church Extension Society, so that the outside walls had remained at the height of about three or four feet for several years. But in the year above-named the church was finished and consecrated, and is one of the few local churches which remain open every day for private devotion. The "priest-in-charge," the Rev. J. S. Pollock, has, on several occasions, been the subject of unfavourable criticism ; and in one instance called forth the indignation of the people in an unusual degree. On the 17th of September, 1866, Mr Pollock, from some cause not explained, publicly excommunicated a girl who had been a member of his church and congregation, named Letitia Taylor, an act which led to a series of meetings and lectures, and memorials were presented to the Bishop of the diocese, but with no satisfactory result. About a month afterwards, on the 13th of October, the excommunicated Miss Taylor, accompanied by Mr. and Mrs. T. H. Aston, again presented herself at the church, (the old temporary church, adjoining the site of the present building), and another violent "scene" took place. "The exhibition," says Dr. Langford, "was disgraceful. Men cursed and blasphemed, clambered over the seats, hissing and yelling in the most excited manner. The women screamed and rushed to the door, and at one time fatal results were anticipated. The chapel had to be guarded for some weeks after by the police."

A handsome church was erected in Heath Street, (St. Cuthbert's,) and consecrated March 19th, 1872. It is in the early decorated style, in brick and stone, and consists of nave, (with clerestory and open-timbered roof,) chancel, aisles, and tower.

On the 1st of May, 1874, a new church was consecrated at Hockley, (St. Saviour's,) at the junction of Bridge Street with Villa Street, just within the borough boundary. It is a brick building, Gothic in style, consisting of nave, chancel, and apse, with three stained windows. The pulpit, of Bath stone, and font, of Caen stone are beautifully carved, by Peter Hollins, by whom the latter was presented. The cost of the building amounted to about £5,500.

After the death of the Rev. Joseph Oldknow, who had, during his many years ministerial duties at Holy Trinity Church, won the affection and esteem of his parishioners, a meeting was held in the schools in connection with that church, on the 8th of September, 1874, presided over by the Very Rev. the (late) Dean of Worcester, at which it was resolved "to commemorate the worth, learning, and work" of the late Vicar, "to carry out his dying wishes by erecting a church, with a legally assigned district, in the thickly-populated neighbourhood of Small Heath." A temporary church was immediately afterwards commenced, and a site purchased for the permanent building, at a joint cost of £1,000. The temporary church was opened July 7th, 1875, and it is still used (1879); it has an excellent organ by Bevington and Sons, which cost £310.

A third church was provided for the Ladywood district in the same year. It is dedicated to St. Margaret, and consists of nave, chancel, aisles, and baptistery. The style adopted being that of the 12th century. It was consecrated October 2nd, 1875.

In 1878 a new ecclesiastical district was formed out of the parish of St. Clement's, Nechells, and a church erected, to accommodate 750 persons. It was dedicated to St. Cathterine, and consecrated November 8th, 1878.

Having now completed the records of church work done in Birmingham within the pale of the Establishment, we now come to the later history of the Dissenters.

As being the oldest nonconforming sect in Birmingham (which must be our only order of preference), we deal first with the Unitarian Society.

In the year 1860 the Society worshipping at the New Meeting resolved upon building a new church, nearer to Edgbaston, and a site was selected,— not on *terra firma*, but over the Birmingham and Worcester canal,—in Broad Street, the first stone being laid by Mr. Timothy Kenrick, on the 11th of August, 1860. The new chapel, which is called the Church of the Messiah, was opened on New Year's Day, 1862, the memorials to Dr. Priestley, the Rev. John Kentish, and others, having been carefully removed from the old building. It is built on strong massive arches spanning the canal, and is a beautiful example of geometrical Gothic. The principal entrance is a triple-arched portico, with granite columns, above which is a fine five-light traceried window and a gable, and from the angle nearest St. Peter's Place rises a lofty and well-proportioned spire, about 150 feet in height. Internally the church has a fine open timber roof, and several stained glass windows. The architect of this beautiful structure, (of which an engraving appears on page 559,) was Mr. J. J. Bateman.

After the vacation of the Moor Street meeting, whereby, in the opinion of the more energetic workers among the poorer classes, a valuable mission station was abandaned, a new society arose, called the Birmingham Free Christian Association, who opened a mission-room in Fazeley Street, and subsequently erected a neat little chapel on the same site. The Unitarians have also three other places of worship in Birmingham, viz. : The chapel of the Birmingham

Unitarian Domestic Mission Society, Hurst Street ; the chapel of the Church of the Messiah Ministry to the Poor, Lawrence Street ; and the Newhall Hill Chapel.

Next in point of antiquity to the Unitarians in Birmingham are the Baptists. We have previously recorded the erection of the principal modern chapel of this denomination, " Mount Zion," in Graham Street ; but the chief events in its history have occurred during the period covered by the present chapter. In 1844 Mr. George Dawson was elected to the pastorate of this church, but after two years of work among the Baptists he found himself out of accordance with many of the doctrines held by this sect and resigned his irksome post for one more congenial to his taste, as pastor of a free church, unfettered by any doctrinal tests whatsoever. In 1852 Mr Charles Vince was elected pastor of Mount Zion Chapel, and held that position until his death, which occurred on the 22nd of October, 1874. This is not the place for his biography, but we may appropriately quote the epitome of his life which is inscribed on the handsome Gothic memorial erected over his grave in the Old Cemetery : " As a preacher of the Gospel of the Lord Jesus Christ, his teaching was especially characterised by perfect faith in the infinite love and mercy of God, and by deep and tender sympathy with the hopes, the sorrows, and the struggles of men. As a citizen, his generous zeal for the poor, the suffering, and the oppressed, made him the strenuous advocate of all efforts for social and political reform. The sweetness of his nature, the purity of his life, and the manliness and simplicity of his character, compelled the respect and attracted the friendship of those who differed from him. His courage, integrity, courtesy, and charity, won the affection, and his eloquence commanded the admiration of all classes of his fellow-townsmen, by whom this memorial is erected as a tribute to his personal worth and public services."

In 1848 the large building in Bradford Street,

previously known as "Ryan's Circus," was purchased by the Baptists, having fallen into disuse as a circus, and was converted into a chapel at a cost of £1,200. It was opened, under the new name of the "Circus Chapel," October 24th, 1849, with the Rev. W. Landels (now of London), as the minister.

The most beautiful of the later chapels erected by the Baptists is Wycliffe Chapel, Bristol Street, which was erected by Mr. W. Middlemore, who laid the foundation stone November 8th, 1859. The style adopted is very appropriately that of the 14th Century, the age of Wycliffe, and it was designed by Mr. Cranston. " In plan it is a parallelogram, with nave and aisles, and a tower and spire at the north-west angle. Externally the building is entirely of stone. The principal elevation has a central entrance, divided. In the tympanum of the arch a statuette of Wycliffe is introduced with very good effect. Above is a large traceried window surmounted by the usual gable, terminated with a rich cross. The sides have two stories of traceried windows, each window in the upper tier having a separate gable. The tower to the level of the roof is square, above it is octagonal and surrounded with clustered pinnacles and flying buttresses, above which is a richly crocketted spire, carried (with the tower) to a height of about 140 feet. Internally the nave is separated from the aisles by iron columns, each column having a central shaft with smaller ones around. The capitals to the shafts are also of iron, with foliage of the same metal. The ceilings or roofs are entirely of wood, the central one having principals with arched braces, the spaces between each principal being panelled. The ceiling to the aisles is groined in wood with moulded ribs to the angles. At the east-end is the baptistery, elliptical in plan, divided from the nave by a lofty moulded archway, having piers with detached shafts, and enriched capitals. The baptistery proper is of marble, the pavement around being of encaustic tiles, the whole being raised a few steps above the general

level. The east wall is pierced with a series of small traceried windows, the panels being carved with fruit, flowers, &c. Above these windows is a small gallery containing the organ and seats for the choristers. There are galleries on three sides, having enriched panelled fronts. The seats are all uniform, and are of a substantial and massive character." We give an illustration of this beautiful structure on page 562.

The Baptists have nine other chapels (besides those mentioned in earlier chapters of this narrative,) within the boundaries of the borough, viz., Heneage Street, (opened 1841), Great King Street, (1848), Hope Street, Lodge Road, Longmore Street, Priestley Road, (Sparkbrook) Warwick Street, (Deritend) ; the General Baptist Chapel in Longmore Street, (first opened in 1786), and the Particular Baptist Chapel, Frederick Street, Newhall Hill.

In 1877 the Baptist Church Meeting in Cannon Street invited the Rev. Arthur Mursell to become its pastor, and that gentleman entered upon a probationary ministry of six months, in January, 1878, concluding at Midsummer of the same year. An interval of about nine months then elapsed previous to his entering permanently upon the pastorate of that church, in April, 1879. The building being condemned under the Birmingham Improvement Scheme, the last Sunday service was conducted therein on the 5th of October in the same year, on which occasion the pastor, having selected as his subject, "Last Echoes among Old Walls," gave a brief outline of the history of the chapel. The Cannon Street church are at the present time (October, 1879), therefore, without a home, their Sunday Services being held in the Town Hall.

Next in chronological order among the Dissenters of Birmingham are the Independents ; and our first duty is to the older churches, the earlier history of which has already been given in these pages.

The principal matter to be recorded in connection with the parent church of this denomination, during the first two decades of the period under notice, is the pastorate of the Rev. John Angell James, to which we have already referred in previous chapters. "As he approached the autumn of life," says Elihu Burritt, "his power in the pulpit became more perceptible and impressive. It was when the autumnal tints of those concluding years had touched his great bushy head and beard and strongly-marked features, that I first saw and heard him. The earnestness of his soul in his work, his voice, mellowed like a sabbath bell that had called a dozen generations to the sanctuary, the deep solemnity of his manner, the sheen of a godly life that seemed to surround him like a halo, the very reflection of the thoughts he had put forth upon the world through his books—all gave to his discourse a power which I had never seen equalled in any other minister on either side of the Atlantic. . . But however large his congregation," continues Burritt, "and however often he may be able to address other audiences, the most eloquent minister can reach but a comparatively few persons with his voice. He must put his thoughts to press in order to reach and move the million. This John Angell James did, to a degree and effect which no other minister, of any denomination, has attained for the last century. It is doubtful if Baxter or even Bunyan has been so widely read. Mr. James gave to the world, as the best legacy of his life, seventeen volumes, some of which have had a vast circulation. His 'Anxious Inquirer after Salvation Directed and Encouraged' must rank only second to Bunyan's 'Pilgrim's Progress' in number of copies printed and circulated in different languages and countries. No man in writing a book could be more deeply impressed with the conviction that he was moved by the spirit of God than was the author of this remarkable volume. That conviction seemed to be deeper at the end than at the beginning of the work. He charges its readers to 'take it up with something of the awe that warns you how you touch a holy thing.'

Thousands on both sides of the Atlantic have taken it up in this way to all the benefit which its author hoped of it."*

Mr. James retained his pastorate for more than half-a-century, and in 1855, a three days' jubilee celebration was held, commencing September 9th, on which occasion Mr. James presented to each of the 2,000 children in the Sunday and Day Schools, a copy of his little book, "A Jubilee Memorial," and on the 11th of the same month, he laid the foundation stone of the Jubilee Chapel, Francis Road, Edgbaston. He died on the 1st of October, 1859, and was buried under the pulpit he had so long filled. Mr. R. W. Dale, who had been admitted as co-pastor, November 22nd, 1855, succeeded Mr. James in the pastorate, and has held that position up to the present time, having won the admiration and esteem of the great body of Nonconformists throughout the world.

The chapel was restored and enlarged in 1871, and now contains accommodation for about 2,000 persons.

In reference to the Steelhouse Lane Chapel, (described in an earlier chapter,) we may mention that during the period under notice the eloquent and thoughtful young preacher and author, Robert Alfred Vaughan, son of the late Dr. R. Vaughan, was for a few years pastor of that church. His death, at an early age, was mourned, not only by all who had enjoyed the rare privilege of personal friendship with him, but by admirers of his writings (copies of which are now very scarce) throughout the country.

In 1844 a neat chapel was erected in Graham Street, called Highbury Chapel, at which, for some time, the Rev. Brewin Grant officiated.

The chapel in Francis Road, referred to above, was completed in 1856, and opened on the 8th of October in that year. It was built from the designs of Mr. Yeoville Thomason, at a cost of £5,000, and comprises nave, transepts, vestries, and a tower and spire 170 feet in height. Internally the building has an open timbered roof,

* Walks in the Black Country, pp. 61-63.

THE COUNCIL HOUSE, ANN STREET.

and is an exceedingly neat and graceful structure. It may interest some of our lady readers (if such there be) to know that the prolific authoress known to the world as Miss Emma Jane Worboise was for some years a member of the Francis Road Church.

There are also places of worship belonging to this denomination in Legge Street, Palmer Street, Bordesley Street, Small Heath, Gooch Street, and all the principal suburbs of the town.

In 1840 a fund was started for the erection of a new College in place of the small and incommodious building at Spring Hill. A donation of £500 was presented anonymously through the Rev. J. A. James ; John Lea, of Kidderminster, and John Barker, of Wolverhampton, also gave £500 each ; and several other donations of £250, £200, and £100 were given, and at the close of the year 1856 the building fund amounted to £12,985.* A beautiful and picturesque site was purchased on Moseley Common for the new building and grounds, commanding a fine and extensive prospect of the surrounding country, and the building was commenced in 1854, from the designs of Mr. Joseph James, of London, and opened on the 24th of June, 1857. "The style," says Dr. Langford, "is that of the early part of the fifteenth century, the details inclining more to the decorated period than to the perpendicular. The building forms three sides of a quadrangle, the main front being to the south. In the centre of the south front is a battlemented tower, 78 feet in height, flanked by a bell turret carried 14 feet higher. In this tower is the principal entrance to the building. The doorway is exceedingly beautiful, the carving with which the face of the arch is enriched being a clever combination of many of the best examples, all brought out with scrupulous care. One of the bands bears the inscription, 'The fear of the Lord is the beginning of wisdom'; and on each side are shields, on which are inscribed, 'On

*I am indebted to Dr. Langford's *Handbook* for these
figue   —R. K. D.

earth peace, goodwill to men,' and 'Glory to God in the highest.' Above the main entrance rise, in succession, three bay windows, for the lighting respectively of Council room, museum, and laboratory. The tracery of these widows is of a very elaborate character, a buttress to the right of the doorway being decidedly original and beautiful in form. To the west of the tower is the library, on the exterior of which a large amount of ornament has been lavished. It is lighted by four very large moulded windows of stained glass, supplied by the Messrs. Chance, of Spon Lane. Over the tracery of these is a rich pierced parapet, surmounted by four elegantly-carved pinnacles. Immediately beyond the library, and forming the west angle, is the Warden's house, flanked by an octagon turret, on the summit of which is a water tank for the use of the establishment. To the east of the tower is the dining hall, with lecture room over it ; and beyond these the matron's residence. The wings, which are two-storied and have transomed windows, are in keeping with the main front, though not so rich in decoration. At the end of each wing is a bell turret. Inside is a handsome entrance hall, paved with encaustic tiles, and having in one of the walls a most elaborate piece of carving, in Caen stone, intended to serve as a frame for a metallic tablet to be erected to the memory of the original founders of Spring Hill College, Mr. G. S. Mansfield, Mr. Charles Glover, Mrs. Sarah Glover, and Miss Elizabeth Mansfield. A corridor window, immediately fronting the entrance hall, is fitted with stained glass and contains the Mansfield and Glover arms, together with those of the three county towns, Warwick, Worcester, and Stafford. The library, the entrance to which is from the hall, is a fine, lofty apartment, open roofed, the principals resting on corbels of winged angels. Bookshelves are carried round three sides of the room, and over these is a small gallery. As regards detail, the most noteworthy feature of the library is the chimney-piece at either end. Both are of Caen stone ; they have the appropriate motto, 'Scientia potentia est;' and they are covered with the most delicate carving which human hands ever executed. Each flower or bit of foliage introduced is worthy of special study. Imagine a lily-of-the-valley, for instance, executed in high relief, with nearly as much delicacy as nature's self could give it. The carver could not have been more successful if wax or Parian marble had been his material, instead of stone dug out of the quarries of Normandy. One chimney-piece is surmounted by a bust of Dr. Joseph Fletcher, formerly of Stepney, the other by a bust of Dr. Pye Smith, who may, we suppose, be regarded as the "representative man" of Nonconforming collegiate life. The dining-room has also two fine chimney-pieces, more massive in style, but with carving equally beautiful. None of the other public rooms call for special remark. Along the north side of the principal building runs a lengthy corridor, with pointed arches, the perspective effect of which is a very fine one. The wings are appropriated to the students; the studies being on the first floor, and the dormitories overhead. Each study has an area of ten feet by eleven feet, and is nine feet in height. There is at present accommodation for thirty-six students; but at the cost of a couple of thousand pounds this could be easily doubled by running a centre building into the quadrangle. The kitchens, etc., are in the basement story of the east wing. All the internal arrangements seem complete, and not the least satisfactory is the apparatus which heats the building."*

"It has," says Elihu Burritt, in his *Walks in the Black Country*, "an able corps of professors, not only of Theology and Ecclesiastical History and Polity, but of Philosophy, Classical and Oriental Languages. It supplies studios and dormitories for thirty-six students, and, adopting a figure pertaining to water-works, it acts as a very important feeder to the pulpits of the Independents throughout the kingdom."

The history of the Methodists during this

*Dr. Langford's *Handbook*, pp. 53-55.

period is one of great progress. In addition to the older chapels, and those erected during the two decades last treated of (1821—1840),* chapels have been erected in Nechells Park Road, Coventry Road, New John Street West, Summer Hill, and in all the principal suburbs of the town. A new and handsome structure has been erected in St. Martin Street, Islington, in place of the older chapel; a Gothic building of stone and ornamental brickwork, designed by Mr. J. H Chamberlain, and erected at a cost of nearly £8,000. The annual Conference of the Wesleyan Connexion has been held in Birmingham several times during this period.

The Wesleyan Societies of Birmingham are divided into five "Circuits," each of which is presided over by three or four stationed ministers, who are changed every three years. The Circuits are arranged as follows :—-

First Circuit, (Cherry Street): Cherry Street, Moseley Road, Inge Street, Knutsford Street, and King's Heath.
Second Circuit, (Belmont Row): Belmont Row, Bradford Street, Coventry Road, Lord Street, and Bloomsbury Mission Room.
Third Circuit, (Newtown Row): Newtown Row, Nechells Park Road, Lichfield Road (Aston), and Erdington.
Fourth Circuit, (Wesley): Constitution Hill, ("Wesley Chapel,") Summer Hill, (Icknield Street West,) New John Street West, Aston Villa, (George Street, Lozells), and Nineveh.
Fifth Circuit, (Islington): St. Martin's Street (Islington), Bristol Road, Harborne and Selly Oak; with preaching stations at Holliday Street, "British Workman," St. Vincent Street, Osler Street, and Icknield Port Road.

The history of Methodism does not end with the records of the Wesleyan Connexion; the Methodist church has perhaps been more fertile in what we may term outgrowths than any other religious community in England. The first of these departures took place very soon after the death of the founder of the Society, when Mr. Kilham, a minister at that time stationed in the Newcastle circuit, appeared as the advocate and champion of separation from

* Viz., Islington (1825), Constitution Hill (1828), Bristol Road (1834), and Newtown Row (1837).

the Church of England, of which the early Methodists considered themselves still apart. Mr. Kilham advocated the celebration of the Lord's Supper in their own chapels, instead of being compelled to receive it at the parish church, and for this he was expelled from the ministry, at the conference of 1796, and soon afterwards formed a new organization which was called "The Methodist New Connexion." This society obtained a small footing in Birmingham as early as 1809, but no permanent place of worship was erected by them until 1838, when a chapel was opened in Unett Street, which was considerably enlarged and improved in 1842. They have now, besides this, chapels in Moseley Street, Heath Street, Ladywood, and at Balsall Heath.

In 1835 the Wesleyan Methodist Association was formed, as a result of a secession from the Old Connexion, on account of the increased authority given by the Conference to the itinerant ministers; and a chapel was built by the new society in this town, in Bath Street, which was opened in 1839. In 1850 the parent society (the Old Connexion) suffered greater losses by secession than they had ever before experienced. At the Conference of that year the Revds. Samuel Dunn, James Everett, and William Griffith were expelled from the Connexion on account of their supposed complicity in the authorship of the notorious "Fly-Sheets," in which the Methodist system had been severely criticised; and, as a result, a large secession took place, especially of lay members of the society, and these, afterwards amalgamating with the older seceders, formed the new society known as the United Methodist Free Churches, who have now two circuits in Birmingham, of the Northern of which Rocky Lane Chapel is the centre, and of the southern Bath Street Chapel.

The Primitive Methodists have also two circuits here, but their influence is chiefly felt in the outside districts. Their principal town chapel is in Gooch Street.

After the erection of St. Chad's Cathedral,

recorded in a foregoing chapter, Birmingham became the centre of the Roman Catholic faith in England, and held that position for many years, partly owing to the proximity of the great collegiate institution at Oscott, of which Cardinal Wiseman was at one time president. The town became, in 1848, a See of Rome, a Papal rescript appointing the Rev. Dr. Ullathorne "Bishop of Birmingham;" and he was enthroned in St. Chad's, on the 30th of August in that year.

Two conventual and monastic orders were established during the same decade, the one in Bath Street and the other in Hunter's Lane; to the latter a chapel was attached, which was opened for public worship on the 28th of July, 1847.

Shortly afterwards a new and more important society of a similar character was founded in Birmingham by the eloquent and zealous convert, John Henry Newman, D.D. This was the Oratory of St. Phillip Neri, which found a temporary home in Alcester Street, and numbered among its earliest inmates Father Faber and Austin Mills. "Their long black cloaks and peculiar habit of the Order were conspicuous objects in the streets until the fulmination of an edict against them by the Government in 1852, incidental to the agitation on the Papal aggression movement." * In 1852 they erected a large and commodious building in Hagley Road, to which is attached a church "dedicated to our Blessed Lady, under the title of her Immaculate Conception." To many persons who have no sympathy with Roman Catholicism the Birmingham Oratory has become endeared by its associations; and the names of John Henry Newman and Edward Caswell will long be remembered in connection therewith.

In 1862 the Roman Catholics purchased from the Unitarians the building long known as the New Meeting House, the successor of that in which Dr. Priestley preached, from 1780 to 1791, and which was burnt by the rioters in the latter

* Hints for a History of Birmingham, [by James Jaffray.]

year. It is now known as St. Michael's, and during the year 1878 a red-brick manse was erected in front, thus obscuring the view of this historic edifice. Two handsome churches have been erected by the Catholics during the past ten years; St. Joseph's, at Nechells, and St. Catherine of Sienna, in the Horse Fair. The other places belonging to the Roman Catholics are : St. Anne's, Alcester Street; the Convent of St. Anne, Lowe Street ; St. Mary's, Brougham Street; and St. Mary's Retreat, Harborne.

Of the Swedenborgians, we have only to record here that on the 16th of June, 1875, the first stone of a new church was laid in Wretham Road, Soho, and the building was opened for worship on the 22nd of November, 1875, at which date the society vacated their old meeting-house in Summer Lane, and so passed out of the history of the religious sects of the borough. The new church, which is built in the early English style, and consists of nave, aisles, and chancel, with a spire, cost £10,000.

Another of the smaller sects have also migrated from their old quarters in the town, viz., the Catholic Apostolic Church, who have erected for themselves a new church in Summer Hill Terrace. The old building in Newhall Street was removed in 1877 to make way for the new Assay Offices.

The withdrawal of Mr. George Dawson from the Baptist Church of Mount Zion in 1846 (to which we have referred in our notice of that denomination), led to the formation of a new unsectarian church, called the "Church of the Saviour." This course was resolved upon at a meeting held on the 23rd of February, 1846, at Mount Zion Chapel, at which a report, drawn up by Mr. Dawson, was adopted, declaring "That as a Catholic Church it is not their intention to have any doctrinal test as a church or as a congregation. They regard fixed views, embodied as professions of faith, as productive of mischief. The preacher should not be retained as an advocate of certain opinions. It is not the fair and manly mode, as all men differ ;

and no man has a right to judge another, further than by the Scriptural rule, 'by their fruits ye shall know them.' A man's own conscience is the arbiter of his fitness to join the Church of God; more especially as they are known to differ in opinion. The preacher is to give the results of his study ; and the people are not bound to believe him further than appears consistent to themselves as inquirers after truth ; their bond being a common end and purpose,—to clothe the naked, to feed the hungry, and to instruct the ignorant."

On the 13th of July, in the same year, the first turf on the site of the new Church was turned, and the building was completed and opened August 8th, 1847, two eloquent discourses being delivered on that occasion, by Mr. Dawson. The morning discourse was afterwards published under the title of " The Demands of the Age on the Church," and earned for the preacher the doubtful distinction of a place in the Rev. George Gilfillan's " Gallery of Literary Portraits."

The Church was built from the designs of Messrs. Bateman and Drury, and is, in plan, a parallelogram, with a circular end. It has a massive cemented front, in the Corinthian order, the entrance being beneath a fine ornamented arch, supported by two enriched columns. In a niche at the upper end of the Church, behind the preacher's platform, is a rich-toned organ.

Mr. Dawson remained minister of the Church of the Saviour until his death, which occurred on the 30th of November, 1876, and was succeeded by his former assistant in the ministry, Mr. G. St. Clair, F.G S.

In 1856 the Jews of Birmingham removed from the old Synagogue in Severn Street to a new and handsome structure in Blucher Street, Singer's Hill, the first stone of which was laid on April 12th, 1855. The new Synagogue, which was consecrated on September 24th, 1856, was erected from designs by Mr. Yeoville Thomason, in the Byzantine style of architecture. It is divided into nave and aisles by arcades of seven arches on each side, the lower order of which support the galleries, and the upper a beautiful semicircular ceiling. The sanctuary opens to the main building by a fine arch, supported by four columns.

The old Meeting House of the Quakers, or Society of Friends, in Bull Street (erected in 1703, and enlarged in 1778), is also among the buildings which have passed away, having given place, in 1856, to the present not inelegant Meeting House, which was erected from the plans of Mr. T. Plevins, and was opened on the 25th of January, 1857.

In 1848 the Presbyterians, finding their original chapel (erected in 1834) too small for their increasing numbers, erected a substantial church in Broad Street, the first stone of which was laid on the 25th of July in that year. The style adopted in the building is Italian, the principal front being occupied by a tower, vestibules, and staircases. It has a somewhat heavy appearance externally, owing to the absence of windows, the church being lighted from the roof.

A second church was erected by the Presbyterians in 1869, in Camp Hill, and was opened on the 3rd of June in that year. It was built from the designs of Mr. T. Naden, in the Decorated Gothic style, and consists of nave and side aisles, with tower and spire.

The Christadelphians first obtained a footing in Birmingham, we believe, in 1866, holding their services in the Athenæum Hall, Temple Row. On the removal of the Swedenborgians to Wretham Road, Handsworth, the Christadelphians took possession of their old meeting house in Summer Lane, which they still hold. Services are also held by this denomination every Sunday, in the Temperance Hall, Temple Street.

The Plymouth Brethren, Disciples of Christ, Lady Huntingdon's Connexion, Latter Day Saints, Spiritualists, and other minor sects, have also places of worship in Birmingham.

"This is not the place"—says Mr. Bates in concluding his notices of the religious edifice of town*—"to expatiate on the necessity of a rigid performance of our religious duties, or to trace the strict connection between religious sentiment and our moral and social condition. Enough that, in the words of Burke, 'we know, and what is better, feel inwardly that religion is the basis of civil society, and the source of all good and all comfort,' and with this conviction, and rejoicing in the knowledge that the Clergy of Birmingham of every denomination are distinguished as a body no less for the fervency with which they labour in their holy ministration, than their exemplary conduct in private life, we trust that, while the visitor in surveying the physical aspect of our town may exclaim with Sir Roger de Coverley, 'that the fifty new churches do very much mend the prospect,'† it may also be apparent in the manners and habits of our people, that the frequent temples of the Almighty subserve a higher and nobler purpose."

*Pictorial Guide to Birmingham, p. 80.
† Spectator, No. 383.

CHAPTER V.

EDUCATION, LITERATURE, AND LITERARY AND SCIENTIFIC SOCIETIES IN BIRMINGHAM; 1841—1879.

The Queen's College—The Birmingham and Midland Institute—Charles Dickens's Readings—Mason's College—The Grammar School——Birmingham Books and their Authors—Local Periodical Literature—Elementary Education—The Board Schools—Literary and Scientific Societies of Birmingham.

WE come now to the history of the educational and literary progress of our town during the past forty years.

In 1828 Mr. W. Sands Cox founded a school of Medicine and Surgery which, by his watchfulness and care grew, in time, into the useful and valuable institution now known as the Queen's College. The present building was erected in 1843-44, and consists of seventy students' rooms, laboratories, anatomical rooms, library, museum, chapel, and a large and handsome dining hall. The principal elevation consists of a centre and wings, each having an entrance doorway, above each of which is a lofty oriel window, extending to the height of two stories ; between each of these are two other traceried windows of the same height, and the whole is surmounted by a gabled parapet, with pinnacles. This façade is evidently copied from that of the Free Grammar School. The chapel, which was consecrated in 1845, contains a stained glass window ("Christ Healing the Sick") designed by Mr. Brooke Smith, junr., and executed by Messrs. Pemberton. The altarpiece contains a fine work of art in silver, designed by Flaxman, and executed by the late Sir Edward Thomason, the subject being the 'Shield of Faith.' In the dining hall are three noteworthy pictures by the great French artist, David, presented by the late Vice-Principal, the Rev. Chancellor Law, one of which, "The Return of the Prodigal," merits special attention. There are also portraits of W. Sand Cox, Esq., the Rev. Chancellor Law, Dr. Johnson, and of the great benefactor to the college, the Rev. Samuel Wilson, Warnford, LL.D.

After a long and troublous conflict between the founder, the professors, and the supporters of the institution, the College was incorporated by Act of Parliament, and has since done much good work. "It is divided into three faculties : 1, Theology ; 2, Medicine ; 3, Arts. The courses of study qualify for the degrees of B.A., M.A., B.C.L., D.C.L., M.B., and M.D., in the University of London, and for the diplomas of the Royal College of Surgeons, and the Society of Apothecaries."[*]

We have already referred, in the chapter on Public Life and Events, to the proposal which was set on foot, in the winter of 1852-3, to establish a Literary and Scientific Institute in the town. The cordial approval of Charles Dickens served to encourage the projectors of the movement, and they were still further encouraged by his offer, made to Mr. Banks on the occasion of his visit to receive the testimonial, to give a public reading of his Christmas Carol, on behalf of the institution. "There would be some novelty in the thing,"—he wrote, on the following day, to Mr. Arthur Ryland—"as I have never done it in public, though I have in private, and (if I may say so) with a great effect on the hearers."

A meeting was held in the Lecture Theatre of the old Philosophical Institution, Cannon Street, on Monday, January 10th, 1853, the result of which was the foundation of the Birmingham and Midland Institute. The first list of donations was issued on the 11th of June, showing that

LANGFORD *Handbook*, p. 48.

the sum of £4,730 had been promised, but of this, £495 was contingent upon the total amount reaching £8,000. The committee announced further that they had applied to the Town Council for permission to erect the building on a piece of vacant land near the Town Hall, not required for Corporation purposes.

This application came before the Council on the 16th, of June and was referred to the Estates and Buildings' Committee, who, on September 6th, reported thereon recommending that the application of the Institute Committee be granted, subject to the sanction of Parliament.

A public meeting in support of the proposed Institute was held in the Town Hall on the 17th of November, and resolutions were passed in support of the project with great enthusiasm. On the 10th of December a fourth list of donations was published, whereby it appeared that the total amount had reached £7,000.

At Christmas the readings so long looked forward to, were given by Mr. Dickens in the Town Hall; on the 27th of December he read the *Christmas Carol*, as promised; on the 29th, *The Cricket on the Hearth;* and on the 30th, (when at his special desire the price of admission was reduced to sixpence, in order to afford the working classes an opportunity of being present,) he repeated the *Carol*. Although this was in reality the first appearance of Charles Dickens as a reader before any large audience, he had thought proper, in the interval between the promise and its fulfilment, to make an experiment of his powers before a less intelligent and and exacting audience at the dull little Cathedral-city of Peterborough. "Here was an opportunity," he argued, "for testing the matter without risk; an antediluvian country town; an audience of farmers' sons and daughters, rural shop-keepers, and a few parsons—if interest could be excited in the stolid minds of such a Bœotian assemblage, the success of the reader would be assured wherever the English tongue was spoken. On the other hand if failure

resulted, none would be the wiser outside this Sleepy-Hollow circle." One who was present at this first reading of the immortal *Carol* says :

"As the clock struck the appointed hour, a red, jovial face, unrelieved by the heavy moustache which the novelist has since assumed, a broad, high forehead, and a perfectly Micawber-like expanse of shirt-collar and front appeared above the red baize box, and a full, sonorous voice rang out the words, '*Marley-was-dead-to-begin-with*'—then paused, as if to take in the character of the audience. No need of further hesitation. The voice held all spell-bound. Its depth of quiet feeling when the ghost of past Christmases led the dreamer through the long-forgotten scenes of his boyhood—its embodiment of burly good nature when old Fezziwig's calves were twinkling in the dance—its tearful suggestiveness when the spirit of Christmases to come pointed to the nettle-grown, neglected grave of the unloved man —its exquisite pathos by the death-bed of Tiny Tim, dwell yet in memory like a long-known tune. That one night's reading in the quaint little city, so curiously brought about, so ludicrous almost in its surroundings, committed Mr. Dickens to the career of a public reader ; and he has since derived nearly as large an income from his readings as from the copyright of his novels."

On the morning after the repetition of the *Christmas Carol*, Mr. Dickens was entertained at breakfast by the committee, when an elegant flower-stand, manufactured by Messrs. Elkington, was presented to Mrs. Dickens, and a bronze inkstand to Mr. Charles Dickens, junr., in acknowledgment of the services rendered to the Institute by Mr. Dickens. The proceeds of the three readings amounted to £227 19s. 9d.

The bill enabling the Town Council to grant the land received the Royal assent on the 3rd of July, 1854, and the foundation stone of the building was laid by H.R.H. the Prince Consort, on the 22nd of November, 1855, and the Institute portion of the building (which was intended, when completed, to provide accommodation also for the Central Reference and Lending Libraries), was opened in 1856. It is in the Italian style, and was designed by Mr. E. M. Barry ; the principal elevation is of Hollington stone, and consists of a rusticated basement with square-headed windows inserted, surmounted by a colonnade of Corinthian pillars, and the usual entablature.

The scheme included two departments, the

SIR JOSIAH MASON'S ORPHANAGE, AT ERDINGTON.

General and the Industrial; the former embracing the usual privileges of a first-class literary society, —a News Room, an admirable Lecture Programme, English History and Literature Classes, and an annual Conversazione,—for the annual subscription of one guinea; the latter consisting of classes for the study of Languages, Literature, and Science, at exceedingly low fees. There has also been added to the Institute an Archæological Section, of which Mr. Sam: Timmins is President, the conditions of membership being a yearly subscription of five shilling in addition to the usual guinea subscription to the Institute itself. This Section has done good work in the publication of valuable papers on local antiquities, with illustrative drawings; and we venture to express the hope that at no very distant period its members may unite in the production of a corrected and enlarged edition of Dugdale's great county history Such a work would be a lasting monument to the present officers and members of the society.

The Birmingham and Midland Institute has numbered amongst its presidents some of the most distinguished writers and thinkers of the present generation, all of whom have delivered the customary inaugural address at the commencement of the session. What an interesting volume might be made of these annual addresses, delivered by Charles Dickens, Charles Kingsley, Professors Huxley, Tyndall, and Fawcett, John Morley, Sir Henry Rowlinson, Sir John Lubbock, Dean Stanley, and others of note. Surely they would repay the trouble of collecting and publishing!

At the present time the Institute building is undergoing considerable alteration and enlargement, at a cost of nearly £18,000. When completed it will be, to a fuller extent, what Charles Dickens has termed it, "one of the most remarkable schemes ever devised for the educational behoof of the artisan" . . . which has "educated education all around it."

On the 23rd of February, 1875, the first stone was laid of a magnificent Science College, founded and endowed by Sir Josiah Mason, the founder of the noble orphanage at Erdington, and, as the building is now nearly completed and will be opened during 1880, we may properly include here some notice of the institution. It is to be governed by a bailiff and six trustees, the founder himself being the bailiff, and the present trustees Messrs. J. Thackray Bunce, J. G. Blake, M.D., T. P. Heslop, M.D., G. J. Johnson, G. Shaw, and M. J. Smith. After the founder's death the Town Council is to elect five other trustees, and vacancies are to be filled up as they occur by the Council and the trustees respectively. The trustees are to be laymen and Protestants; no theological test or qualification is to be imposed upon, or required from, any professor or teacher in the College; and neither sex, creed, or birthplace is to hinder any student from admission thereto. Preference, however, is to be given to students from the Orphanage at Erdington, and a second preference to natives of Birmingham and Kidderminster.

"Apart from the value it is likely to have as an educational institution," says the *Daily Mail*, "it is architecturally a building which everyone in the town may point to with pride.

As a specimen of Gothic architecture, it is one of the finest the town possesses. With the gradual pulling down of the scaffolding one is enabled more fully to appreciate the beautiful proportions and bold dignity of the structure. The lofty hipped roof rises in the central block over a building five storeys high, the façade of which is massive in appearance, varied, and picturesque. The front is built of red brick, with Portland stone details, which have been inserted without any minute ornamentation, but in the best manner possible to produce the most genuinely artistic effect Divided into five parts, the elevation rises in the centre to a considerable height, and the walls of the upper floor recede from the line of the front enough to allow of a passage, guarded by a pierced parapet. In the centre of this block is the entrance gateway, in the form of a deeply recessed arch raised on shafted jambs. Over this is a projecting stone balcony, and on the next floor six large windows, which will give light to the chemical lecture room. From this point rises a large oriel window of two storeys high, and above this a gable, the terminal of which—a mermaid—is 122 feet above the level of the street. From the predominant central block portions recede on each side, and at the extremities of each of these are projecting wings terminating in lofty turreted gables. These projecting wings are 90 feet in height, and on each storey have three windows grouped together. The portions between the centre and wings are much lower, being about 55 feet in height and having but three storeys. The whole of the central block has a frontage to Edmund Street of 148 feet, and is 36 feet wide. The buildings now in progress of erection cover an area of about 2,400 square yards, but in the course of time, when the original plan of the founder is fully carried out, they will occupy nearly double that area, the extention, of course, being made in the rear. At right angles from the block fronting Edmund Street, three parallel blocks recede on the sides of two open courts, and these are joined at the south-west end by a wing parallel with the front block. From this it will be seen that the buildings are arranged something in the shape of a double parallelogram, the cental block extending from Edmund Street in the direction of Great Charles Street doing double duty in forming one of the sides for each.

"Upon entering the gateway in the central block we find ourselves in a large and lofty vestibule, whose groined arches with moulded ribs resting on dwarf columns, carved capitals, and spandrils, and geometrical tracery are in admirable harmony with the exterior of the building. From the vestibule a broad flight of steps leads to a landing on the ground floor, which is six feet above the level of the street, and from this landing a wide central corridor extends from the front to the back of the buildings, while another corridor, in a transverse direction from the first, runs along that part of the college fronting Edmund Street, at each end of which is a staircase from the basement to the top of the building. The principal staircase opens to the right half way down the central corridor with an arcade of four arches on granite columns, and communications with every storey. The central corridor, further down, passes into the back range of buildings, the doors on one side opening to a library and reading room of large dimensions, and on the other to the physical laboratory. On the first floor are the chemical lecture theatre already spoken of, three large lecture rooms, chemical preparation rooms, professors' apartments, class rooms for magnetism, rooms for chemical collections, models and apparatus, and in the south-west block at the back are several large rooms for drawing. The floors above are entirely devoted to chemistry. A commodious apartment in the front block is set apart as a professor's laboratory, and here also are rooms for the study of organic chemistry, and for gas, water, and spectrum analysis. Above these is a large and lofty room to be used as a museum. In addition to the rooms already mentioned, there are on the several floors about 25 smaller rooms for professors, assistants, classes, &c., and on each floor opposite the principal staircase are the necessary coat-rooms and lavatories. Altogether the building contains nearly a hundred rooms. The several laboratories will be fitted up with small and large evaporation niches and with every appliance and fitting that the modern professor can suggest or the student require,"

The Grammar School has undergone considerable change in its constitution during this period.

After several unsuccessful attempts at reform, a new scheme for the government and conduct of the school, drawn up by the Charity Commissioners, was approved. By the original Charter the governors of the School were self-elected; but under the new scheme, they are elected as follows :—Eight by the Town Council, one each by the three Universites of Oxford, Cambridge, and London, by the teachers of the school, and the remainder are what is termed co-optative. The Head Master must be a graduate of one of the Universities, but need not now be in Holy Orders. The old distinctions of classical, commerical, and elementary schools are now abolished, giving place to what are termed the High, Middle, and Lower Middle Schools, and except in case of foundation scholarships (to the extent of one-third of the whole number of scholars) and King Edward's Scholarships, fees are paid varying from £2 to £7 per annum, which will be increased after June 24th, 1880, to a scale varying from £2 10s. to £8 per annum ; and again, after Midsummer, 1881, from £3 to £9 per annum. The present number of children being educated under this foundation is about 1,560.

During the past forty years the literature of Birmingham has been somewhat extensive, and among the books thus issued from the metropolis of the Midlands have been not a few which have taken high rank in the literature of our time, and have been read not only among those who have enjoyed the personal acquaintance and friendship of their authors, but by readers everywhere. Among these may be mentioned the charming prose writings of Elihu Burritt, the poems of Dr Sebastian Evans and Dr. J. A. Langford, the " Prison books and their authors," " Pleasant Spots and Famous Places," and the four chatty and interesting volumes of local history of the latter gentleman, who received the degree of LL.D., in 1869 from the senate and trustees of Greenville and Tusculum College, Tennesse, " as a mark of their high appreciation of the value of his literary labours." Dr. C. M. Ingleby, Dr. J

H. Newman, John Angell James, R. W. Dale, George Dawson, W. Lucas Sargant, J. Thackray Bunce, Sam: Timmins, J. Toulmin Smith, T. H. Gill, Thomas Ragg, Bessie Rayner Parkes, and other names might also be mentioned of local authors who have found many readers outside the radius of their personal influence. Mention should also be made here of several well-known authors whose works have not been issued from the local press, but who have special claims upon us as natives of or residents in Birmingham, as, for instance, Mr. Edward A. Freeman, the historian of the Norman Conquest, who is a native of Harborne; Mr. Edward Capern, the Devonshire postman poet, who has taken up his residence in the same pleasant suburb; Mr. George Mogridge, better known as "Old Humphrey," who lies buried at Handsworth; and Mrs. Emma Jane Worboise, who was for many years a resident in this locality. The department of prose fiction has also been enriched by the writings of Miss Julia Goddard, daughter of our townsman, Mr. S. A. Goddard, who laboured so hard in the cause of freedom, both in the Reform agitation of 1830 and in the Anti-Corn Law struggle of later years. But he is perhaps better known to modern Birmingham men by his letters during the American War, advocating the cause of the North, which have since been republished in two volumes.

In the history of local periodical literature we must go back to the year 1836, in which, during the month of July, a new weekly newspaper—the *Midland Counties' Herald*—was commenced, on the plan of a gratuitous circulation, and is for the most part an advertising medium, chiefly devoted to the land interests, farming, agriculture, etc. It is neutral in politics, and has a very extensive circulation. On the 30th of December, 1848, the Birmingham *Mercury* was established, on democratic principles.

The first daily newspaper published in Birmingham appeared on the 7th of May, 1855, under the title of the *Birmingham Daily Press.*

It was not a successful venture, and lived only about two years.

In 1857, the *Birmingham Daily Post* was established by the proprietors of the *Birmingham Journal*; the first number was issued on the 4th of December. The *Daily Post* has remained, throughout its career, loyal to the principles of Liberalism, and by enterprise and good management has become the leading journal in the Midland Counties, having a daily circulation of upwards of 40,000 copies. In connection with this journal was issued for the first time, during the same month, a weekly newspaper for the working classes—the *Saturday Evening Post*, which, in addition to the news of the week, contained serial stories and other special contributions. The title was subsequently altered, on the discontinuance of the *Journal*, in 1869, to that of the *Birmingham Weekly Post*. It has a circulation of 52,000 copies weekly.

On the first of January, 1861, a monthly satirical publication, entitled the *Town Crier*, was commenced, which has held its own against subsequent competitors up to the present time. It had at first occasional woodcuts, but the art of wood engraving was not at that time in a flourishing condition in Birmingham, and these embellishments were wisely discontinued.

In May, 1862, a second daily newspaper, Conservative in politics, was established in connection with the venerable *Birmingham Gazette*, founded by Mr. Aris in 1741, and bearing the same name. The Saturday issue still bears the name of the original founder, and thus preserves a link between the days of George the Second and the Victorian era.

The political campaign of 1868 brought into existence several 'comic' weeklies, to which we have already made reference in a previous chapter. *The Third Member*, the organ of the Conservatives, and *Toby*, that of the Liberals, lived only during the election contest, (about three months), both were illustrated, the former with lithographed cartoons, and the latter with woodcuts. The

Gridiron, a third publication of the same class, lived only about three weeks.

In September, 1869, one of the most important journalistic experiments ever attempted in the provinces was commenced in the publication of the first number of the *Illustrated Midland News*, a weekly publication conducted by Mr. Joseph Hatton, the well-known novelist and journalist. It consisted of sixteen folio pages, of the same size and general appearance as its successful proto-type, the *Illustrated London News*, and con-tained from eight to twelve fairly executed wood engravings every week.   But the proprietors laboured under the disadvantage of being com-pelled to send their best work to the London engravers, as there was at that time no competent engraver on wood in the town, and although this difficulty was at length to some extent obviated, the local work was of manifestly inferior quality, and this, together with the introduction of by far too many borrowed electrotypes, uninteresting to midland readers, caused the local interest in the venture to die out, and after sixteen months' existence, it became, practically, a London pub-lication, and soon afterwards altered its title, becoming the *Illustrated Newspaper*.   With the increased local facilities for producing such a journal, and the probability of securing a larger circle of subscribers, it is a matter of surprise that no attempt has yet been made to repeat the experiment.

During the same week in which the *Illustrated Midland News* was commenced, the first number of a new weekly satirical journal was published, entitled *Brum*, edited by "Old Sarbot," and illus-trated with coloured lithographic cartoons drawn by Mr. G. H. Bernasconi.   This periodical lasted scarcely four months, expiring in the following December.

Soon after the outbreak of the war between France and Germany, when the London *Echo* (a halfpenny evening newspaper) was selling in large numbers in Birmingham, the first local even-ing journal was issued, at the same price—the

Birmingham Daily Mail—which speedily won for itself a large circulation, both by its fearless and outspoken Liberalism and by the ability of its "special" articles on all topics of general interest. As a pleasant and chatty newspaper, appearing at an hour when the majority of business men have leisure for reading, it has become one of the most popular and widely-read journals in the Midland Counties, having at the present time a circulation of 56,000 copies.

A more ambitious, but less successful, daily newspaper was issued for the first time on the 2nd of January, 1871, under the editorship of the late Mr. George Dawson, M.A., with Dr. J. A. Langford as "local editor," bearing the simple title of the *Birmingham Morning News*.   The policy of this journal was that of "advanced Liberalism," but its special feature consisted in the contributions of the editor, whose popularity ob-tained for the new journal a considerable circula-tion.   Owing, however, to some differences with the proprietor, Mr. Dawson did not long retain the editorship, and when it became known that he had resigned the circulation began to fall off, and the paper was no longer able to hold its own against the powerful *Post*, and, after a chequered career of about five years (during the last six months of which it appeared both morning and evening as a halfpenny journal), it ceased to exist.

During the year 1876 a monthly periodical, entitled the *Birmingham Examiner*, was pub-lished, and gave promise of a high class serial for local readers, which should represent the thought and culture of the town.   After about a twelve months' existence, however, the publication ceased from want of sufficient support.   More successful have been the attempts to establish periodicals of this class representing special departments of knowledge, as in the case of the *Birmingham Medical Review*, the *Midland Naturalist*, and the *Central Literary Magazine*, the latter of which has now been in existence about seven years

In October, 1876, a weekly "Journal of Sense and Satire," entitled the *Dart*, was commenced as a Liberal organ, freely criticising the action of public men, and giving each week a cartoon portrait or caricature sketch, drawn by Mr. G. H. Bernasconi. In the following January, 1877, the *Lion*, a Conservative journal of a similar character, was commenced, but lived only a few months. In February of the present year the *Owl* was established, on the old lines of the *Dart*, which had ceased to represent the Liberal party, and the artist, Mr. Bernasconi, joined the new venture, his place on the *Dart* being filled by Mr. Sershall. A halfpenny journal of a similar character, also in the Liberal interest, has since been established under the resuscitated title of *The Gridiron*.

At the time of writing (October, 1879), we hear of changes in the proprietorship of the *Daily Gazette*, which has been purchased by the present editor, Mr. A. A. Sylvester, and Mr. E. W. Simkin; and of the projected issue of a new evening journal in connection therewith, under the title of the *Birmingham Daily Globe*.

Another attempt is about to be made to establish a high-class local magazine, in the publication of *Mid-England: A Magazine of Literature, Science, Art, and Archæology*, the first number of which is announced to appear in November (1879), with contributions by Miss Julia Goddard, Llewellynn Jewitt, Sam: Timmins, W. Bates, B.A., W. G. Fretton, and others.

If the periodical literature of Birmingham has been productive of many failures, it has also been distinguished by a few great successes. The *Birmingham Daily Post* has taken a place among the best-conducted provincial newspapers of our time, and its opinions are received with attention and respect throughout the country; while its contemporary, the *Gazette*, has the honour of being one of the oldest newspapers in the kingdom, and few journals could have been of greater assistance to the historian than this, which has now figured in the course of our history nearly a hundred and forty years.

The two great national scientific associations have held several of their annual gatherings in Birmingham during this period. The British Association (which had first visited Birmingham in 1839) came again in 1849. Among those who took part in this meeting were Prince Lucien Bonaparte, the Bishop of Oxford, Sir Charles Lyell, Dr. Buckland, Sir Roderick Murchison, the Chevalier Bunsen, Sir David Brewster, Professors Owen, Forbes, Playfair, Sedgwick, and Percy, Robert Stephenson, and many others of note.

A third visit was paid by the Association in 1865, on which occasion an important volume of reports was collected and published, respecting the Resources, Products, and Manufactures of Birmingham and the Midland Hardware District, edited by Mr. Sam: Timmins.

The kindred society—the National Association for the Promotion of Social Science—was born in Birmingham, the first Congress being held here in October, 1857 On the 12th of that month the inaugural address of the Association was delivered in the Town Hall by Lord Brougham. Papers were afterwards read on the three following days on Jurisprudence and Amendment of the Law, on Punishment and Reformation, on Public Health, Education, and Social Economy, by the ablest exponents of the new science.

In 1868 the Association again visited Birmingham, the meetings commencing on September 30th. The proceedings were opened by a sermon, preached in St. Philip's Church, by the Bishop of Worcester; and in the evening the Inaugural Address was delivered by the President, the Earl of Carnarvon. Two soirées were held in the Town Hall, one on the 1st of October and the other on the 5th; and on the 2nd, after the unveiling of the Watt statue by the Mayor, Mr. Sam: Timmins delivered an eloquent address on the life of the great inventor.

We come now to the elementary schools of the town. An important addition was made in 1849 to the school accommodation of the town by the erection of the Birminghom Free Industrial School in Gem Street, the first stone of which was laid on the 12th of April in that year by the late Recorder of Birmingham, Matthew Davenport Hill. Mr. C. W. Orford was the architect. For some years the school was principally devoted to the education of the children of soldiers killed in the Crimean War, who were maintained out of the Royal Patriotic Fund. After these had grown up out of the school, and the school became more strictly devoted to the work of local education, an application was made for a certificate under the Industrial Schools Act of 1866, and after the usual examinations it was granted, and the institution became a duly certified Industrial School in March, 1868.

As early as 1850 the people of Birmingham formed themselves into an association for the introduction of a free, secular, and compulsory system of National Education, supported by the rates. The Society—which was called the Birmingham School Association—had for its secretaries Mr. William Harris and Mr. H. B. S. Thompson; and sent a deputation to the Educational Conference held at Manchester in that year. A National Public School Association was formed, as the result of their deliberations, of which the Birmingham Association became a branch, and the question of a national system of education was agitated in the town with great vigour and energy during the year 1851.

In January, 1861, a conference was held in Birmingham with reference to the education of neglected and destitute children. Mr. Recorder Hill, Mr. W. Scholefield, M.P., Miss Carpenter, of Bristol; Dr. Miller, and others interested in the cause of education, took part in the deliberations.

Although nothing of importance was accomplished as the result of these conferences, they prepared the way, to some extent, for the conferences of 1867, held at the suggestion of Mr. George Dixon, then Mayor of Birmingham, which, in their turn, were the prelude to the organisation of the National Education League.

The Mayor moved, and the Rev. C. Evans seconded :—

That in the opinion of this meeting increased powers are necessary for the extension of the means of education ; and that for this purpose it is desirable to apply to Parliament for an Act empowering municipal corporations to levy rates for educational purposes.

Mr. W. L. Sargant then moved, and Mr. J. T. Bunce seconded :—

That this meeting approves of the principle that children of tender age shall not be employed unless due provision be made for their instruction at school.

The adjourned Conference was held on the 24th of the same month, at the Chamber of Commerce, Exchange Buildings, when the following resolutions were passed :—

That, whereas it has been ascertained that there are large numbers of persons who are able to send their children to school and yet who do not do so, either from apathy or from selfish considerations, it is the opinion of this meeting that a due regard for the interests of those children, thus neglected, imposes on the Government the duty of passing a law, inflicting penalties on the parents of children for whose continued absence from school there is not, in the opinion of the magistrates, a sufficient reason given.

That this meeting declines to recommend any general system of compulsory instruction, but that it is of opinion that the Industrial Schools Act, extended by the light of experience, may prove a means of securing the instruction of neglected children.

The third and last meeting of the Conference was held in the Council Chamber, March 5th, when similar resolutions were passed, and as a result of the meetings the " Birmingham Education Society" was formed. The report of the society was published on the 31st of December, and from that we learn the following particulars :— The population was 343,948, there was school accommodation for 29,275, and the attendance at schools was 18,561, or 8·41 average per cent. on the whole population.

The first annual meeting of the society was held on the 17th of April, 1868. From the report then read we find that the Society had already done good work in the cause of free education. The report states that :—

There are now 80 schools on the list of the society to which children are sent free. This comprises four-fifths of the whole number in Birmingham. The cases of the children have been strictly examined before grants have been made, in order to avoid the demoralisation resulting from giving aid to those who could afford to educate their own children. In this matter the committee have been guided, in a great measure, by the number of persons in each family and their aggregate weekly earnings.

In 1869, through the society's efforts, an undenominational school was erected at Brookfields; and the same year saw the formation of the National Education League, which was founded at a private meeting held at the residence of Mr. G. Dixon, M.P. The basis of the League was as follows :—

1.—Local authorities shall be compelled by law to see that sufficient school accommodation is provided for every child in their district. 2.—The cost of founding and maintaining such schools as may be required shall be provided out of the local rates, supplemented by Governmental grants. 3.—All schools aided by local rates shall be under the management of local authorities, and subject to Government inspection. 4.— All schools aided by local rates shall be unsectarian. 5.—To all schools aided by local rates admission shall be free. 6.— School accommodation being provided, the State or the local authorities shall have power to compel the attendance of children of suitable age not otherwise receiving education.

In order to carry out the objects of the League, large sums were subscribed by many gentlemen interested in the cause of education throughout the country. Among these we may mention the following sums subscribed by Birmingham men :—

Mr. G. Dixon, M.P	..	...	...	£1,000
Mr. R. L. Chance	..	..	...	1,000
Mr. J. Chamberlain	..	...	...	1,000
Mr. Joseph Chamb'ain		...	..	1,000
Mr. G. B. Lloyd	...	...	...	1,000
Mr. A. Field	...	...	...	1,000
Mr. Follett Osler, F.R.S.		...	...	1,000
Mr. W. Middlemore	...	...	...	1,000
Mr. Archibald Kenrick		...	...	1,000
Mr. F. S. Bolton	...	...	...	1,000
Mr. T. Kenrick	...	...	..	500
Mr. William Kenrick	...	...	...	500
Mr. J. Arthur Kenrick	...	...	...	500
Mr. John Jaffray	...	...	...	500
Mr. William Dudley	...	...	...	200
Mr. John Webster	..	...	...	200

The work of the League was commenced in real earnest by the publication of a Monthly Paper, and of pamphlets, leaflets, and other publications, to educate the people of England on this important subject. Meetings were held in all parts of the country, with the result that, in 1870, the Government passed an Elementary Education Act, as recorded in our last chapter of Political History.

By this Act each district was empowered to elect a School Board, and that of Birmingham was elected in November, 1870. Nearly £350,000 have been expended by the Board in the erection of school buildings, and twenty-four handsome sets of schools have been added to the town thereby, from the designs of Messrs. Martin and Chamberlain, whose names are a guarantee for good sound architectural work.

Besides these there are in the town fifty-seven elementary schools belonging to the various religious denominations, providing accommodation for nearly 30,000 children, giving, with the 24,638 provided for by the Board, a complete total of school accommodation for nearly 55,000 children.

Nor must the older institutions noticed in previous chapters be overlooked. The Blue Coat School, the four elementary or Lower Middle Schools in connection with King Edward the Sixth's foundation, and the numerous well-conducted private schools in the town, all help to swell the provision for elementary education of the children of Birmingham. And although, even yet, we cannot regard that provision as adequate and complete, we may with pride and gratitude contrast our present condition with that of the period immediately preceding the commencement of this period, and, surveying our great Free Libraries, Midland Institute, School of Design, and Colleges, as the means of continuing the great work of education begun in the schools, and feel that not only have the Birmingham men and women of the future an opportunity of becoming fairly grounded in the rudiments of knowledge, but that they may have the best possible education which can be devised, and thus, as Elihu Burritt observes, "a large and broad basis has been laid on which to erect the structure of public opinion

FORWARD

A. R. GAUL.

PHOTOGRAPHED BY WHITLOCK.

BIRMINGHAM: HOUGHTON & CO., LIMITED SCOTLAND PASSAGE.

in Birmingham, and to increase its force and effect upon the country and its government."

We need only mention briefly here the Diocesan Training College for Schoolmasters at Saltley; a handsome building in the Gothic of the period of Edward I., which contains accommodation for 100 students. The College was opened in 1852, and since that time nearly a thousand schoolmasters have been trained within its walls.

From the ashes of the old Mechanics' Institute (established in 1825, at the schoolrooms in connection with the Old Meeting and Ebenezer Chapel), arose, in 1843, the Polytechnic Institution, which occupied the building afterwards used as the Children's Hospital, and here classes were held for instruction in the various branches of knowledge, including Latin, German, French, and other languages. Lectures were also given frequently during the winter season, by some of the eminent and popular lecturers of that day. A library of about 4,000 volumes was attached to this institution, together with news and reading rooms, in which the principal newspapers and literary periodicals of the time were supplied. It was in connection with this institution Charles Dickens delivered his first Birmingham speech, on the 28th of February, 1844.

The Polytechnic Institution, however, like all the predecessors of the Midland Institute, had a hard fight for existence, and at length succumbed to its fate in September, 1853, dying, however, almost at the hour of victory of its more fortunate successor.

The Athenic Institute was established, in 1841, in Suffolk Street, "its object being to provide its members with the means by which may be obtained mental, moral, and physical improvement, together with rational amusement."* In 1846, according to the fifth Annual Report, the Institute numbered eighty members, and the receipts for the past year had amounted to upwards of £132.

The Central Literary Association was founded in 1856, the first meeting being held on the 28th

of November in that year. Meetings are held weekly during the session, at which readings are given, papers read, and literary topics discussed. We have already made reference to the quarterly magazine issued in connection with this Society, in our notice of the periodical literature of this period.

In the same year the Birmingham Amateur Dramatic Society was formed by Mr. John Steeple (the artist), Mr. S. W. Hill, and Mr. H. J. Whitlock. The first meeting of the Association was held at the Assembly Rooms, Broad Street, January 26, 1857, when the farce entitled "Done on Both Sides," was performed. The first public performance took place on the 3rd of June, 1859, at the Theatre Royal, on behalf of the funds of the Midland Institute, the pieces performed being Tom Taylor's "Plot and Passion," "Le Pauvre Jacques," (with new music by T. Anderton), and the farce, "I've Eaten my Friend." The second public performance, on behalf of the same institution, was given on October 17, 1861, at the same house, the pieces being "All that Glitters is not Gold," "Bombastes Furioso," and "A Wonderful Woman." But the most successful public performance of this Society was that given on the 23rd of April, 1868, in aid of the Shakespeare Memorial Fund, when the amateurs were assisted by Mr. Sothern and Miss Madge Robertson (now Mrs. Kendal). The representation consisted of Sheridan's brilliant comedy "The School for Scandal," and the farce entitled "A Thumping Legacy." The performance, although highly successful from an artistic point of view, was nevertheless, commercially, a failure, only a few pounds being realized. The Society has since given several other public performances for various charitable purposes.

Among the literary institutions of the town we may appropriately notice here the great reform effected in the management of the Birmingham [Old] Library, by Mr. G. Jabet in 1860. Previous to that date the shareholders only had been

---

* W. Bates, *Pictorial Guide*, p. 153.

permitted to make use of the library, the subscription being 30s. per annum ; consequently the institution was in anything but a flourishing condition, but, by Mr. Jabet's efforts, the committee were induced to lower the annual subscription to one guinea, and to throw the library open to all who chose to become members, irrespective of proprietorship. The result has been that this institution has become one of the most flourishing and successful subscription libraries in the provinces.

Of the Society of Artists we may only add here, that a Spring Exhibition of Water-Colour Drawings has been established in connection therewith, so that its rooms are now open to the public eight months of the year.

The Royal Birmingham and Midland Counties' Art Union has its offices in the Society's Rooms, and from its walls the winners select their art-prizes.

Of the other literary and scientific societies in our midst, we need only here enumerate the Birmingham and Edgbaston Debating Society, the Birmingham Law Society (which has a valuable law library), the Birmingham Medical Institute, (this institution also possesses a valuable library), the Birmingham Natural History and Microscopical Society, and the Birmingham Philosophical Society. There are now Literary Institutes on the plan of the Birmingham and Midland Institute, at Perry Barr, Harborne, Moseley and Balsall Heath, and King's Heath.

CHAPTER VI.

CHARITABLE INSTITUTIONS; 1841—1879.

The General Hospital ; new wing erected—The Queen's Hospital—Lying-in Charity—The Ear and Throat Infirmary—The Orthopædic and Spinal Hospital—The Homœopathic Hospital—General Institution for the Blind—The Children's Hospital—The Eye Infirmary —Women's Hospital—Sir Josiah Mason's Orphanage and Almshouse—The James Memorial Almhouses at Nechells.

THE history of the local charities during the period under notice is one of the pleasantest records of prosperity in well-doing which it can fall to the lot of a town historian to chronicle.

In connection with the General Hospital we have here to record that in 1857 a new wing was erected (chiefly out of the funds realised by the Aston Hall Fêtes) from the designs of Messrs. Martin and Chamberlain, making provision for 20 additional beds, and for a dispensary, physicians' and surgeons' room, and other offices. The 20 beds and the furniture of the ward were generously provided by Mr. J. C. Cohen ; and these increased the total number of beds to about 240. We cannot here enter into minute detail as to the work of the hospital ; but may state, from the last published annual report, that the number of in-patients admitted during 1878 was 3,041—

2,266 of which were admitted without tickets ; the out-patients of the same year numbered 25,655. The amount derived from the Triennial Musical Festivals during this period will be found in the history of the Festivals.

One of the first charitable movements in this period, and one which resulted in the founding of an institution second only to the General Hospital, was that set on foot by Mr. W. Sands Cox for the establishment of a Clinical Hospital in connection with the Royal School of Medicine and Surgery, now better known as the Queen's College. The proposal was first made in a letter from Mr. Cox to the Rev. J. T. Law, the then Chancellor of the Diocese of Lichfield, in November, 1839 ; and that gentleman responded by contributing £1,000 rent-charge on land in Bath Row. The Rev. Dr. Warneford seconded the liberality of Mr. Law by a donation of £1,000 towards the proposed institution, and public subscriptions flowed in to a sufficiently large extent to justify the promoters in commencing operations. The first stone of the Queen's Hospital, as it came to be called, was laid by Earl Howe on the 18th of June, 1840, and the wards were opened for the reception of patients in the year. The building was erected from the designs of Messrs. Bateman and Drury, and consisted of a centre and two wings, approached by a portico, surmounted by the arms of the Rev. Dr. Warneford. The entire cost was £8,746.

In 1847 a penny subscription was undertaken by the artisans of Birmingham (who have always taken special interest in this charity) which realised the noble sum of £935 1s. 3d., and on the 28th of December, 1848, the funds of the charity were further augmented by the noble sum of £1,070 as the result of a special concert at the Town Hall, gratuitously given for that purpose by the "Swedish Nightingale," Jenny Lind.

We have already recorded the efforts of Mr. J. W. Walsh on behalf of this institution, in organising the great Aston Fêtes in 1856, and we need only mention here the great assistance rendered by the Hospital Sunday and Hospital Saturday movements to this, among other institutions. In 1867 the Hospital Committee entered into an agreement for the purchase of the house and grounds of St. Martin's Rectory, adjoining the Hospital, for the extension of the building, in order to provide for the increasing necessities of the Out-patient Department. The great proportion of the cost of this extension was contributed by the working classes of the town; and the first stone of the new building was laid by Lord Leigh, on the 4th of December, 1871. A hymn, specially written for the occasion by the late Canon Kingsley, was sung by a choir of 1,000 children from the Birmingham Schools' Choral Union; and after the ceremony of the stone-laying, the event was celebrated by a luncheon. The new building was opened on the 7th of November, 1873, and on the 1st of

January, 1876, partly in consideration of the noble assistance which had been so willingly rendered by the working classes, the Hospital was made free. Nearly 40,000 patients have been received by this Hospital since its foundation, and the total income during last year amounted to £10,771 6s. and the expenditure to £7,703 5s.

In 1842 the Lying-in Hospital was instituted, for the reception of poor women during their confinement. The work of the charity was carried on in the building now used as the Children's Hospital, in Broad Street, but in 1868 it was resolved to change it into a Lying-in Charity for the provision of medical attendance for poor married women during confinements at their own homes, free of expense, and the building in Broad Street was vacated. The business of the charity is now carried on in Newhall Street.

In 1844 an Institution for the Relief of Deafness was founded by Mr. William Dufton, and was first carried on in Cannon Street; afterwards it was removed to Cherry Street, and subsequently to 45, Ann Street, where the Eye and Ear Dispensary was amalgamated with it, and, as there was already an excellent Eye Hospital in existence, that department of the treatment was discontinued; and as great attention was at that time being devoted to the various diseases of the throat, as being intimately associated with the organ of hearing, the energies of the staff were directed entirely to the subject of ear and throat diseases, and the amalgamated institutions took the new name of the Ear and Throat Infirmary. The institution was again removed, and now has its home in Newhall Street under the same roof as the Orthopædic and Spinal Hospital.

Of the last-named charity, which has already been noticed in a preceding chapter, we have only to mention here that it was removed from place to place, and at length found a home in Great Charles Street, in 1858, "and from that time," says Dr. Warden, "its progress and prosperity

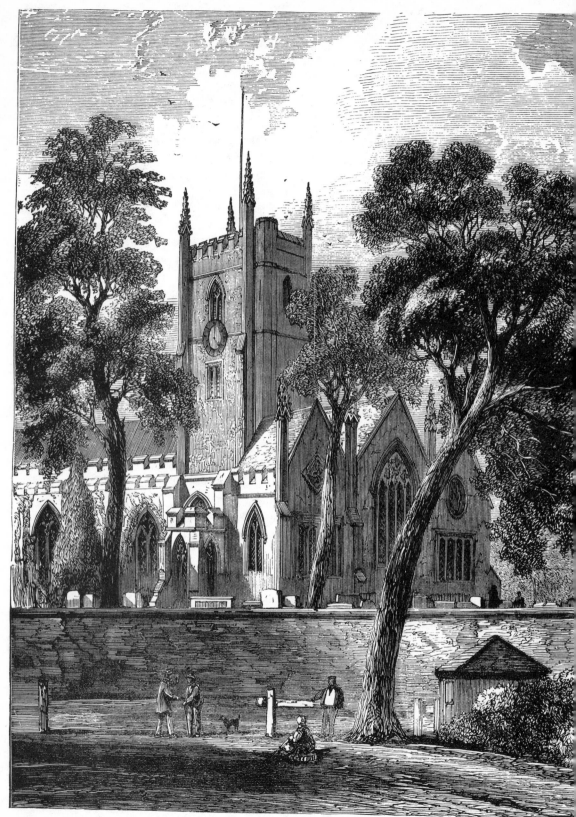

HANDSWORTH OLD CHURCH.

may be dated." The premises formerly occupied by the Institution of Mechanical Engineers, at the corner of Newhall Street and Great Charles Street, were obtained in 1877 for the purposes of this and the last-mentioned charity.

Homœopathy was first introduced into Birmingham in 1845; a Dispensary was opened in Great Charles Street in the same year, but larger and more convenient premises being required, a house was in the Old Square opened as a Homœopathic Hospital and Dispensary, in May, 1847. In 1866, the friends of the institution, encouraged by the liberality of Sir Josiah Mason and Mr. R. L. Chance, who offered to contribute £1,000 each towards the erection of a new building, resolved at a fitting time to commence a vigorous canvass for that purpose; and in 1873, a suitable site having been obtained in Easy Row, at a cost of £7,000, one-half of the new building was erected from a design by Mr. Yeoville Thomason, and opened on the 23rd of November in the same year.

The General Institution for the Blind (commenced originally as a private establishment by two ladies in 1816), was formed into a public institution on the 24th of April, 1848, and occupied premises in Broad Street. On the third anniversary of its establishment, April 23rd, 1851, the first stone was laid. of a new and more suitable building, in Carpenter Road, Edgbaston, and the institution entered upon its new abode on the 22nd of July, 1852. The building was erected in the Elizabethan style, and cost upwards of £12,000; and there are excellent playgrounds and gardens adjoining. The course of instruction given to the inmates, includes music (special attention being given to the organ), reading, and arithmetic, the latter by means of pegs and boards; geography is taught by the aid of raised maps and globe; and the useful arts of brush and basket making are also taught. In the year ending June, 1879, the number of indoor pupils had been 76,—48 males and 28 females; the sales of articles made by the inmates during the same year, had realised £1,922 5s. 11d., the income for the year, was £4,159 17s. 10d., and the expenditure £4,252 7s. 5d.

In June, 1861, a private meeting was held at the instance of Dr. T. P. Heslop, and presided over by the Mayor (the late Mr. A. Ryland), out of the deliberations of which arose one of the most successful of our modern local charities, the Free Hospital for Sick Children. Early in the following month a more public meeting was held in the Council Chamber, Moor Street, presided over by the Rev. Dr. Miller, at which the work was formally resolved upon, and a provisional committee appointed to make arrangements for the opening of the Hospital. After some deliberation, the Committee obtained a suitable building—that formerly used for the purposes of the Polytechnic Institution, for which they paid £2,100. At the first annual meeting of the Hospital, it was stated that, although no canvass had been made, donations had been sent in to the amount of £1,100.

In 1867-8 a handsome building was erected as a separate out-patient department, on the opposite side of the street, on a piece of land leased from the trustees of Lench's Trust. The new building was erected from designs by Martin and Chamberlain, at a cost of about £3,000, and was opened on the 11th of January, 1869. In this year, too, the Committee obtained from the managers of the Lying-in Charity, the commodious building in Broad Street, formerly used as a Hospital, and after being considerably improved in appearance (a handsome gateway entrance and boundary railing being erected at the joint expense of Dr. Heslop and Mr. C. E. Mathews, the honorary secretary), it was opened as an in-patient department, and the old building, in Steelhouse Lane, was vacated. A new wing was added in 1875, for the reception of infection cases, and the building now forms, with its pleasant grounds facing the street, one of the brightest and pleasantest objects in that neighbourhood. The income in

1878 was £3,289 6s. 9d., and the expenditure £4,190 16s. 3d., and since this noble institution was founded it has received 10,365 patients within its walls, and has further relieved out-patients to the number of 191,830, and home-patients to the number of 2,527, making a grand total of 204,722.

The Eye Infirmary, originally established in Cannon Street, was, after the decease of the Polytechnic Institution, removed to its premises in Steelhouse Lane, and subsequently to the front portion of the almost historic Royal Hotel, in Temple Row, which they still occupy.

In 1871 a Hospital was founded for the reception and treatment of Women afflicted with diseases peculiar to their sex. " It consists," says Dr. Langford, " of an Out and In-patient free and paying department. All women whose average weekly family earnings do not exceed 30s. ; all women having more than three children whose average weekly family earnings do not exceed 40s. are at once admitted. All paupers and all women whose earnings are beyond these limits, have their cases submitted to the decision of the House Committee. The hospital was opened for out-patients in October, 1871, and for in-patients in December of the same year. The building was at that time in the Crescent ; but in 1878 the In-patient Department was removed to more convenient premises at Spark Hill, in which the necessary alterations and additions having been made, the work of the charity is carried on under the most favourable conditions as to situation and surroundings. Miss Ryland, to whom the house at Spark Hill belongs, gave £500 towards the alterations, and a lease at a nominal rental for 42 years. The number of beds is eighteen. In the same year the Out-patient Department was removed to the Upper Priory—a building tasteful in design, and admirably adapted for its purpose."*

We have already recorded the endowment of Sir Josiah Mason's Orphanage, at Erdington, and

it may here suffice to quote from the *Birmingham Red Book* the following interesting account of this institution, and of the Almshouses founded by the same large-hearted philanthropist:—

" The Almshouses are situate on the turnpike road from Birmingham to Sutton, at the corner of Sheep Street, and were built in the year 1858, one portion as Almshouses, and the other for an Orphanage. There is accommodation in the Almshouse portion for 30 women, spinsters or widows of the age of fifty years or more. Each inmate is provided with a furnished house, coal, gas, and other advantages. The portion which was originally the Orphanage is now converted into a home for girls educated at the Orphanage, who may be out of service or suffering from sickness, and is under the care of a matron. The new Orphanage, erected on part of the Orphanage estates, is a noble building, situate a short distance from the Chester Road, at Erdington. The foundation stone was laid by Josiah Mason himself, privately, on the 19th of September, 1860, and the building was finished and first occupied in 1868. In addition to the expenditure of £60,000 on the building, the founder has endowed the institutions with land and building estates of the estimated value of £200,000. No publicity was given to this munificent gift until the twelve months prescribed by the statute had elapsed after the date of the deed, when, on the 29th of July, 1869, the institution and the estates were handed over to seven trustees, who, together with the founder, compose the present board of management. On his death, the trustees will be increased by the appointment of seven others by the Town Council of Birmingham. The inmates of the Orphanage are to be "lodged, clothed, fed, maintained, educated," and brought up at the exclusive cost of " the Orphanage income." There is no restriction whatever as to locality, nationality, or religious persuasion. In the year 1874 an additional separate wing was built, consisting of dormitories and a schoolroom for 150 boys, connected with the main building by a large dining hall capable of accommodating 500 inmates. The Institution is now capable of accommodating 300 girls, 150 boys, and 50 infants, boys, who all meet together for meals and prayers, but are separated as to school and dormitories. The number of inmates admitted to the Institution since its commencement has been as follows :—Girls, 312, of whom 27 have died, 153 have been sent to service or returned to friends, and 202 are now in the Orphanage ; boys, 223, of whom 5 have died, 103 have been sent to employment or returned to friends and 113 now remain in the Orphanage. The rules permit the admission of boys from 7 to 10 years old, and girls from 4 to 10 years. Certificates are required of marriage, death of father, death of mother, and birth of child."

A neat block of almshouses or memorial cottages have been erected at Nechells by the daughters of the late Mr. Howell James, in memory of their father, and of their brother, John Howell James. They are capable of accommodating 31 inmates, widows, single women, and married couples—whose age is above 60, and who are also natives of, or resident in, Birmingham, or within a distance of five miles.

CHAPTER VII.

THE TRIENNIAL MUSICAL FESTIVALS:

Third Period, 1834-1879.

The first Festival in the Town Hall—Mendelssohn in Birmingham—" St. Paul "—The " Lobgesang "—First Performance of the " Elijah "—Bust of Mendelssohn—The Mendelssohn Fragments—" Eli "—Testimonial to Costa—" Judith "—" Naaman "—" The Woman of Samaria "—" St. Peter "—" The Light of the World "—Macfarren's " Resurrection "—Wagner's " Holy Supper "—Rossini's " Moses in Egypt," etc.

WE turn now once more to the Musical Festivals, and proceed to record the principal events in the third and most important period in their history. The last Festival held in St. Philip's Church took place in 1829, and, according to custom, the next should have been held in 1832, but, as the new Town Hall was at that time in course of erection, its was decided to wait for its completion, in order that the Festival might be held therein. It was not until 1834, therefore, that the building was sufficiently advanced to allow of the holding of the first Festival within its walls. The performances consisted of a new oratorio by Neukomm, entitled " David," a portion of the same composer's " Mount Sinai," the " Messiah," and the closing part of Spohr's " Last Judgment ;" two evening concerts comprising the usual miscellaneous selections, and a performance at the theatre of scenes from " Otello " and " Anna Boleyn." The Festival commenced on the 7th of October, and on this occasion the prices of admission were first raised to the present standard. The receipts were £13,527, and the profits £5,489, out of which £1,200 was paid for lengthening the Town Hall to form an organ recess, and £254 towards the expenses connected with the organ; so that the sum actually paid to the treasurers of the Hospital was £4,035.

The Festival of 1837 is memorable on account of the first appearance of Mendelssohn here, and the performance of his oratorio " St. Paul." A short new oratorio by Neukomm, on the subject of the " Ascension," was also given, and on the Wednesday evening the opera of " Semiramide " was performed at the Theatre, Madame Grisi sustaining the leading character. A new oratorio, " The Triumph of Faith," (founded on the story of Peter the Hermit), by Hæser, was also performed at this Festival. The produce of this year's celebration (which commenced on the 19th of September,) was £11,900, but the profit only amounted to £2,776 in consequence of the numerous and costly engagements.

In 1840 the " Lobgesang " of Mendelssohn was performed, and among other works, new to the Birmingham Festivals, Rossini's " La Gazza Ladra," and Gnecco's " La Prova," Mendelssohn's overture to the Midsummer Night's Dream." The proceeds were £11,613, and the profits £4,503.

The Festival of 1843 does not call for special mention, no complete oratorio being performed except the " Messiah." It commenced on the 19th of September ; the proceeds fell lower than usual, amounting only to £8,822, and the profits to £2,916.

The most important of all the series of Festivals was that of 1846, to which attaches the special interest arising out of the first performance of Mendelssohn's great masterpiece, the " Elijah," thereat (on the 26th of August), which evoked the greatest enthusiasm, perhaps, ever manifested at a musical performance in this country.

"At the close of the performance, the long pent-up excitement, which had been gathering strength with every new feature in the oratorio, burst forth in a torrent of applause, renewed again and again. Conventional rules were forgotten; the frigidity of etiquette is a feeble barrier to the expression of feeling, intense and long suppressed. Hearts that had not melted, save by the heavenly potency of 'the Messiah,' acknowledged a kindred power in this new development of the resources of art. Fair hands and earnest voices paid homage to the genius of the age. By the universal fiat of the vast assembly the composition was placed high on the roll of Fame, with the hallowed glories of Handel, of Beethoven, and of Haydn. The illustrious composer bowed his acknowledgments, and his agitation was visible. He descended and tried to escape from the torrent of approbation; but another roar, in which audience and orchestra joined, called him again before them, and with a modest air he responded to the greeting of the assembly."

There can be no doubt that much of the instantaneous appreciation of this great work on its first performance was due, as the *Times* pointed out, to "the zealous and artist-like unanimity" of the band and chorus, and for the latter, we read, "Mendelssohn, after thanking them, expressed his particular obligation to Mr. Stimpson, the Birmingham professor, who had for two months previously so well and effectively trained the local choir." The produce of this unique Festival was £11,638, and the net profit £5,508.

In 1849 the "Elijah" was repeated, and the "Messiah" occupied its usual place; "Israel in Egypt," the "Creation," and other well-known works were also performed. The receipts were £10,334, and the profits £2,448. Previous to this Festival, and shortly after the death of Mendelssohn, a bust of the great composer was executed by Mr. Peter Hollins, and was placed in front of the orchestra during the performances, and is now located on the landing of the principal staircase of the Town Hall.

The performances in 1852 included, besides the now traditional "Messiah" and "Elijah," Mendelssohn's fragment of an unfinished oratorio, the "Christus," his "Walpurgis Night," and the unfinished "Loreley," Haydn's "Creation,"

"Samson," and other works. The receipts were £11,925 and the profits £4,704.

The novelty of the Festival of 1855 was the new oratorio of "Eli," composed expressly for Birmingham by Mr. Costa, without fee or reward; desiring that the sum intended to be paid him should be given as a contribution to the funds of the General Hospital. It "proved a great success, both musically and in the marked applause which it elicited—the composer at the close of the performance being greeted with tumultuous applause, which was renewed when he appeared at the conductor's desk to begin the evening concert."* A silver group commemorative of a scene from the work was afterwards presented to him by the Committee "as a record of his disinterested liberality." Two new cantatas were also performed at the evening concerts during the Festival —Macfarren's "Leonora," and Mr. Howard Glover's "Tam o'Shanter." The receipts were £12,745 and the profits £4,090.

In 1858 a new oratorio, "Judith," by Mr. Henry Leslie, was performed. The other morning performances consisted of the "Elijah," "Eli," and the "Messiah." The gross receipts amounted to £11,141, and the profits to £2,731. "The meeting," says Mr. Bunce, "was arranged on a scale of unprecedented completeness, whether as regards the works selected for performance or the artistes to whom their interpretation was entrusted."

The Festival of 1861 may also be regarded as a most successful one; to the traditional performances of Tuesday and Thursday may be added the following list of works performed:—Handel's "Samson," Hummel's "Alma Virgo," Beethoven's Mass in D, Haydn's "Creation," "Judas Maccabæus," and a portion of "Israel in Egypt." The performance of Beethoven's Mass was warmly commended by the *Times* and obtained for the chorus the proud title (bestowed upon them by the leading journal) of "the champion choristers of England." The proceeds were £11,453, and the profits £3,043.

J. T. Bunce.

At the Festival of 1864 new laurels were added to the Birmingham wreath by the masterly performance of Beethoven's "Mount of Olives," in which Mdlle. Tietjens, Mr. Sims Reeves, and Mr. Santley sustained the solo parts. Besides the "Elijah" and "Messiah," a new oratorio, "Naaman," by Mr. Costa, was produced with great success. Mr. H. Smart's dramatic cantata "The Bride of Dunkerron," and Mr. A. Sullivan's "Kenilworth" formed the principal attractions of the evening concerts. The proceeds were £13,777, and the profits £5,256.

In 1867 the principal novelties comprised a sacred cantata, "The Woman of Samaria," by Rigby, appeared for the first time at a Birmingham Festival on this occasion.

The year 1873 was signalised by the greatest financial success ever attained by the Festival, the receipts being £16,076, and the profits, £6,577. The principal new work produced at this Festival was Mr. A. Sullivan's oratorio, "The Light of the World," and on this occasion H.R.H. the Duke of Edinburgh paid a visit to Birmingham for the express purpose of hearing this work.

The new works produced at the Festival of 1876 were Mr. F. Cowen's cantata, "The Corsair;" Professor G. A. Macfarren's oratorio, "The Resurrection;" Gade's sacred cantata,

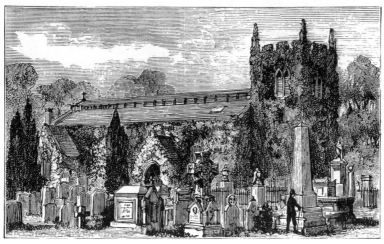

EDGBASTON OLD CHURCH.

Dr. Sterndale Bennett, Gounod's "Mass in G." (for the first time in Birmingham), Benedict's cantata, "The Legend of St. Cecilia," and Mr. J. F. Barnett's cantata, "The Ancient Mariner." The receipts amounted to £14,397, and the profits to £5,541.

In 1870 the new works were Benedict's oratorio, "St. Peter"; Dr. Ferdinand Hiller's cantata, "Nala and Damayanti;" and Mr. Barnett's cantata, "Paradise and the Peri." The receipts were £14,635, and the profits £6,195. Our gifted townsman, Mr. Vernon "Zion," and his secular cantata (performed here for the first time in England), "The Crusaders." Richard Wagner's Biblical scene, "The Holy Supper," was also produced, for the first time in this country, at this Festival. The proceeds amounted to £15,374, and the net profits, £6,071.

In 1879, the special features of the Festival consisted of the performance of Rossini's "Moses in Egypt," and of two new cantatas, "The Lay of the Bell," by Max Bruch, and "The Lyre and the Harp," by Saint Saens.

77

We have not space to mention the names of all the principal vocalists who have taken part in the festivals during the period under notice, but some idea of the completeness of the arrangements in this department may be gathered from the following list of a few of those who have graced these almost world-famous gatherings. At the earlier meetings of this period Madame Grisi, Clara Novello, Madame Caradori-Allan, Herr Staudigl, (the first and greatest representative of *Elijah*,) Signors Mario and Lablache, and Mr. Braham appeared ; and among the vocalists at the later meetings have been Mdlle. Adelina Patti, Mdlle. Tietjens, Mesdames Sainton-Dolby, Rudersdorff, Lemmens-Sherrington, Patey, Mdlle. Christine Nilsson, Mdlle. Ilma di Murska, and Miss Edith Wynne ; Messrs. Sims Reeves, Santley, Cummings, Weiss, Vernon Rigby, and Signor Foli.

We subjoin the usual tabulated statement of the financial results of the third period of the Festivals :

	Gross Produce. £		Net Profits. £
1834	...	13,527	...	5,489
1837	...	11,900	...	2,776
1840	...	11,613	...	4,503
1843	...	8,822	...	2,916
1846	...	11,638	...	5,508
1849	...	10,334	...	2,448
1852	...	11,925	...	4,704
1855	...	12,745	...	4,091
1858	...	11,141	...	2,731
1861	...	11,453	...	3,043
1864	...	13,777	...	5,256
1867	...	14,397	...	5,541
1870	...	14,635	...	6,195
1873	...	16,076	...	6,577
1876	...	15,374	...	6,071
1879	about 12,000	...	[Not yet ascertained.]

CHAPTER VIII.

AMUSEMENTS OF THE PEOPLE, 1841—1879
(Including the History of the Theatres during that period).

The Theatre Royal—Macready—First appearance of Mr. Sims Reeves—Hackett as Falstaff—Charles Dickens and the Amateurs—The Guild of Literature and Art—Madame Ristori—J. L. Toole—Tonk's Colosseum—Gustavus v. Brooke—The Moor Street Theatre—The Music Hall, Broad Street—Prince of Wales' Theatre—Shakesperian Revivals—Aston Lower Grounds—The Holte Theatre—Musical Societies—Miscellaneous Amusements.

IN the limited space now at our disposal, it will be impossible to attempt a full and complete history of the local stage or of the other public amusements during the past forty years : such a work would of itself require a goodly volume, and would well repay in its interest the labour bestowed upon it. All we propose to do in this chapter is to pick out a few examples of the amusements of the forty years comprised in our present record, and to notice the various places of amusement now in existence.

First, then, as to the " Old Theatre,"—as it is sometimes lovingly called—the early history of which has already been given in these pages. During the first year of this period the boards were once more graced by one whose first appearance had been made thereon—Mr. Macready—who commenced a five nights' engagement on the 12th of April, during which he appeared in " Hamlet," " Macbeth," " Richelieu," " Virginius," and " Werner." Later on (June 25th), he appeared for one night, sustaining the part of *Claude Melnotte*, in the " Lady of Lyons," for the first time in Birmingham.

Passing on to the year 1843, we pause for a moment to notice the first appearance in Birmingham of a vocalist of great promise, named Reeves,—the now world-famous tenor, Mr. Sims Reeves—of whom a contemporary critic observes : " This gentleman possesses a fine tenor voice, and sings with great purity of style; there is, however, a deficiency in his articulation, which requires correction."

In 1852 Mr. James Hackett, the celebrated American *Falstaff*, made his first appearance here in that impersonation.

The efforts on behalf of the national fund for the purchase of Shakespeare's House brought about that "Splendid Strolling" of which Mr. Forster makes record in his *Life of Charles Dickens*, and gave the people of Birmingham an opportunity of witnessing the performances of perhaps the most famous company of amateurs who ever "trod the boards." They appeared at the Theatre Royal on the 6th of June, 1848, in Ben Jonson's comedy of "Every Man in his Humour," in which Charles Dickens sustained the part of *Captain Bobadil*. This successful impersonation, with its picturesque make-up, has been immortalised on canvas by Mr. W. P. Frith, R.A.

The part of Old *Knowall* (which tradition assigns to Shakespeare as its original representative), was sustained on this occasion by Mr. Dudley Costello; Mr. Frederick Dickens sustained that of *Edward Knowall*; and among the other actors were Mark Lemon, John Forster, George Cruikshank, Frank Stone, Augustus Egg, G. Scharf, and Mrs. Cowden Clarke. The performance concluded with the farce entitled "Animal Magnetism," by Mrs. Inchbald, in which Dickens, Lemon, Cruikshank, G. H. Lewes, Miss A. Romer, and Miss Emmeline Montague appeared. The gross receipts amounted to £327.

A second performance was given by the amateurs, on the 27th of the same month, the piece selected on this occasion being the "Merry Wives of Windsor." The character of the fat knight was worthily sustained by Mark Lemon, (who in later years became somewhat famous in the same impersonation); to Charles Dickens was assigned the part of *Justice Shallow*, and to John Leech that of his cousin *Slender*. Other parts in the mirthful comedy were

sustained by Frank Stone, Augustus Egg, John Forster, G. H. Lewes, Dudley Costello, Frederick Dickens, F. W. Topham, Mrs. Cowden Clarke, and other members of the brilliant coterie, but in the whole comedy there was surely nothing more richly humorous than the representation of the character of the blustering swashbuckler, *Ancient Pistol*, by teetotal George Cruikshank! The receipts on this occasion amounted to £262.

A still more famous company of amateurs (with which Charles Dickens was also connected), appeared in Birmingham, on the 12th and 13th of May, 1852,—the Amateur Company of the Guild of Literature and Art. The play was a new one by Lord (then Sir E. Bulwer) Lytton, entitled "Not So Bad as We Seem," written expressly for the Members of the Guild; and the cast included the names of Charles Dickens, Wilkie Collins, John Forster, Mark Lemon, John Tenniel, Frank Stone, Augustus Egg, Charles Knight, Dudley Costello, R. H. Horne, and other well-known *littérateurs*. The piece was splendidly mounted, the scenes having been specially painted by Clarkson Stanfield, Louis Haghe, David Roberts, Telbin, John Absolon, and other eminent artists. Following Lord Lytton's brilliant comedy came a most amusing farce, produced under the joint authorship of Charles Dickens and Mark Lemon, entitled "Mr. Nightingale's Diary,"— a piece which the play-going public would be glad to see revived. In it, Mr. Dickens impersonated 'a half-waiter and a sort of a half-boots,' closely resembling our old friend Sam Weller; and further performed the remarkable feat of 'doubling'—or should we not say *sextupling*— that character with five others; while Mark Lemon, the other principal actor in the piece, undertook three parts. The price of admission to this noteworthy performance (which had previously been given before Her Majesty the Queen,) was seven shillings.

Another famous performance during this decade took place on the 5th of August, 1858, when

Madame Ristori appeared at the Theatre Royal, "for one night only," sustaining the part of *Elizabetha*, in "Elizabetha, Regina d'Inghleterra." She was supported by Mdlles. Ferroni and Tessero, and Signors Marjeroni, Bocconini, Glech, Tessero, and Bellotti Bon. Madame Ristori again appeared, on the 14th of July 1863, in her grand impersonation of *Medea*.

On October 25th, 1864, the most popular comedian of the present day, Mr. J. L. Toole, made his first appearance in Birmingham, in three pieces,—"The Pretty Horsebreaker," "Ici on Parle Francais," and "Oliver Twist." He subsequently appeared in the "Cricket on the Hearth," as *Caleb Plummer*, and in other of his now famous impersonations.

Of the many other eminent actors who have appeared at the Theatre Royal during the long period covered by the present chapter, we cannot further speak here, but it may suffice to say that, under the long and prosperous managerial career of the Messrs. Simpson (the late Mr. Mercer H. Simpson, senr., and his son, the present manager,) nearly every artist of note has fulfilled engagements at this house, and that almost every class of dramatic entertainment has, at one time or other, been presented therein ; so that the complete history of this classic theatre would be, in reality, the history of the English stage itself during this period.

In December, 1853, Mr. John Tonks opened Bingley Hall with an equestrian company, that building having been fitted up as an amphitheatre capable of holding 4,500 persons ; it bore the name of "Tonks's Colosseum. In the April of the following year Lord Byron's *Sardanapalus* was produced at this house ; and in July, Mr. Gustavus V. Brooke made his farewell bow here prior to his trip to Australia and California. He appeared as *Sir Giles Overreach* in "A New Way to pay Old Debts," also in the "Hunchback," "The Merchant of Venice," "The Lady of Lyons," "Romeo and Juliet," "Richelieu," "Othello," "The Wife," "Ham-

let," "The Stranger," and a new tragedy entitled "Unarno."

An application was made to the Magistrates in 1860 for a license to perform plays in the Amphitheatre in Moor Street, but was refused. On the 19th of March, 1861, however, the renewed application (made on behalf of Mr. J. C. Chute, who had taken the building at a rent of £475 per annum) was granted. The principal fare at the new house consisted of pieces of a sensational or melodramatic character, such as "Pauline ; or, the Children of the Night ; " "The Pirate of the Gulph," "Nick of the Woods," "Cartouche," and similar productions.

In 1856 a Music Hall was erected in Broad Street (on the front portion of the grounds of the late Bingley House), by a joint-stock company, at a cost (including the organ) of £12,000. It was intended to be used for concerts of high-class music, and was opened under distinguished patronage, with two oratorio performances, in which Madame Clara Novello, Madame Weiss, Messrs. Sims Reeves, Montem Smith, and Alfred Mellon took part, on the 3rd and 4th of September, 1856. It did not, however, prove very successful as a Music Hall, and on the 13th of May, 1862, a theatrical license was applied for and granted, on the understanding that only such entertainments as those of Mr. and Mrs. Howard Paul, Mr. and Mrs. German Reed, and others, should be given. In October of the same year the newly licensed theatre was taken by Mr. James Scott, of the Belfast, Theatre, but he only retained the management a few weeks, being succeeded in November by Mr. W. H. Swanborough who opened it as the Royal Music Hall Operetta House, for the performance of vaudevilles, operettas, and light pieces generally. In the following April Mr. Charles Mathews appeared at this house, and here Mr. H. J. Byron made his first appearance in Birmingham, in his own burlesque of "Ali Baba, or the Thirty-nine Thieves." This theatre (which in commemoration of the Royal Wedding on the 10th of March in this year, had taken the name of "the Prince of Wales' Operetta House,") is also noteworthy as the one at which Mr. Sothern's unique impersonation of Lord Dundreary was first presented to a Birmingham audience.

For some time, however, the fortunes of the Prince of Wales' Theatre, as it came afterwards to be called, were not of the brightest, and after several changes it passed into the hands of the present lessee, Mr. James Rodgers, in November 1866, and under his judicious management it has become one of the most prosperous and successful theatres in the provinces. In 1876 it was entirely reconstructed; the old low front was removed, and handsome shops erected in its place, and the interior of the theatre, having been re-modelled and decorated, was rendered more perfect in its acoustic properties, and brighter and more cheerful in appearance. This house has been distinguished of late years by the brilliant Shakesperian and other revivals produced thereat, among which special mention should be made of the late Mr. Charles Calvert's revivals of "Henry the Fifth," "Henry the Eight," and "Sardana-palus," and Mr. Coleman's revival of "Henry the Fifth." Mr. Henry Irving usually appears at this house, when on his provincial tours, and has performed here in "Hamlet," "Richard III.," "Louis XI.," "The Bells," and other of his great impersonations. Mr. and Mrs. Kendal, Mr. Hare, Mr. J. L. Toole, and many other leading artists have also appeared from time to time at this theatre.

In connection with the beautiful pleasure grounds laid out by Mr. H. G. Quilter, at Aston, known as the Aston Lower Grounds, a third local theatre (the "Holte") was established in April, 1879. A handsome block of buildings (on the model of the Alexandra Palace, Muswell Hill,) have been erected by the Lower Grounds Company, in the centre of the increasingly popular grounds, comprising a large and complete Aquarium, with a series of Fine Art Galleries over it, and (at right angles therewith), a Great Hall 220 feet long, by 90 feet wide, suitable either for concerts or theatrical performances. On three sides of this splendid hall are broad galleries, and at the further end is a handsome stage, suitable either for modern comedy or for elaborate spectacular pieces. When the building is used for theatrical performances the floor is raised, and about three-fourths of the hall enclosed, leaving the portion nearest the entrance as a commodious vestibule or promenade. By this means the theatre proper is shut off from noise and interruption, and the acoustic proper-ties of the house are thereby greatly improved. During the present year (1879), theatrical performances have been given by the late Mr. Craven Robertson's comedy company, Mr. and Mrs. Billington, Mr. Joseph Eldred, Mr. J. W. Ryley, Mr. T. W. Robertson's *Caste* Company, Mr. Durand's EnglishOpera Company, and others. Musical performances have been given from time to time, and among the works performed by the Holte Choral Society have been Rossini's "Stabat Mater," Mendelssohn's "Loreley," the "Messiah," Gade's cantata, "Zion," and Mr. T. Anderton's cantata, "John Gilpin." A series of ballad concerts have also been given. We have not space to describe at length all the attractions of this most popular resort, but it may suffice to say that it has taken the position of a "people's palace," similar to the large establish-ments of Sydenham and Muswell Hill, and bids fair to become in future the most popular place of amusement in the midland counties. Views of the grounds and buildings are given on page 575.

As in former periods already noticed in these pages the miscellaneous entertainments of the forty years covered by this chapter have been numerous and very varied, from the high-class concert to the performances of the so-called Concert Halls. Birmingham is in a marked degree a musical town, and hence we may say of musical societies and performances that thei name is Legion. The Festival Choral Society give a series of high-class Concerts every season; another series is given by Messrs. Harrison, at which nearly every vocalist of note has appeared; a third series (chiefly of orchestral music), is given under the direction of Mr. Stockley; a fourth is given by the Philharmonic Society; and within the last few weeks (Nov. 1879), an association has been formed at the suggestion of the Mayor (Jesse Collings, Esq.,) called the Birmingham Musical Association, for the purpose of providing cheap concerts for the people, the first of which was given on Saturday evening, November 8th.

Of miscellaneous entertainments we can only mention a few here. We have already referred to the first readings by Charles Dickens, on behalf of the Birmingham and Midland Institute, and these, as most of our readers are doubtless aware, were the precursors of a series of public readings given by the great novelist at intervals from that date until within a few months of his death. He appeared in Birmingham as a public reader on several sub-sequent occasions, the last being during his farewell tour, on the 1st and 2nd of April, 1869.

On the 27th of December, 1850, Albert Smith paid us a visit, and gave his entertainment entitled "The Overland Route," at the Royal Hotel. In January, 1857, William Brough lectured on "Burlesque." The notorious P. T. Barnum also paid us a visit, in February, 1859, and imparted to the shrewd, money-making "Brums" his notions on the "Science of Money-making, and of Humbug generally." On the 25th of February, 1862, the genial editor of Punch, Mr. Mark Lemon, appeared at the Music Hall, Broad Street, and delivered his Lecture, "About London and Westminster," illustrating his discourse with views of some of the places referred to. The second part of the Lecture was delivered on March 4th.

The same gentleman, in February, 1869, appeared for the first time in Birmingham in his impersonation of *Falstaff*,—a character which

he had essayed in the golden days of the "splendid strollers,"—but this time the fat knight's adventures were those of the road rather than of his Windsor amours. The scenes were selected from the two parts of "Henry the Fourth," in which the editor of *Punch* was supported by Messrs. Herbert Crellin, W. L. Branscombe, Harry Lemon, (his son), W. B. Clarke, Master Couran, and Miss Rose Garland. The merry little company paid us another visit in the following October, on which occasion Birmingham was honoured by the presence on one evening of three noteworthy entertainers; Charles Dickens addressing the members of the Midland Institute, Mark Lemon playing in the scenes from "Henry the Fourth," at the Exchange, and Benjamin Webster in the "Willow Copse," at the Theatre Royal.

Other entertainers of divers sorts have fre-quently appeared in our midst: Frederic Maccabe, issuing the pleasing mandate, "Begone Dull Care!" George Grossmith, opening up un-explored mines of English humour; J. C. M. Bellew and Walter Montgomery have charmed their large circles of admirers by their rendering of the masterpieces of literature; "drawing-room entertainments" innumerable have been given, by Mr. and Mrs. Howard Paul, Thurton, Woodin, Charles Du-Val, George Grossmith, junr., and many others of note; Panoramas, Negro Minstrels, Conjurors, Ventrilo-quists, and every variety of diversion, have helped to swell the catalogue of the amusements of the people. And on all holidays and throughout the summer months, the "iron horse" has carried out into the pure country air, or away to the seaside, thousands of the toiling artisans of Birmingham; and excursions are now made in a single day to far-off places which in the 'good old times' would have taken weeks to reach. There are few Birmingham artisans nowadays who have not paid more than one visit to the seaside, or who have not climbed the hills of Wales, or explored the little world of the metropolis.

CHAPTER IX.

LOCAL TRADE AND COMMERCE, 1841—1879.

Brassfoundry—The Gun Trade—Coining—The Button Trade—Electro-Plating—Glass Manufacture—The Steel Pen Trade—Pin-making—
Miscellaneous Trades—The Coffee Houses—Birmingham Banks.

WE cannot bring to a close this history of our town and its people without some notice of the trade and commerce of Birmingham during the second half of the nineteenth century. It would be out of place, however, in a general work of this character, to enter into minute details respecting each branch of industry; it will suffice, therefore, to give here an outline of the principal industries of the town as they now exists.

First among our local trades come the various departments of brassfoundry, in which about 11,000 persons are employed, and in which metal to the value of upwards of £2,300,000 is used in a single year. The various articles made from this metal comprise bells and general household fittings, plumbers' brassfoundry, tubes, lamps, chandeliers, gas-fittings, wire and sheathing, bedsteads, ordnance and naval brassfoundry, and ecclesiastical brass-work. Messrs. Winfield are the principal manufacturers of general brass-work; Messrs. S. B. Whitfield, Greening and Fardon, and Brierley and Co., of brass bedsteads; Messenger and Sons, and Hinks and Son, of lamps and chandeliers; Hardman and Co., Camm Brothers, and Jones and Willis, of ecclesiastical brass-work; and Martineau and Smith, of brass taps, etc.

The gun trade, which employs about 10,000 persons, may rank second among our industries, and although not in so flourishing a condition now, as it was before the establishment of the Enfield Small Arms Factory, it still maintains an important position, as may be seen from the annual reports of the Guardians of the Proof House, from which we learn that in 1878 the number of gun-barrels proved was 558,815, an increase of 100,000 over the returns of the preceding year. It is difficult to mention even all the principal manufacturers in so extensive a branch of industry, but perhaps the largest firm is that of the Birmingham Small Arms Company, Small Heath. Mr. W. Greener, Messrs. Cooper and Goodman, Westley Richards and Co., and W. L. Sargant are also well-known firms.

The industry introduced by Matthew Boulton, of making good current coin of the realm, (as distinguished from those counterfeits which were 'coin'd by stealth' and brought the town into evil repute), is still carried on by Ralph Heaton and Co., at the Mint, in Icknield Street, where coins are struck for the British and other Governments, including China, Turkey, Italy, and the Republics of South America.

Buttons are still manufactured in Birmingham in large quantities by many well-known firms, principal among which may be mentioned Messrs. Green, Cadbury, and Richards, Smith and Wright, Watts and Manton, and Hammond, Turner and Sons.

Perhaps the most interesting of the modern industries of Birmingham is that of electro-plating, which was introduced in 1838 by Messrs. Elkington, Mason, and Co., whose show-rooms form one of the greatest attractions to every intelligent stranger visiting the town, and whose productions have contributed so much to the interest of the great international exhibitions. Here the artistic workmanship of former ages is reproduced as if by magic; the choice productions of a Cellini or a Ghiberti are copied in the most faithful manner. " Here are more than ' apples of gold in pictures of silver' ; here are the trees that bear both, and the leaves that guard and garnish them, all done to Nature's best truth, life, and beauty. Here are her most exquisite ferns, with their crinkly foliage in tracery as delicate as she herself could work. Here are the master thoughts and master touches of artistic genius in designs of infinite variety."* It is not merely in reproduction that this firm has been successful, but in the production of original designs, in the variety of prize cups, shields, and other articles they have from time to time produced. Mention may also be made of the bronze statues of Burke and Goldsmith, by the late Mr. Foley, and of the beautiful *cloisonné* enamels produced at this famous manufactory. There are now many other firms in the electro-plate trade, among whom may be mentioned Messrs. Horace Woodward and Co., Wm. Spurrier, Johnson and Co., and Collis and Co.

Next to the electro-plate trade in point of interest is the now very extensive glass manufacturing industry of Birmingham, in which the firms of Chance Brothers and Co., F. and C. Osler, Stone, Fawdry, and Stone, and Lloyd and Summerfield are best known. The word " glass " calls up various and widely different associations, from the humble but useful article which admits light to the dwelling of the cottager and artisan to the finely cut and richly ornamented objects of art for which Venice has been celebrated for centuries ; thence to the powerful lenses used in lighthouses, and to the material used in the erection of the great Crystal Palace at Sydenham ; and above all, perhaps, to the

> " Storied windows, richly dight,
> Casting a dim religious light,"

which adorn alike both the stately cathedral and the humble village church. For the latter Messrs. Hardman and Mr. Swaine Bourne are

---

* BURRITT : *Walks in the Black Country*, p 118.

famous. Messrs. Osler have almost a world-wide reputation for ornamental glass. " If the vote were taken," says Elihu Burritt, " of the million of different countries who saw what that first Crystal Palace contained, as to the most impressive, attractive, and best remembered object, a majority would say that it was Osler's Crystal Fountain. It was a magnificent centre-piece for all the splendid surroundings of art and industry within those walls. It seemed a gorgeous stalactite from that concave sea of glass which gave translucent roofage to the great spectacle of human skill and toil. But that fairy fountain was only the beginning of productions which have excited equal admiration."

If a stranger were asked for what particular article of manufacture Birmingham had become most famous, he would in all probability select the steel pen as the representative of local industry, and when it is mentioned that twenty millions of these useful articles are made here every week it will be readily conceded that such a guess would be pretty near the mark. In its early days the steel pen was an expensive article, costing as much as twelve shillings a dozen, and they were, in proportion, more valued than at the present time. With a single steel pen, presented to him by Mr. Gillott, Charles Reade wrote the whole of his powerful story, " It is Never too late to Mend," though, in all probability the poor ill-used (or should we say well-used) nib must have been almost past mending by the time it had completed its task. A curious anecdote is quoted by Dr. Langford in his *Handbook*, from the *Manchester Examiner*, as to the destination of some of the Birmingham-made pens. Writing from Geneva, in the present year (1879) a correspondent of that journal says : " I went the other day into a stationer's shop to buy a box of pens. I asked for English pens. ' *Ma foi*,' said the shopman, ' we have hardly anything but English pens.' ' But these are German,' I remarked. ' Not a bit of it ; they have a German name, it is true, but they all come from Birmingham. You have Ruder, of Berlin ; Schmidt, of Frankfort ; Schneider, of Bremen ; but they make no pens, these fellows, they buy them in England. Even our *Plume Federali* (Federal pen), so much used here, and which all the world believes to be Swiss, is English made. Make your choice, Monsieur, every one of these boxes is from Birmingham." Of course the principal manufacturers of this article are the world-famous Gillotts, and Perry & Co.. (late Josiah Mason) ; but there are now many other well-known firms, as Messrs. Hinks and Wells, John Mitchell, and Brandauer & Co.

After the pen trade comes that of pin-making, of which also Birmingham is the centre. Every schoolboy will recollect the old descriptions of pin making, in which we learned that it required ten persons to make a single pin,—though strictly speaking *fourteen* persons were employed in the various stages of its manufacture—but all this has long been changed, by the invention by an American named Lemuel Wright, of a machine for making a perfect pin during the revolution of a single wheel. This machine, which was introduced in 1824, has since been perfected, and these useful but sometimes dangerous articles are now turned out in such quantities as to add new force every day to the wonder as to " where all the pins go."

There are many other local trades of which we cannot speak fully here ; as, for instance, the manufacture of wood screws, of which Messrs. Nettlefold (late Nettlefold and Chamberlain) turn out about 200,000 gross a week ; cut nail making, die sinking (specially represented by Mr. Joseph Moore, of whose work there are some fine specimens in the Corporation Art Gallery) ; Jewellery, which, in good times is a very important trade, (in which Messrs. Bragg are famous) ; Wire Drawing, in which branch of industry Messrs. Horsfall, of Hay Mills, (where the first Atlantic Cable was made) are perhaps the largest manufacturers in the world ; Rope-making ; Tin Plate Work ; the Papier-Mâché

trade, (already described in these pages) ; and many others. We must not omit a brief reference to the famous establishment of Messrs. Tangye Brothers, (manufacturers of Hydraulic and General Machinery), whose hydraulic jacks were used in launching the *Great Eastern*, and in raising the huge Monolith, recently erected ' on the banks of Thames.'

Mention may not inappropriately be made here, as it affects the condition of the artisan population of the town, of the enterprise of the Birmingham Coffee House Company, Limited, in providing for the necessities of the people by the establishment of handsome and attractive Coffee Houses, in all the principal thoroughfares, in which tea, coffee, milk and cocoa are provided at a cheap rate, and every means adopted to render these houses a counter-attraction to the public house or the gin palace. More than a dozen of these useful establishments have now been opened by the Company, and the fact that all are doing well is a sufficient evidence that already much has been done to ameliorate the condition of the toiling multitude in this great hive of industry.

The banking companies of Birmingham are as follows :—The Birmingham Branch of the Bank of England, Bennett's Hill ; Lloyds Banking Company, Limited, which has its head office in the handsome building erected in 1869, in Ann Street, but also continues to occupy the old premises in High Street, and has branch establishments in Deritend, Great Hampton Street, Five Ways, and Aston Road ; the Birmingham Banking Company, Bennett's Hill ; the National Provincial Bank of England, which now occupies the handsome modern building erected on the site of the old premises in 1869, at the corner of Bennett's Hill and Waterloo Street ; the Birmingham and Midland Bank, a handsome building in New Street and Stephenson Place, erected in 1867-8 ; the Birmingham, Dudley, and District (formerly the Birmingham and District) Bank, in Colmore Row, (erected in 1868-69,) of which there is also a branch establishment in

Hockley Hill; the Birmingham Joint Stock Bank (formerly Attwood, Spooner and Marshall's) in New Street, the premises of which have been rebuilt very recently, (with branches in Temple Row West and Great Hampton Street); the Birmingham, Worcester City and County Banking Company, Limited, Cherry Street, for whom new premises are now being erected in Ann Street; the Union Bank of Birmingham, Waterloo Street; the Staffordshire Joint Stock Bank, New Street; and Messrs. Goode, Marr, & Co., Upper Priory.

CHAPTER X.

PUBLIC BUILDINGS, AND APPEARANCE OF THE TOWN, 1841—1879.

Old Streets swept away—Snow Hill Station—The Old Inkleys—Ann Street and Colmore Row—The Council House—The Post Office—New Churches—Private Improvements--Street-paving—Street Gardens—The Suburbs—Aston—Handsworth—Edgbaston—Harborne—Saltley—Small Heath and Spark Brook—Moseley and Balsall Heath.

OUR task is now almost completed. We have endeavoured in this portion of the work, to note the development of the town from its incorporation to the present time, and we may appropriately, in conclusion, gather up the threads of the nine foregoing chapters and notice briefly the modern public buildings and the appearance and extent of the town.

Since we took our last survey in 1832 the entire appearance of Birmingham has undergone considerable change Many of the old narrow streets have been swept away; a group of narrow streets and lanes were removed to make way for the central railway station, and others followed in the clearing of the site of the Snow Hill station. The latter structure was itself rebuilt in 1870, and is now a light and elegant building worthy of the Great Western Company. On its completion the old buildings in Little Charles Street and Edmund Street were removed, and the line of the last-named street altered and continued. It now bears the name of "New Edmund Street" and extends from the Livery Street front of the station to Broad Street Corner.

The Old Inkleys, too, have for the most part been removed, as also many of the old buildings in Moor Street, and on the site of Albert Street. A portion of the new street undertaken by the Town Council, called Corporation Street, has been laid out, and is now being built upon. The old line of Ann Street and Colmore Row has been altered, and the whole of the north side rebuilt, forming one of the finest thoroughfares in the town. Two large hotels and other public buildings have been erected therein, and the line is appropriately finished by the noble Council House.

This noble structure rises (in the dome) to the height of 162 feet, and is 296 feet in length along the principal front, in Ann Street. The Congreve Street front is 122 feet and the Eden Place 153 feet. The height to the top of the cornice is 65 feet, and to the top of the pediment over the principal entrance is 90 feet. The central pediment contains a sculptured group representing "Britannia rewarding the Birmingham Manufacturers." Under the circular arch beneath this group is a figure subject in glass mosaic, by the Venice and Murano Company, and in the four pediments at each angle of the front portion of the building are other sculptured groups representing literature, art, and science in their relation to manufactures. The windows are divided by a row of columns, so as to harmonise with the adjacent Town Hall, which has also guided the Council in their choice of the classic style of architecture, and in the height of the building. Internally the building comprises offices for all the various departments of the work of the Corporation, a handsome and commodious Council Chamber, with ante-rooms thereto, the Mayor's Parlour, and a series of noble Reception Rooms. To these, as well as to the Council Chamber, access is obtained from the great central staircase, immediately under the dome. The hand rails of the balustrade are all of marble, of various colours; and the return flight of the staircase is supported on polished marble columns. The Reception Rooms, or State Apartments are so arranged as, by the opening of a pair of massive folding doors, to form one noble apartment nearly 160 feet in length. The central portion is separated from the western by an open screen of marble columns. The floor is of oak, with parquet border, and along the northern wall are niches in which it is intended to place statues. The southern side consists of a double row of windows; the upper of which will be filled with stained glass. The Council Chamber is at the western end of the building; it is semicircular in plan, and around the western end is the spectators' gallery, raised somewhat above the level of the portion alloted to members, and divided therefrom by an open screen of marble columns. The members' seats are arranged in a semicircular form, the Mayor's chair being at the eastern end of the chamber, on a daïs. Behind this is a handsome screen of Riga oak, with panels of Italian walnut, richly carved, with the arms of the Borough emblazoned in the centre. The upper tier of windows are filled with stained glass, and both the walls and the ceiling are ornamented with frescoes emblematical of Birmingham industry. The whole of this noble building reflects the highest credit upon the architect, Mr. Yeoville Thomason, who has designed and superintended every detail during its erection.

The Post Office has twice been removed during this period. First, from the corner of Bennett's Hill to the building formerly known as the New Royal Hotel; and subsequently, in 1874, to the new building erected for the purpose opposite the Town Hall. The old building was thereupon taken down, and with it passed away one of the old-fashioned *suburban* mansions of New Street, "Portugal House," which was built by the once-celebrated "Beau Green."

New churches have been erected in all parts of the town, as described in the last chapter on the "Churches and Sects of Birmingham." Palatial buildings have taken the place of the old-fashioned country banks, some of them enriched with stained glass and marble sculpture, and all of a highly ornamental description. Even the retail shopkeeper has kept pace with the times, and many of these establishments in the principal streets are elegantly fitted up and decorated with the utmost taste.

Nor are the tasteful buildings of the town confined to the principal thoroughfares. The handsome school buildings erected in every part of the town are ornaments to their respective neighbourhoods, and the artistic work displayed in their erection has been emulated and copied in many of the more modern manufactories, warehouses, and other buildings of each locality.

Great attention has been paid by the Town Council, of late years, to the paving of the streets; nearly all the footways are now paved either with flags or blue bricks, and the old-fashioned "petrified kidneys," have now, for the most part, been abolished; the roadways in the principal streets have been paved with wood, and in many others with granite blocks. The thick, black, greasy mud with which the streets used to be flooded during the winter, and of which visitors from the country carried home extensive samples on their attire, as *souvenirs* of their annual excursion to the cattle show, is now to a great extent unknown.

Improvements have been effected in open spaces by the planting of shrubs and flowers thereon, and the Corporation have now undertaken the care of the town churchyards ; so that bright green spots are even more frequently to be met with in the heart of the town nowadays than at the date of our last survey, more than forty years ago.

The old pleasant suburbs, as they were in 1832, have now become thickly populated districts, which, except in name, are in reality portions of the great midland metropolis. Most of these are now governed by Local Boards of Health, exercising many of the functions of Town Councils.

While the old suburbs, such as Aston, Ashted, Bloomsbury, Nechells, Balsall Heath, and other adjoining districts have become small towns, the suburban residents have found new homes further from the town; and now outlying districts, such as Acock's Green, King's Heath, Moseley, King's Norton, Harborne, Perry Barr, Erdington, and even as far as Sutton Coldfield have become new suburbs to Birmingham, and as the present exodus still continues, it is difficult to say how far the local influence, so to speak, of the town, will yet extend. With the view of reaching these outlying suburbs, and of making them contribute to the public expenditure of the town, a scheme was published in December, 1877, by the Town Council, for extending the boundaries of the borough so as to include them all ; but no action, has, as yet, been taken in the matter, and although most of the residents therein are Birmingham men, the districts themselves are beyond the radius of the town, and do not, therefore, come within the scope of the present work.

At Aston and Handsworth the Local Boards have adopted the Free Libraries' Act, and in the former a temporary Library has been in working since February, 1878. The Library contains about 4,500 volumes and about 3,500 of the inhabitants have availed themselves of its pro- visions. At Handsworth a handsome building has been erected from the designs of Messrs. Alexander & Henman for the use of the Library

and other departments of the Local Board. There are also Local Boards at Saltley, Balsall Heath, and Harborne.

In 1875 the Manor of Aston adopted the Elementary Education Act, the first School Board being elected in the July of that year. Mr. J. A. Cooper is the Chairman of the Board, and Mr. T. G. Pratt the clerk ; and during the four years of the Board's existence five handsome sets of school buildings have been erected in Aston, one at Saltley, and one at Water Orton.

Aston Parish Church is one of the most interesting of the old churches of Birmingham, and contains a fine series of monuments to mem- bers of the Holte family, and several very fine altar tombs. The church is built in various English styles, from Edward II. to Henry VII. but the principal feature of the building is the massive tower, surmounted by its tall and graceful spire. The latter was carefully restored and slightly increased in height under the direc- tion of Mr. J. A. Chatwin, in 1878, and the church itself is now undergoing restoration under that gentleman's able direction.

There are also handsome modern chapels in this suburb, belonging to the Baptists, Indepen- dents, and Wesleyans. The Independent Chapel in Wheeler Street, Lozells, is one of the largest and most commodious nonconformist chapels in the neighbourhood.

The still pleasant suburb of Handsworth has a fine old Parish Church, dedicated to St. Mary, which has been called by Elihu Burritt, "a kind of Westminster Abbey to Birmingham, conse- crated to the memory of its great dead, whose names have won illustrious fame." Here is Chantrey's noble statue of James Watt, and Flaxman's bust of Matthew Boulton, and the remains of both of these illustrious partners lie buried here. William Murdoch is also com- memorated by a memorial bust executed by Chantrey, and he, too, lies near the other heroes of the Soho factory. The church was completely restored, and partly rebuilt, under the direction of Mr. J. A. Chatwin, in 1876, at a cost of upwards of £7,000.

There are two other churches in the parish of Handsworth: St. James's, and St. Michael, and All Angels', Soho Hill.

Edgbaston is one of the few suburbs close to the town which has maintained its semi-rural appearance, mainly from the fact that it is the aristocratic suburb of Birmingham—literally, our " West-end "—and also because it is, for the most part, the property of one landlord, Lord Calthorpe, who has exercised the strictest care in preventing the erection of such buildings as would destroy the present character of the locality. The old Parish Church is one of the most beautiful little churches in England. " Its beauty," says Elihu Burritt, " is not in architectural proportions or pretensions, but in the charm which nature has given it. In the first place, it is picturesquely situated under the eaves of a stately grove that veils Edgbastan Hall and its park and pool from the road. Then it is completely netted to the very top of its tower with ivy. Hardly a square inch of its bare walls can be seen at a few rods distance. . . . Robed thus by nature in the best vestment she could weave for a sanctuary, it seems to have a more sacred consecration to the worship of God than an archbishop could give it." *

Besides the parish church there are at Edgbaston three other churches of the Establishment. *St. George's*, in Calthorpe Road, was erected in 1838, in the early English style, and was enlarged, in 1856, by the addition of the chancel. *St. James's*, Charlotte Road, was consecrated in 1852, in the decorated style, and is cruciform in plan, with a dwarf spire. *St. Augustine's*, in the Hagley Road, is one of the handsomest churches in the neighbourhood. It was built by subscription at a cost of £9,000, and was consecrated in 1868. The tower and spire were added, at a cost of £4,000, in 1876.

Passing through Edgbaston we come to Harborne, which, like Edgbaston, has a beautifully situated Parish Church, which was carefully restored in 1867, and contains a fine stained window to the memory of David Cox. There is a School Board for Harborne and Smethwick, but no new school-buildings have been erected by the Board in this suburb.

The village of Saltley has little of special interest, except the Training College already described. There is a neat church dedicated to St. Saviour, to which was added in 1870, a massive square tower, in the Norman style of architecture.

Small Heath and Sparkbrook are now portions of the Borough ; at the former the principal object of interest is the Small Arms Factory and there is besides a church, dedicated to St. Andrew, and handsome places of worship belonging to the Congregationalists and the Wesleyans. The church at Sparkbrook, (called Christ Church) is an excellent example of ecclesiastical Gothic, and was opened in October, 1867.

At Moseley the principal objects of interest are, the Independent College, (already described in these pages) ; and the Hall and Park, on the site of the old building destroyed in the riots of 1791. Several other old houses injured in the riots were also situated in this neighbourhood. The Parish Church has an old square tower erected in the reign of Henry VIII, and as it is for the most part clad in ivy, this sacred edifice has an appearance of rare antiquity. There is also a modern church, dedicated to St. Anne, which was erected at the expense of Miss Anderton, of Moseley Wake Green, in 1874.

At Balsall Heath, (which connects Moseley with Birmingham) is a modern church dedicated to St. Paul. It is built of brick, and has a massive square tower which may be seen for several miles round.

We have now completed our survey of the town and its suburbs, and have thereby brought our notices of New Birmingham to a close.

---

* *Walks in the Black Country,* pp. 95-6.

We have travelled through eight centuries of Birmingham life, and have traced the growth of the town from its cradle to the fulness of manhood ; and if the reader has carefully noted the facts of this history, and has marked the steady improvement in every department of our public life, he will have felt that, like the great Apostle of the Gentiles, the Birmingham man may claim with truth to be a " citizen of no mean city." Calling to mind the long list of worthies of whom we have imperfectly spoken herein, he will feel that it is no small honour to be able to say, " I, too, am a Birmingham man."

APPENDIX.

EDWARD BERMINGHAM IN THE TOWER (p. 7).

The following very curious and interesting document (copied from the original in the Library of Lord Lyttelton at Hagley, by Mr. Hamper), throws considerable light on the manner in which the estates of Edward Bermingham were divided, and more especially as to the character of the man John Prattye or Prety, and the means by which he obtained this "remarkable Lease," as Mr. Toulmin Smith terms it. If the testimony of the second witness, Edward Taylour, be true, the lease was a forgery, executed after the death of Edward Bermingham.

" 28 Oct. 3 & 4 Philip & Mary, Thomas & John Prattye children of John Prattye deceased, & Alce late wife of the elder John Prattye, complained in Chancery against Edward Lytelton Esqre's title to the Heath Mill &c. alledging that Edward Brymyngham Esq: by Indenture dated 11 Oct. 24 Henr: VIII. did demise & let to farm to the said John Prattye senior the said Mill, also the Connygre containing 160 acres, a Meddow called the Lake Meadow containing 80 acres, and a pasture called Dod-walles containing 80 acres, to hold for fourscore & nineteen years, at the yearly rent of £6. 13. 4: where-upon a Commission issued & many Witnesses were examined ; inter alia, the following :—

" John Ellsone of Yardeley in the countie of Wigorn " yoman of the age of threscore fyftene yeres or there "aboutes deposeth & saythe that he this Examynat " aboutes twentie yeres paste, repayred to London aboutes " certayne his busynes there to do, & being there was re-" quested by John Prattye to go with hym into the Tower of " London to speake with one Edward Brymyngham who at " that present remayned there as a prysoner at whiche " their comyng to saide E.B. after salutacions hadd " betwene theym the saide E. B. spake unto the saide " Prattye in the presence of this Examynat theis wordes " Alas ! John Prattye what wante of grace hadd I to lose " my landes and goodes after this sorte, it was by keaping of " light company, and the saide Prattye answeared that he " hadd the lesse grace, and then the saide Byrmyngham " declared unto the saide Prattye that he wanted money, " and prayed the saide Prattye to helpe hym to some, " whereunto the said Prattye answeared that there was " no cause whye he shulde do so for that he hadd no " benefytt at his handes, saying further that he the saide " Prattye dyvers tymes desired some lyving at his handes, " whiche he coulde never obteigne, and further saide to " the saide E. B. yet Sir if youe will make me a lease for " yeres of the Heathe Mylne, the Lake meadowe, the " Conyngre, and the Dudwales, in Byrmyngham, I will " helpe youe to some money although I borrough some to " bringe me home, whereunto the saide E. B. annswered " Alas ! John Prattye lyttell shall it avayle thee any " lease that I can make to thee, for that my landes are in " the Kyng his handes, and then the saide J. P. saide, for " to have soche a lease as youe can make me I will give " youe here twentie shillings, and further you shall have " a Colte when youe will sende for hym, whiche the saide " Prattye saide he wolde gyve more for pyttie then for " any advanntage he shulde have by the same lease, and " then the saide E.B. promysed the said P. he wolde " make hym so good assurance as he coulde devise."—

" Edwarde Taylour of Kythermynster in the Countie of " Wigorn yoman of the age of threscore twelfe yeres— " saythe that the saide John Prattye aboutes eightene " yeres paste sent for this examynant to his house & at his " comyng the saide P. declared to hym that he shulde " before his departure engrosse a lease in parchement to be " made betwixte Edwarde Byrmyngham then deceassed a " lyttle before that tyme, & the same J. P., and that this " deponent shulde be well recompensed for his paynes, " whiche this deponent was very lothe to doo, albeit for " fere of bodylie hurte there did engrosse an Indenture in " parchement made betwixte the saide E. B. & the saide " J.P. by the informacion of the said J.P. of certayne " parcelles of grounde within the lordeshipp of Byrmyng-" ham, the names whereof he remembreth not, & when " he was wryting the same one came in and loked uppon " hym whose name he knewe not, whereat the said J. P. " was angry, and further this deponent saythe that the " same Indenture he dated with an antedate, but howe " longe before the makyng he remembreth not, and after " this deponent hadd engrossed the same and sett thereto " labelles the said P. set-to waxe and sett fourth a Signett " whiche he sayde was the Seale of Armes of the saide " E. B. & sayde he founde it in his purse whiche he toke " from hym when the saide Byrmyngham was dying, and " then and there in the presence of this deponent the " saide Prattye did seale the saide lease & wolde have " hadd this examynant to have counterfayted the hande " of the saide E.B. and to wryte *by me Edwarde Byr-*" *myngham* whiche this deponent sayde he coulde not doo, " and then the saide J. P. wrote [with] his owne handes " under the saide lease *by me Edwarde Byrmyngham*, and " saythe further when this was done there were no more " present but this examynant and the saide Prettye, and " saythe further that the saide P. earnestlye willed this " deponent to keape his counsaill touching the premysses, " and so this deponent deperted, and remembreth that he " hadd for parte of his rewarde a Colte skynne tanned, " and also saythe that dyvers tymes longe after the saide " lease so made the said Prettye sent for this deponent by " his frendes to come to his house and make merry with " hym, and also when he mett this examynant in any " towne wolde have hadd hym to the Wyne and Taverne " to have made hym chere, and to have hadd talke with " hym, albeit this deponent weying his corrupte practyce " as bifore wold never after the making of the saide lease " come in his company, nor talke with hym."

STRATFORD HOUSE.—(pp. 49, 54.)

We give on the following page another view of this interesting half-timbered house, which was built by Ambrose Rotton, A.D. 1601, and is now the property of Mr. J. W. Simcox, of Hall Green. This fine old-fashioned homestead has been in the Simcox family since 1696, and the present owner has in his possession the conveyance thereof, in that year, to William Simcox, together with all subsequent deeds relating thereto. The engraving is copied from an old lithographed drawing by Mr. W. Hawkes Smith, in the possession of Mr. Simcox. It is taken from the east end of the building, and does not therefore show the fine west wing which has since been taken down ; the chimney stack and the ridge of the roof of that wing are, however, visible in the picture. The sketch on page 49 was taken in 1878.

STRATFORD HOUSE, *from an old lithographed print by W. Hawkes Smith, published about 1820.*

(See previous page.)

FORWARD

R. K. DENT.

PHOTOGRAPHED BY WHITLOCK.

BIRMINGHAM: HOUGHTON & CO., LIMITED SCOTLAND PASSAGE.

EARLY HISTORY OF THE SOCIETY OF FRIENDS IN BIRMINGHAM—(p. 53).

From Mr. William White's interesting little volume, *Friends in Warwickshire in the 17th and 18th centuries,* we glean the following additional facts respecting the early history of Quakerism in Birmingham. The earliest notice of the Birmingham Friends is in *Besse's Sufferings,* when the meeting was held at the house of William Bayliss. George Fox, the founder of the Society, held a meeting in Birmingham in 1667; and during the same decade we read that at Birmingham, "William Dewsbury, being in a meeting at the house of William Reynolds, a constable came with a rude multitude, armed with swords and staves, who pulled Friends out of the house, and beat and abused some of them; they also broke the windows of the house in the constable's presence. The like treatment Friends met with when religiously assembled in the house of William Bayley." We further read, previous to the close of the seventeenth century, that "the Spring Quarter Meeting [of the Societies in Warwickshire] hath ever been held in Birmingham."

The view from the site of the original Meeting House in Monmouth Street is thus described by Mr. White: "Looking north, the hill would slope away in gentle undulations to Hockley woods; its brook flowing in freshness and purity, and widening into a considerable sheet of water, called Hockley pool. The gables and roofs of the newly-erected Aston Hall would be seen with the church spire a little more to the right, and behind would rise, beyond the windings of the The Tame, the 'gravelly hill,' and the bare and bleak heath on which Erdington now stands, and known as the Coldfield; while the background would be filled up by the tower of Sutton church, the woods of its spacious park, and the long-backed eminence of Barr Beacon. Looking due east, the most distant objects were the Meriden Hills, half way to Coventry, and nearer, the gentle eminences crowned by the semi-castellated mansion of Castle Bromwich; and in the foreground the valleys of the Rea and Tame, 'the way to Coleshill,' now Coleshill Street, and the shady trees of the 'Dale End.' South-west and south would be seen portions of the upper part of the town, the spire of St. Martin's, and rising above the trees of the cherry orchard, the homely turret crowning the roof of King Edward's School, which had been founded then upwards of a hundred years, but which still stood on the edge of the town. The woods of Bordesley park, overlooked by the suburban Park Street, and bounded by the quaint gabled houses of 'Deergate-end,' would complete the picture."

LENCHS' TRUST—(p. 76).

At the period to which our former remarks upon Lench's Trust extended (p. 76) the whole of the rents amounted to about £40 only, of which more than one-half was derived from the property left by William Lench, and the remainder from the other charitable foundations embraced by the Trust. It is significant of the great increase in the value of Birmingham properties that at the present time (less than two centuries having elapsed) the yearly rents have increased to upwards of £3000, a very considerable portion being still the small rents derived from old building leases. As the income has gradually expanded so has the usefulness of the Charity. The original Trust "for the repairing of the ruinous ways and bridges in and about the Town of Birmingham," before noticed, was carried out with unvarying regularity. Few of the present inhabitants know the extent of the obligations of their forefathers to William Lench.

Camden properly described Birmingham as "very watery." Few towns were more so; the parish comprised or covered a hill between two hills, and its two main streams—the Rea and Hockley Brook, had numerous small rivulets or streams for feeders. The great fall on the slope from Holloway Head and Bells Barn gave Clay Brook and Pudding Brook running to the Moat; that from Broad Street, Easy Hill, and Paradise Street, a stream by the Parsonage, near Lady Well, there swelled by that spring. The high ground now occupied by St. Philip's Church drained through Cherry Orchard, across High Street, and formed a stream anciently called "Hersum's dyche" or "Hassam's ditch," and continuously identified by those names from the 12th to 15th century, passing Moor Street at the side of the Woolpack Hotel, where the space remains to the present day, and on across Park Street. The Priory Grounds, of great extent and traditionally well wooded, washed down to the Butts—as witness "the ditch" behind Stafford Street—hence across the Dale, which formed a stream for distinction from Deriend—Deergate End—became the Dale End of the town, on towards Park Street and through Lake Meadow, where it was joined by Hersum's dyche, and ran past the present Bull's Head, across Digbeth (Dyg's bath), dividing the parish from Aston, where a bridge, commonly called the Little Bridge, was erected over it ere it joined the Rea, again to pass Digbeth by the larger bridge of stone. Thus the surface waters of one side of the hill gave bridges to be repaired and fords to be maintained at Dudley Street (Dudwall Lane), the Parsonage, Edgbaston Street, Moor (or Moul) Street, Park Street, Dale End—where, as at Deritend, the bridge was barred, and kept chained and locked, with an attendant bar-keeper. The waters on the other side of the slope through the New Hall estate formed the pool recorded by Water Street, then flowed across Snow Hill (Sandy Lane) and Walmer (Wall Moor) Lane, with a bridge and ford at at each, others again were found at the Sandpits, at Hockley, Aston, Bournbrook, Watery Lane, Lawley Street, a very ancient road, and at other points, on all of which, when ruinous, the bailiff or treasurer of the Trust regularly disbursed the funds at his disposal in such repairs as were needed.

Gravel and stones also were purchased and brought from Winson Green, and carters, labourers, and paviours were constantly employed. At times a paviour had to be brought from Lichfield or other distant place.

Timber was largely employed in staking up the rude footpaths, and now and again a bridge was washed away in a flood. The badly-made roads were, in hilly situations such as Digbeth and Carr's Lane, easily destroyed by heavy rains, the functions, therefore, of the bailiff assimilated to those of the modern borough surveyor, and he shared the official importance of the town bailiff and constable.

Contract work was unknown, every job was ordered and paid for in detail, even to the ale which was an invariable accompaniment to the work.

With the growing importance and better government of the town was this expenditure gradually diminished, and by about 1840 entirely died away.

Another ancient Trust was for making love or peace between those who quarrelled. Loveday Street attests the source of this. Two persons quarrelled, and a lawyer made them friends, gave a receipt to the bailiff for 2s. 6d. and probably retained the oyster. This practice, though of long standing, was too absurd for continuance and became obsolete about 100 years since. Amongst other quaint appropriation of the funds was the yearly payment for bell ropes to St. Martin's Church, still in force. Indeed the Charity has been uniformly marked by a stedfast regard to its original foundation—the early Trust "in default of other uses, the rents to the poor living within the town" having always been kept in view and constantly extended. Thus, in 1764 were built the Steelhouse Lane almshouses, and subsequently others in Park Street and Dudley Street, which having fallen into disuse have been replaced by others in Hospital Street, Ravenhurst Street, and Ladywood, the comfort of the inhabitants, being the study and aim of the stewards of this wellmanaged Charity.

Mr. Toulmin Smith who, shortly before his death, compiled a calender of the very interesting records of the Trust in bearing testimony to the management of the Charity past and present has recorded that "the 'works of charity' ordained by William Lench in 1525 to be done in Birmingham still continue to be done there by his feoffees in the spirit and as near as can be to the letter of these old ordinances,"[*] and he desired to say that "with a very wide acquaintance with the ordinances and history of English Gilds, I am aware of no instance in which there has been such a steady adherence to the original

purposes of the endowment and such an unbroken course of sound management and well-kept accounts, as I have found to be the case from an examination of the long series of the records of Lench's Trust."[†]

The work of the Charity is still being expanded, another block of almshouses being projected at Highgate from designs by Mr. J. A. Chatwin.

The inmates for the houses are always selected from the most urgent cases, and to some 170 aged widows and spinsters is the evening of life thus rendered pleasant. The applicants for the benefits of the Charity are, however, always largely in excess of its means, and any charitable person who has a desire to help the poor and distressed may here find a sure and economical mode of carrying out his wishes.

[*] English Gilds, p. 250.
[†] Introduction to the Calendar.

RESULTS OF PARLIAMENTARY ELECTIONS : 1832-1876.

December 12, 1832.

Thomas Attwood, L. } Elected without opposition.
Joshua Scholefield, L.

January, 1835.

Thomas Attwood, L. - - - - - 1718
Joshua Scholefield, L. - - - - 1660
Richard Spooner, C. - - - - - 915

August, 1837.

Thomas Attwood, L. - - - - - 2145
Joshua Scholefield, L. - - - - 2114
A. G. Stapleton, C. - - - - - 1046

On Mr. Attwood's retirement, Jan. 1840.

George Frederick Muntz, L. - - - 1454
Sir Charles Wetherell, C. - - - 915

July, 1841.

George Frederick Muntz, L. - - - 2175
Joshua Scholefield, L. - - - - 1963
Richard Spooner, C. - - - - - 1825

On Mr. Scholefield's death, July, 1844.

Richard Spooner, C. - - - - - 2095
William Scholefield, L. - - - - 1735
Joseph Sturge, L. - - - - - 346

August, 1847.

George Frederick Muntz, L. - - - 2830
William Scholefield, L. - - - - 2824
Richard Spooner, C. - - - - - 2302
Mr. Serjeant Allen, C. - - - - 89

July, 1852.

George Frederick Muntz, L. } Elected without
William Scholefield, L. } opposition.

March, 1857.

George Frederick Muntz, L. } Elected without
William Scholefield, L. } opposition.

On the death of Mr. Muntz, August, 1857.

John Bright, L., elected without opposition.

April, 1859.

William Scholefield, L. - - - - 4425
John Bright, L. - - - - - 4282
Thomas D. Acland, C. - - - - 1544

July, 1865.

William Scholefield, L. } Elected without opposition.
John Bright, L.

On the death of Mr. William Scholefield, July, 1867.

George Dixon, L. - - - - - 5819
Sampson S. Lloyd, C. - - - - 4214

November, 17, 1868.

George Dixon, L. - - - - - 15,198
Philip Henry Muntz, L. - - - - 14,614
John Bright, L. - - - - - 14,601
Sampson S. Lloyd, C. - - - - 8,700
Sebastian Evans, C. - - - - 7,061

December 21, 1868.

John Bright, L. } Elected without opposition on taking office as President of Board of Trade under Mr. Gladstone.

October 18, 1873.

John Bright, L. } Elected without opposition on accepting the office of Chancellor of the Duchy of Lancaster.

January 30, 1874.

Messrs. Bright, L., Dixon, L., and Muntz, L. } Re-elected without opposition.

June 27, 1876.

Joseph Chamberlain, L., elected without opposition on the retirement of Mr. G. Dixon.

Mayors of Birmingham—

Elected, December 27th—	Elected, November 9th—	Elected, November 9th—
1838 William Scholefield	1852 Henry Hawkes	1867 Thomas Avery
Elected, November 9th—	1853 James Baldwin	1868 Henry Holland
1839 Philip Hy. Muntz	1854 John Palmer	1869 Thomas Prime
1840 Philip Hy. Muntz	1855 T. R. T. Hodgson	1870 G. B. Lloyd
1841 Samuel Beale	*1856 John Ratcliff	1871 J. Sadler
1842 James James	1857 John Ratcliff	1872 Ambrose Biggs
1843 Thomas Weston	1858 Sir J. Ratcliff, Knt.	*1873 J. Chamberlain
1844 Thomas Phillips	1859 Thomas Lloyd	1874 J. Chamberlain
*1845 Henry Smith	1860 Arthur Ryland	1875 J. Chamberlain
1846 Robert Martineau	1861 Henry Manton	1876 George Baker
1847 Charles Geach	*1862 Charles Sturge	1877 W. Kenrick
1848 Samuel Thornton	1863 William Holliday	1878 Jesse Collings
1849 William Lucy	1864 Henry Wiggin	*1879 R. Chamberlain
1850 William Lucy	1865 Edwin Yates	
*1851 Henry Smith	1866 George Dixon	

In the years marked thus * Nov. 9th fell on Sunday.

List of Local Periodicals—(exclusive of Newspapers, Trade Journals, and Sporting Papers). *Those marked with an asterisk are still in existence.*

The Birmingham Register and Entertaining Museum, 2 vols. (was 2nd ever completed ?). Sketchley, 1765.

The Medical Miscellany, by J. Tomlinson. This only extended to one volume : a second edition, with an appendix, was published by S. Aris, 1774.

The Birmingham Inspector, edited and published by W. Hawkes Smith ; 1 vol. 8vo, 1817.

The Searcher. Jabet, 1817.

Edmond's Weekly Recorder : 4to, 4d. per number. Vale, 1819. Last number, Aug. 14, 1819 ; (8 nos.).

The Saturday's Register ; 8vo, by J. Edmonds, and published by him, 6d. per no. Jan., 1820.

Edmond's Weekly Register ; 4to, 19 nos. Last, 8th Jan., 1820.

The Comet Magazine, or Literary Wanderer ; 12mo., 6d. per number. Bloomer, 1820.

The Theatrical Looker-On : 4to, 3d. No. 1, June 26, 1823. (About 47 nos.).

The Birmingham Bazaar ; 4to, 3d. No. 1, June 26, 1823. (About 47 nos.).

The Birmingham Reporter and Theatrical Review. Printed by Hodgetts, published by Buckton, edited by Francis Lloyd ; 1823. (14 nos.).

The Theatrical John Bull ; 2 vols. 12mo, 1824. Edited by Edward Allday, printed by Cooper.

The Mouse-Trap ; 12mo., 1824. Printed by T. Dewson. (Query edited or written by Alfred Bunn ?)

The Review. Printed by Butterworth : said in "Mouse Trap," page 2, to be 'still-born.'

The Note Book.

The Birmingham Spectator ; 1 vol. 12mo, 1824. Drake.

The Lounger. Drake. 1825.

The Dramatic Censor or Theatrical Recorder ; 1826, 12mo, price 2½d.

The Birmingham Independent ; 1827.

The Birmingham Magazine ; edited by Rev. Hugh Hutton, 1 vol. 8vo. Drake, 1828.

The Hazlewood Magazine ; 12mo, 1828, &c.

The Monthly Argus and Public Censor ; 8vo, from 1828 to 1834.

The Iris ; 9 nos. 8vo. Moore, 1830.

The Literary Phœnix ; 4 nos. only, 8vo. Belcher, 1830.

The Political Companion. Oct,, 1830, 8vo, 3d. W. Plastans, Dale End.

The Political Union Monthly Register, or the Reformers' Magazine. No. 1, March, 1832. Charles Watson, Church Street.

The Wasp ; 8vo, July, 1832, 1d. R. Jenkinson, Church Street.

The Midland Chronicle ; 1 vol. 12mo. Hudson, 1833.

The Analyst ; 8vo, 1834, &c.

The Oscotian ; 2 vols. and odd nos. Edited by the Rev. John Moore, &c.

The Birmingham Monthly Magazine ; 12mo. Allen, High Street. 6 numbers, August, 1834, to Jan. 1835 ; pp. 144.

The Birmingham Penny Magazine. Harding, 1835. (Probably not more than one number published.)

The Naturalist ; edited by Hall.

The Botanic Garden ; edited by G. B. Knowles.

The People's Watchman ; 8vo. Wright, 1838. 32 nos.

The Birmingham Iris ; edited and published by T. J. Ouseley, 1839, 8vo. 4 nos., 1s. per no.

The Free School, or King Edward's Magazine ; 6 nos., edited by Wescott and Evans. Published by Davis, 1840.

The Midland Counties Standard ; edited by Joseph Allday. 6 vols. 4to, 1842.

The Birmingham and Edgbaston Proprietary School Magazine ; 8vo, 1845. Belcher.

The Birmingham Musical Examiner and Dramatic Review ; edited by Mr. Stimpson, 8vo, 19 nos., 2d. each. 1845-6.

The Protestant Watchman ; 12mo. Ragg. 1848, &c.

The Reform League Circular ; by Muntz, Weston, &c. 2 nos., 8vo. ; merged into the *Mercury,* 1848.

The Remembrancer of the Presbyterian Church, Broad Street ; 1848, 8vo. 1d. per no.

The Recorder ; 4 nos., small 4to, 1849.

The Town Crier ; 4to. Commenced January, 1861. (*First few numbers illustrated.*)

The Bazaar Gazette of Wisdom, Wit, and Humour. Issued during the Volunteers' Bazaar, October 14, 15, 16, and 17, 1863 ; folio. *Illustrated.*

The Protestant Record of Birmingham and neighbourhood ; 1863-6. (24 nos.) 8vo.

Birmingham Protestant Association Record ; 1866-8. (12 nos.) 8vo.

The Midland Metropolis ; June, 1868. (One number only.) 8vo. *Illustrated,* 1s.

The Third Member ; edited by Aunt Jane. (16 nos.) 1868, 8vo. *Illustrated.*

Toby. (About 12 nos.) 1868, 8vo. *Illustrated by Sershall.*

The Gridiron ; edited by Old Sarbot. (4 nos. 1868) 4to. *Illustrated.*

Brum ; edited by Old Sarbot. (16 nos.) 1869, 4to. *Illustrated by Bernasconi.*

The Illustrated Midland News. Conducted by Joseph Hatton. September, 1869, to March, 1871. Folio, 4 vols.

The Torch, (Announced in 1869 but never issued.)

The National Education League Monthly Paper. Commenced December, 1869, 4to. (Continued during the existence of the League.)

The Mutual : A monthly Magazine for Mutual Improvement Societies. 1870. 8vo.

The Birmingham Pulpit ; 1871-3, 4to. 6 vols.

* *The Birmingham Medical Review.* (Quarterly.) Commenced 1872. 8vo.

The Secular Chronicle ; 1872, &c. 4to.

King Edward's School Chronicle ; 1872-3. 4to.

The Birmingham Protestant Association Magazine ; 1872-3. (17 nos.) 8vo.

The Inland Review ; 1872, &c. 4to.

* *The Central Literary Magazine.* (Quarterly.) Commenced January, 1873. 8vo. *Illustrated.*

The Liberal. Published for the Birmingham Liberal Association, 1873. 8vo.

The School Board Election News. Published by the Birmingham Scriptural Education Union. (5 nos.) 1873. 8vo.

The Birmingham Sunday Reporter ; 1874. 8vo.

The Birmingham Examiner, 1876-7. 8vo.

* *The Dart :* A Journal of Sense and Satire. Commenced October, 1876. 4vo. *Illustrated by Bernasconi and Sershall.*

The Lion : (A Satirical Journal.) 1877. Small folio. (Continued about six months.) *Illustrated.*

* *The Midland Naturalist.* 8vo.

* *The Small Heath Literary Magazine.* 8vo.

* *The Owl :* A Journal of Wit and Wisdom. Commenced January 31, 1879. 4to. *Illustrated by Bernasconi.*

* *The Gridiron :* A weekly Grill for Saints and Sinners. Commenced June, 1879. 4to.

* *The Speaker.* (The organ of the Birmingham Parliamentary Debating Society.) Commenced 1879. Small 4to.

* *M.P.* (The organ of the Hockley and Handsworth Parliamentary Debating Society.) Commenced 1879. 4to.

* *Mid-England :* A monthly Magazine of Literature, Science, Art, and Archæology. No. 1, December, 1879. *With Photograph and other Illustrations.*

The earlier portion of this list (previous to 1850), is compiled from the notes of Mr. W. Bates, B.A.

We omitted to mention that in 1879 Mr. Capern had published in Birmingham a second edition of his " Wayside Warbles," with additions, and since then a new volume of his poems, entitled, " Sungleams and Shadows," has been published by Houghton & Co.

The map dated 1750 was copied from an original and scarce plan (size, 30½ × 21in.) in the possession of Mr. John Rabone.

INDEX.

DR. ROOKE'S MEDICINES

THE
ORIENTAL PILLS AND SOLAR ELIXIR

THESE WELL-KNOWN FAMILY MEDICINES have had a continually increasing Sale throughout the United Kingdom and the British Colonies since their introduction in 1836, and are especially noted for their STRENGTHENING and RESTORATIVE Properties. Hence their invariable success in the RELIEF and CURE of

INDIGESTION,	BRONCHITIS,	GOUT.
LIVER COMPLAINTS,	Pulmonary CONSUMPTION	SCROFULA,
ASTHMA,	RHEUMATISM,	General DEBILITY,

And all Diseases of the NERVOUS SYSTEM.

Whether arising from a Sedentary mode of life, unhealthy occupation, insalubrious climate, or other cause whatsoever

THE ORIENTAL PILLS AND SOLAR ELIXIR

Are prepared only by **CHARLES ROOKE, M.D., SCARBOROUGH.** The **Pills** are sold in Boxes at **1s.1½d.** and **4s.6d.** each; the **ELIXIR** in Bottles at **4s.6d.** and **11s.** each, duty included. Around each Box and Bottle are wrapped Directions for the guidance of Patients in all Diseases.

DR. ROOKE'S ANTI-LANCET

All who wish to preserve health, and thus prolong life, should read

DR. ROOKE'S "ANTI-LANCET," or "HANDY GUIDE TO DOMESTIC MEDICINE,"

Which contains 172 pages, and is replete with anecdotes, sketches, biographical matter, portraits of eminent men, &c. It may be obtained GRATIS of any Chemist, or POST FREE from DR. ROOKE, Scarborough, England.

CONCERNING THIS BOOK, THE LATE EMINENT AUTHOR, SHERIDAN KNOWLES, OBSERVED :

It will be an incalculable boon to every person who can read & think.

CROSBY'S
BALSAMIC
COUGH ELIXIR

Is the leading medicine of the day, and is specially recommended by several eminent Physicians. It has been used with the most signal success for Asthma, Bronchitis, Consumption, Coughs, Influenza, Consumptive Night Sweats, Spitting of Blood, Shortness of Breath, &c. ; and is a most valuable adjunct to Dr. Rooke's Medicines in all Affections of the Throat and Chest.

Crosby's Balsamic Cough Elixir is sold everywhere, by all Chemists and Medicine Vendors, at the following prices:— 1s.9d., 4s.6d., and 11s. each Bottle. A saving of THREE SHILLINGS is affected by purchasing the large bottles. Full directions with each Bottle.

NOTICE TO INVALIDS.

A NEW EDITION of the TREATISE on "DISEASES of the LUNGS and AIR-VESSELS," containing full and plain instructions for the relief and cure of those diseases, has just been printed, and may be had GRATIS from any Chemist, or post free from JAMES M. CROSBY, Chemist, Scarborough.

OLD AND NEW BIRMINGHAM.

AN ILLUSTRATED HISTORY OF THE TOWN AND ITS PEOPLE.

PRINTED AND PUBLISHED BY

HOUGHTON & HAMMOND, SCOTLAND PASSAGE,

BIRMINGHAM.

BRITISH WORKMAN'S
ASSURANCE COMPANY,
LIMITED.

CHIEF OFFICES:
BROAD STREET CORNER, BIRMINGHAM.

ESTABLISHED 1866.

The surpassing progress, and great achievements of this Office are the best proofs of the public confidence, and the high esteem placed upon the Company's liberal dealings; especially its promptitude in settling Claims, and its peculiar feature of Surrender Value. Through the Agency of the BRITISH WORKMAN'S ASSURANCE COMPANY, the great Principles and Advantages of Life Assurance become universal in their application. THIS COMPANY EMBRACES ALL CLASSES, AND ALL AGES OF HEALTHY PEOPLE

FROM BIRTH TO 85 YEARS OF AGE.

OVER 80,000 PROPOSALS FOR ASSURANCE WERE RECEIVED IN THE PAST YEAR.

ANY PREMIUM IS NOW TAKEN, FROM 1D. PER WEEK TO £100 PER YEAR.

The Sums Assured increase with the age of the Policy, although the Premium paid must only be 1d. per Week. A person who has paid in 12 years, is justly and fairly entitled to more than a person that has paid in 12 months, only.

THE COMPANY WILL RETURN ONE-FOURTH OF THE PREMIUMS PAID (in the Life Department) to any persons wishing to discontinue their payments after the first three years. Thus the Company not only engages to pay the Sum Assured at Death, or in Lifetime (as agreed upon at the date of entry); but Five Shillings out of every Pound paid in can be withdrawn at will, as stated upon the Policy,

£1,118 WERE RETURNED TO THE WORKING CLASSES

IN THE INDUSTRIAL DEPARTMENT, IN THE PAST YEAR.

Thousands can bear witness, to the Company's prompt and liberal manner, in settling just and proper Claims.

NEARLY £75,000 HAVE ALREADY BEEN PAID.

Claims of £50 and under are paid at once; upon satisfactory proof.

THE PRESENT ANNUAL INCOME EXCEEDS £60,000.

Send for Prospectus. The Table Payable at Death or a given Age should have particular attention.

Mr. WOOLHOUSE, the Actuary, reports that the Funds in hand are in excess of the amount really required to meet the liabilities of the Company.

HENRY PORT, F.S.A., Managing Director.
D. A. BECKETT, Secretary.